PASSAGES 12

LITERATURE AND LANGUAGE

Guy Giroux

Catherine Hay

Barbara Illingworth

Ann Manson

James Stowe

Vetta Vratulis

Peter Yan

CONTRIBUTING WRITERS
Jennifer Connell
Bryan Ellefson
Catherine Reid
Robert Riel
Colleen Shook
Bill Talbot

EDITORIAL TEAM
Joe Banel
Sandra McTavish
Patrice Peterkin
Diane Robitaille
C. Samantha Vrakking
Vivien Young

gagelearning

National Library of Canada Cataloguing in Publication Data

Main entry under title:

Passages 12 : literature and language

ISBN 0-7715-0958-8

1. Readers (Secondary) I. Giroux, Guy

PE1121.P333 2002   428.6   C2001-903081-9

PASSAGES REVIEWERS
Marg Frederickson, Burnaby SD #41, BC
Ashley M. Kelly, Vancouver SB, BC
Kerry Hutchinson, North Vancouver District #44, BC
Remigio Vicente, Richmond School District, BC
Harry Wagner, Parkland School Div. #70, AB
Jane Prosser, Saskatoon Public School Board, SK
Sharron Olson, Winnipeg School Division #1, MB
Robert Riel, Winnipeg School Division #1, MB
Gina Barbosa Tousignant, Dufferin-Peel RCDSB, ON
Sandy Dobec, Ottawa-Carleton Catholic SB, ON
Myra O. Junyk, Toronto Catholic DSB, ON
Ken Oulton, School District #8, NB
Michelle Coleman, Cape Breton Victoria Regional SB, NS
Catherine Reid, Avalon East SB, NF
Jennifer Connell, Eastern School District, PEI

Permissions Editor: Elizabeth Long
Photo Researcher: Patricia Buckley
Design, Art Direction: ArtPlus
Cover Design: Dave Murphy/ArtPlus
Cover Image: Daryl Benson

We acknowledge the financial support of the Government of Canada through the Book Publishing Industry Development Program for our publishing activities.

ISBN 0-7715-**0958-8**
1 2 3 4 5 FP 05 04 03 02 01

Printed and bound in Canada

Passages retains the original spelling, grammar, and punctuation used by each author. Gage Learning editorial style, however, is used throughout for activities and other text generated by Gage Learning writers. Some inconsistency of style results.

Table of Contents

* Canadian Content

Unit 3 Personal Focus: People in Profile

Unit 4 Media and Popular Culture: Behind the Scenes

* **Canadian Content**

* **Canadian Content**

Alternate Table of Contents—Themes and Genres

Unit 1

Communication:
Opening Up Opportunities

Jot down in your notebook jobs that you have had. Note what you liked and disliked about each one. Did any of these jobs give you an inkling of what you want to do for a living?

Early Inklings

Essay by John Updike

"You're hired": sweet words, in this life of getting and spending. I have heard them rather rarely; my last regular paycheck was issued when I was twenty-five and poised to anoint myself as self-employed writer. My first paying job that I can recall was swatting flies ten for a penny on my family's side porch. The pay rate, considering the number and sluggishness of Pennsylvania flies, seems high; perhaps I broke my employers' bank. Though I was keen and eager, at the age of six or so, the job did not open out into a career.

Next, at the age of twelve, I worked for a weekly pass to the local movie theatre. I and some six or eight other boys would gather at the Shillington, with its triangular marquee and slanting lobby, on Saturday mornings, and be entrusted with bundles of little tinted leaflets, folded once like a minimal book, advertising the week's coming attractions. Shows, some of them double features, changed every other day and took Sundays off—gangster films, musicals, Disney cartoons, romantic comedies, Abbott and Costello, Biblical epics, all offering a war-beset, Depression-haunted America ninety minutes of distraction from its troubles. We boys were dispatched in pairs, some of us to territories as remote as Mohnton and Sinking Spring, and scampered up and down the concrete steps of hilly Pennsylvania to leave our slithering beguilements on expectant porches where tin boxes held empty milk bottles and rubber mats said in raised letters "Welcome." When the leaflets were gone—some very bad boys, it was rumored, would dump theirs down a storm drain—we returned to the theatre for our magic pass. More than once, to save the seven cents the movie-house proprietor had given us for the trolley car, my partner and I would saunter the several miles back to Shillington, between the shining tracks.

Next, a dark chapter. I must have been sixteen when I was deemed eligible to work in a lens factory in the gritty city of Reading. They were sunglass lenses, at least in our end of the plant—they came mounted on hemispheres fitted, in turn, onto upright hubs that held them under rotating caps in a long trough full of a red liquid abrasive called "mud." They had to be changed every twenty minutes, as I remember; I was always falling behind, and a foreman kept coming around to chalk rejection marks—white X's—on my overcooked hemispheres, with their blank and slippery eyes. The red sludge got all over you, inexpungeably, into hair, ears, and fingernails. A wan, Dickensian boy about my age tried to teach me the ropes, but my only prowess emerged at the brief lunch break, when a country skill at quoits[1] enabled me to outscore my malnourished city-dwelling co-workers.

On the vast factory floor, various machines mercilessly thrummed around me, and my stomach churned. In my nervous moments of repose, I smoked cigarettes, flipping the butts right onto the scarred old floor. I could smoke all I wanted; the adults around me didn't care. But the consolation fell short: if this thrumming, churning misery marked the entrance to adulthood, childhood wasn't so bad. I quit after three days, promising my parents to work profitably instead at my strawberry patch on the farm to which we had moved. Agricultural labor is as mirthless as industrial, but the strawberry season lasted only three weeks of straddling the wide rows, as the sun baked your bare back and daddy longlegs waltzed up your arms. For the rest of the summer, I tried to write a mystery novel.

When I was eighteen, between high school and college, the editor of the Reading *Eagle* told me I was hired, as a summer copyboy. This was even better than swatting flies. It paid a bit better, too—thirty-four dollars and change in a small brown envelope every Friday. My duties were to hang around the editorial room, doing a breakfast run for the doughnut-prone, coffee-addicted staff and carrying copy into the Linotype room, where men in green eyeshades tickled the keyboards of the towering Mergenthaler Linotype machines. Their activity was noisily industrial, and smelled of hot lead and human confinement, but its product made sense to me. A copyboy's last duty of the day was to bring up a stack of fresh, warm newspapers (the *Eagle* was an afternoon paper) from the roaring pressroom and distribute them, with a touch of ceremony, to the editors, the reporters, and even the paper's owner, a local magnate who sat patiently in his grand front office. He always thanked me. I felt part of a meaningful process, a daily distillation, an installment of life's ceaseless poetry. This was my element, ink on paper.

---

[1] **quoits:** a game similar to horseshoes.

Letterpress Background by Jayme Thornton.

1. Exploring Meaning

a. The title "Early Inklings" is an example of a pun. Explain the pun and the meaning of the title. Do you think it is an effective title for this essay? Explain. How does the last line reinforce the meaning of the pun?

b. What jobs does John Updike tell us he has had?

c. Updike did not enjoy his job at the lens factory. Why?

d. What does Updike mean when he says, "I felt part of a meaningful process, a daily distillation, an installment of life's ceaseless poetry"?

e. What is meant by the statement, "This was my element, ink on paper"? What do you consider your element to be? Do you have a particular career choice that you would consider your element? If so, what is it?

2. Vocabulary Reread "Early Inklings" concentrating on the author's choice of words. Using the context clues in the following lines, write a definition for the underlined words:

> I and some six or eight other boys would gather at the Shillington, with its triangular <u>marquee</u> and slanting lobby, on Saturday mornings, and be <u>entrusted</u> with bundles of little tinted leaflets . . .

> In my nervous moments of <u>repose</u>, I smoked cigarettes, flipping the butts right onto the scarred old floor.

> Agricultural labor is as <u>mirthless</u> as industrial . . .

Compare your definitions with those in a dictionary.
Self-Assessment: How effective do you think you are at working out the definition of words from their context? What strategies do you use effectively? What strategies do you need to build on?

3. Genre Study *Narrative Essay* "Early Inklings" follows the narrative essay form. It tells what, where, and when something takes place, who is involved, and why and how it happens. It uses a chronological order and **transition words** and phrases such as *first, then,* and *later* to reinforce this order. Skim this essay and record examples of its narrative characteristics in your notebook.

Transition words indicate relationships between ideas. Writers use them to suggest links between sentences or paragraphs.

4. Writing *Descriptive Paragraph* Write a brief descriptive paragraph of one of your memories of work. Use vivid details to show rather than tell what the work was like, how you felt at the time, and how you feel looking back on it. Share your paragraph with others and discuss your work experiences.

5. Visual Communication *Assess Image* With a partner, discuss the image that accompanies this essay and assess its effectiveness. What is the mood of the photo? What message does the image send? Share your assessment with a larger group.

"It's easy to lose your dreams," says a character in this story, especially when you're not sure what your dreams should be.

Star Food

Short Story by Ethan Canin

The summer I turned eighteen I disappointed both my parents for the first time. This hadn't happened before, since what disappointed one usually pleased the other. As a child, if I played broom hockey instead of going to school, my mother wept and my father took me outside later to find out how many goals I had scored. On the other hand, if I spent Saturday afternoon on the roof of my parents' grocery store staring up at the clouds instead of counting cracker cartons in the stockroom, my father took me to the back to talk about work and discipline, and my mother told me later to keep looking for things that no one else saw.

This was her theory. My mother felt that men like Leonardo da Vinci and Thomas Edison had simply stared long enough at regular objects until they saw new things, and thus my looking into the sky might someday make me a great man. She believed I had a worldly curiosity. My father believed I wanted to avoid stock work.

Stock work was an issue in our family, as were all the jobs that had to be done in a grocery store. Our store was called Star Food and above it an incandescent star revolved. Its circuits buzzed, and its yellow points, as thick as my knees, drooped with the slow melting of the bulb. On summer nights flying insects flocked in clouds around it, droves of them burning on the glass. One of my jobs was to go out on the roof, the sloping, eaved side that looked over the western half of Arcade, California, and clean them off the star. At night, when their black bodies stood out against the glass, when the wind carried in the marsh smell of the New Jerusalem River, I went into the attic, crawled out the dormer window onto the peaked roof, and slid across the shingles to where the pole rose like a lightning rod into the night. I reached with a wet rag and rubbed away the June bugs and pickerel moths until the star was yellow-white and steaming from the moisture. Then I turned and looked over Arcade, across the bright avenue and my dimly lighted high school in the distance, into the low hills where oak trees grew in rows on the curbs and where girls drove to school in their own convertibles. When my father came up on the roof sometimes to talk about the store, we fixed our eyes on the red tile roofs or the small clouds of blue barbecue smoke that floated above the hills on warm evenings. While the clean bulb buzzed and flickered behind us, we talked about loss leaders or keeping the elephant-ear plums stacked in neat triangles.

The summer I disappointed my parents, though, my father talked to me about a lot of other things. He also made me look in the other direction whenever we were on the roof together, not west to the hills and their clouds of barbecue smoke, but east toward the other part of town. We crawled up one slope of the roof, then down the other so that I could see beyond the back alley where wash hung on lines in the moonlight, down to the neighborhoods across Route 5. These were the neighborhoods where men sat on the curbs on weekday afternoons, where rusted, wheel-less cars lay on blocks in the yards.

"*You're* going to end up on one of those curbs," my father told me.

Usually I stared farther into the clouds when he said something like that. He and my mother argued about what I did on the roof for so many hours at a time, and I hoped that by looking closely at the amazing borders of clouds I could confuse him. My mother believed I was on the verge of discovering something atmospheric, and I was sure she told my father this, so when he came upstairs, made me look across Route 5, and talked to me about how I was going to end up there, I squinted harder at the sky.

"You don't fool me for a second," he said.

He was up on the roof with me because I had been letting someone steal from the store.

From the time we first had the star on the roof, my mother believed her only son was destined for limited fame. Limited because she thought that true vision was distilled and could not be appreciated by everybody. I discovered this shortly after the star was installed, when I spent an hour looking out over the roofs and chimneys instead of helping my father stock a shipment of dairy. It was a hot day and the milk sat on the loading dock while he searched for me in the store and in our apartment next door. When he came up and found me, his neck was red and his footfalls shook the roof joists. At my age I was still allowed certain mistakes, but I'd seen the dairy truck arrive and knew I should have been downstairs, so it surprised me later, after I'd helped unload the milk, when my mother stopped beside me as I was sprinkling the leafy vegetables with a spray bottle.

"Dade, I don't want you to let anyone keep you from what you ought to be doing."

"I'm sorry," I said. "I should have helped with the milk earlier."

"No," she said, "that's not what I mean." Then she told me her theory of limited fame while I sprayed the cabbage and lettuce with the atomizer. It was the first time I had heard her idea. The world's most famous men, she said, presidents and emperors, generals and patriots, were men of vulgar fame, men who ruled the world because their ideas were obvious and could be understood by everybody. But there was also limited fame. Newton and Galileo and Enrico Fermi were men of limited fame, and as I stood there with the atomizer in my hand my mother's eyes watered over and she told me she knew in her heart that one day I was going to be a man of limited fame. I was twelve years old.

After that day I found I could avoid a certain amount of stock work by staying up on the roof and staring into the fine layers of stratus clouds that floated above Arcade. In the *Encyclopedia Americana* I read about cirrus and cumulus and thunderheads, about inversion layers and currents like the currents at sea, and in the afternoons I went upstairs and watched. The sky was a changing thing, I found out. It was more than a blue sheet. Twirling with pollen and sunlight, it began to transform itself.

Often as I stood on the roof my father came outside and swept the sidewalk across the street. Through the telephone poles and crossed power lines he looked up at me, his broom strokes small and fierce as if he were hoeing hard ground. It irked him that my mother encouraged me to stay on the roof. He was a short man with direct habits and an understanding of how to get along in the world, and he believed that God rewarded only two things, courtesy and hard work. God did not reward looking at the sky. In the car my father acknowledged good drivers and in restaurants he left good tips. He knew the names of his customers. He never sold a rotten vegetable. He shook hands often, looked everyone in the eye, and on Friday nights when we went to the movies he made us sit in the front row of the theater. "Why should I pay to look over other people's shoulders?" he said. The movies made him talk. On the way back to the car he walked with his hands clasped behind him and greeted everyone who passed. He smiled. He mentioned the fineness of the evening as if he were the admiral or aviator we had just seen on the screen. "People like it," he said. "It's good for business." My mother was quiet, walking with her slender arms folded in front of her as if she were cold.

I liked the movies because I imagined myself doing everything the heroes did—deciding to invade at daybreak, swimming half the night against the seaward current—but whenever we left the theater I was disappointed. From the front row, life seemed like a clear set of decisions, but on the street afterward I realized that the world existed all around me and I didn't know what I wanted. The quiet of evening and the ordinariness of human voices startled me.

Sometimes on the roof, as I stared into the layers of horizon, the sounds on the street faded into this same ordinariness. One afternoon when I was standing

Man Looking at the Cosmos by Alberto Ruggieri.

under the star my father came outside and looked up at me. "You're in a trance," he called. I glanced down at him, then squinted back at the horizon. For a minute he waited, and then from across the street he threw a rock. He had a pitcher's arm and could have hit me if he wanted, but the rock sailed past me and clattered on the shingles. My mother came right out of the store anyway and stopped him. "I wanted him off the roof," I heard my father tell her later in the same frank voice in which he explained his position to vegetable salesmen. "If someone's throwing rocks at him he'll come down. He's no fool."

I was flattered by this, but my mother won the point and from then on I could stay up on the roof when I wanted. To appease my father I cleaned the electric star, and though he often came outside to sweep, he stopped telling me to come down. I thought about limited fame and spent a lot of time noticing the sky. When I looked closely it was a sea with waves and shifting colors, wind seams and denials of distance, and after a while I learned to look at it so that it entered my eye whole. It was blue liquid. I spent hours looking into its pale wash, looking for things, though I didn't know what. I looked for lines or sectors, the diamond shapes of daylight stars. Sometimes, silver-winged jets from the air force base across the hills turned the right way against the sun and went off like small flash bulbs on the horizon. There was nothing that struck me and stayed, though, nothing with the brilliance of white light or electric explosion that I thought came with discovery, so after a while I changed my idea of discovery. I just stood on the roof and stared. When my mother asked me, I told her that I might be seeing new things but that seeing change took time. "It's slow," I told her. "It may take years."

The first time I let her steal I chalked it up to surprise. I was working the front register when she walked in, a thin, tall woman in a plaid dress that looked wilted. She went right to the standup display of cut-price, nearly expired breads and crackers, where she took a loaf of rye from the shelf. Then she turned and looked me in the eye. We were looking into each other's eyes when she walked out the front door. Through the blue-and-white LOOK UP TO STAR FOOD sign on the window I watched her cross the street.

There were two or three other shoppers in the store, and over the tops of the potato chip packages I could see my mother's broom. My father was in back unloading chicken parts. Nobody else had seen her come in; nobody had seen her leave. I locked the cash drawer and walked to the aisle where my mother was sweeping.

"I think someone just stole."

My mother wheeled a trash receptacle when she swept, and as I stood there she closed it, put down her broom, and wiped her face with her handkerchief. "You couldn't get him?"

"It was a her."

"A lady?"

"I couldn't chase her. She came in and took a loaf of rye and left."

I had chased plenty of shoplifters before. They were kids usually, in sneakers and coats too warm for the weather. I chased them up the aisle and out the door, then to the corner and around it while ahead of me they tried to toss whatever it was—Twinkies, freeze-pops—into the sidewalk hedges. They cried when I caught them, begged me not to tell their parents. First time, my father said, scare them real good. Second time, call the law. I took them back with me to the store, held them by the collar as we walked. Then I set them in the straight-back chair in the stockroom and gave them a speech my father had written. It was printed on a blue index card taped to the door. DO YOU KNOW WHAT YOU HAVE DONE? it began. DO YOU KNOW WHAT IT IS TO STEAL? I learned to pause between the questions, pace the room, check the card. "Give them time to get scared," my father said. He was expert at this. He never talked to them until he had dusted the vegetables or run a couple of women through the register. "Why should I stop my work for a kid who steals from me?" he said. When he finally came into the stockroom he moved and spoke the way policemen do at the scene of an accident. His manner was slow and deliberate. First he asked me what they had stolen. If I had recovered whatever it was, he took it and held it up to the light, turned it over in his fingers as if it were of large value. Then he opened the freezer door and led the kid inside to talk about law and punishment amid the frozen beef carcasses. He paced as he spoke, breathed clouds of vapor into the air.

In the end, though, my mother usually got him to let them off. Once when he wouldn't, when he had called the police to pick up a third-offense boy who sat trembling in the stockroom, my mother called him to the front of the store to talk to a customer. In the stockroom we kept a key to the back door hidden under a silver samovar[1] that had belonged to my grandmother, and when my father was in front that afternoon my mother came to the rear, took it out, and opened the back door. She leaned down to the boy's ear. "Run," she said.

The next time she came in it happened the same way. My father was at the vegetable tier, stacking avocados. My mother was in back listening to the radio. It was afternoon. I rang in a customer, then looked up while I was putting the milk cartons in the bottom of the bag, and there she was. Her gray eyes were looking into mine. She had two cans of pineapple juice in her hands, and on the way out she held the door for an old woman.

---

[1] **samovar:** a metal urn with a tap, used for heating water for tea.

That night I went up to clean the star. The air was clear. It was warm. When I finished wiping the glass I moved out over the edge of the eaves and looked into the distance where little turquoise squares—lighted swimming pools—stood out against the hills.

"Dade—"

It was my father's voice from behind the peak of the roof. "Yes?"

"Come over to this side."

I mounted the shallow-pitched roof, went over the peak, and edged down the other slope to where I could see his silhouette against the lights on Route 5. He was smoking. I got up and we stood together at the edge of the shingled eaves. In front of us trucks rumbled by on the interstate, their trailers lit at the edges like the mast lights of ships. "Look across the highway," he said.

"I am."

"What do you see?"

"Cars."

"What else?"

"Trucks."

For a while he didn't say anything. He dragged a few times on his cigarette, then pinched off the lit end and put the rest back in the pack. A couple of motorcycles went by, a car with one headlight, a bus.

"Do you know what it's like to live in a shack?" he said.

"No."

"You don't want to end up in a place like that. And it's damn easy to do if you don't know what you want. You know how easy it is?"

"Easy," I said.

"You have to know what you want."

For years my father had been trying to teach me competence and industry. Since I was nine I had been squeeze-drying mops before returning them to the closet, double-counting change, sweeping under the lip of the vegetable bins even if the dirt there was invisible to customers. On the basis of industry, my father said, Star Food had grown from a two-aisle, one-freezer corner store to the largest grocery in Arcade. When I was eight he had bought the failing gas station next door and built additions, so that now Star Food had nine aisles, separate coolers for dairy, soda, and beer, a tiered vegetable stand, a glass-fronted butcher counter, a part-time butcher, and, under what used to be the rain roof of the failing gas station, free parking while you shopped. When I started high school we moved into the apartment next door, and at meals we discussed store improvements.

Soon my father invented a grid system for easy location of foods. He stayed up one night and painted, and the next morning there was a new coordinate system on the ceiling of the store. It was a grid, A through J, 1 through 10. For weeks there were drops of blue paint in his eyelashes.

A few days later my mother pasted up fluorescent stars among the grid squares. She knew about the real constellations and was accurate with the ones she stuck to the ceiling, even though she also knew that the aisle lights in Star Food stayed on day and night, so that her stars were going to be invisible. We saw them only once, in fact, in a blackout a few months later, when they lit up in hazy clusters around the store.

"Do you know why I did it?" she asked me the night of the blackout as we stood beneath their pale light.

"No."

"Because of the idea."

She was full of ideas, and one was that I was accomplishing something on the shallow-pitched section of our roof. Sometimes she sat at the dormer window and watched me. Through the glass I could see the slender outlines of her cheekbones. "What do you see?" she asked. On warm nights she leaned over the sill and pointed out the constellations. "They are the illumination of great minds," she said.

After the woman walked out the second time I began to think a lot about what I wanted. I tried to discover what it was, and I had an idea it would come to me on the roof. In the evenings I sat up there and thought. I looked for signs. I threw pebbles down into the street and watched where they hit. I read the newspaper, and stories about ballplayers or jazz musicians began to catch my eye. When he was ten years old, Johnny Unitas strung a tire from a tree limb and spent afternoons throwing a football through it as it swung. Dizzy Gillespie played with an orchestra when he was seven. There was an emperor who ruled China at age eight. What could be said about me? He swept the dirt no one could see under the lip of the vegetable bins.

The day after the woman had walked out the second time, my mother came up on the roof while I was cleaning the star. She usually wore medium heels and stayed away from the shingled roof, but that night she came up. I had been over the glass once when I saw her coming through the dormer window, skirt hem and white shoes lit by moonlight. Most of the insects were cleaned off and steam was drifting up into the night. She came through the window, took off her shoes, and edged down the roof until she was standing next to me at the star. "It's a beautiful night," she said.

"Cool."

"Dade, when you're up here do you ever think about what is in the mind of a great man when he makes a discovery?"

The night was just making its transition from the thin sky to the thick, the air was taking on weight, and at the horizon distances were shortening. I looked out over the plain and tried to think of an answer. That day I had been thinking about a story my father occasionally told. Just before he and my mother were married he took her to the top of the hills that surround Arcade. They stood with the New Jerusalem River, western California, and the sea on their left, and Arcade on their right. My father has always planned things well, and that day as they stood in the hill pass a thunderstorm covered everything west, while Arcade, shielded by hills, was lit by the sun. He asked her which way she wanted to go. She must have realized it was a test, because she thought for a moment and then looked to the right, and when they drove down from the hills that day my father mentioned the idea of a grocery. Star Food didn't open for a year after, but that was its conception, I think, in my father's mind. That afternoon as they stood with the New Jerusalem flowing below them, the plains before them, and my mother in a cotton skirt she had made herself, I think my father must have seen right through to the end of his life.

I had been trying to see right through to the end of my life, too, but these thoughts never led me in any direction. Sometimes I sat and remembered the unusual things that had happened to me. Once I had found the perfect, shed skin of a rattlesnake. My mother told my father that this indicated my potential for science. I was on the roof another time when it hailed apricot-size balls of ice on a summer afternoon. The day was hot and there was only one cloud, but as it approached from the distance it spread a shaft of darkness below it as if it had fallen through itself to the earth, and when it reached the New Jerusalem the river began throwing up spouts of water. Then it crossed onto land and I could see the hailstones denting parked cars. I went back inside the attic and watched it pass, and when I came outside again and picked up the ice balls that rolled between the corrugated roof spouts, their prickly edges melted in my fingers. In a minute they were gone. That was the rarest thing that had ever happened to me. Now I waited for rare things because it seemed to me that if you traced back the lives of men you arrived at some sort of sign, rainstorm at one horizon and sunlight at the other. On the roof I waited for mine. Sometimes I thought about the woman and sometimes I looked for silhouettes in the blue shapes between the clouds.

"Your father thinks you should be thinking about the store," said my mother.

"I know."

"You'll own the store some day."

There was a carpet of cirrus clouds in the distance, and we watched them as their bottom edges were gradually lit by the rising moon. My mother tilted back her head and looked up into the stars. "What beautiful names," she said. "Cassiopeia, Lyra, Aquila."

"The Big Dipper," I said.

"Dade?"

"Yes?"

"I saw the lady come in yesterday."

"I didn't chase her."

"I know."

"What do you think of that?"

"I think you're doing more important things," she said. "Dreams are more important than rye bread." She took the bobby pins from her hair and held them in her palm. "Dade, tell me the truth. What do you think about when you come up here?"

In the distance there were car lights, trees, aluminum power poles. There were several ways I could have answered.

I said, "I think I'm about to make a discovery."

After that my mother began meeting me at the bottom of the stairs when I came down from the roof. She smiled expectantly. I snapped my fingers, tapped my feet. I blinked and looked at my canvas shoe-tips. She kept smiling. I didn't like this so I tried not coming down for entire afternoons, but this only made her look more expectant. On the roof my thoughts piled into one another. I couldn't even think of something that was undiscovered. I stood and thought about the woman.

Then my mother began leaving little snacks on the sill of the dormer window. Crackers, cut apples, apricots. She arranged them in fan shapes or twirls on a plate, and after a few days I started working regular hours again. I wore my smock and checked customers through the register and went upstairs only in the evenings. I came down after my mother had gone to sleep. I was afraid the woman was coming back, but I couldn't face my mother twice a day at the bottom of the stairs. So I worked and looked up at the door whenever customers entered. I did stock work when I could, stayed in back where the air was refrigerated, but I sweated anyway. I unloaded melons, tuna fish, cereal. I counted the cases of freeze-pops, priced the cans of All-American ham. At the swinging door between the stockroom and the back of the store my heart went dizzy. The woman knew something about me.

In the evenings on the roof I tried to think what it was. I saw mysterious new clouds, odd combinations of cirrus and stratus. How did she root me into the linoleum floor with her gray stare? Above me on the roof the sky was simmering. It was blue gas. I knew she was coming back.

It was raining when she did. The door opened and I felt the wet breeze, and when I looked up she was standing with her back to me in front of the shelves of cheese and dairy, and this time I came out from the counter and stopped behind her. She smelled of the rain outside.

"Look," I whispered, "why are you doing this to me?"

She didn't turn around. I moved closer. I was gathering my words, thinking of the blue index card, when the idea of limited fame came into my head. I stopped. How did human beings understand each other across huge spaces except with the lowest of ideas? I have never understood what it is about rain that smells, but as I stood there behind the woman I suddenly realized I was smelling the inside of clouds. What was between us at that moment was an idea we had created ourselves. When she left with a carton of milk in her hand I couldn't speak.

On the roof that evening I looked into the sky, out over the plains, along the uneven horizon. I thought of the view my father had seen when he was a young man. I wondered whether he had imagined Star Food then. The sun was setting. The blues and oranges were mixing into black, and in the distance windows were lighting up along the hillsides.

"Tell me what I want," I said then. I moved closer to the edge of the eaves and repeated it. I looked down over the alley, into the kitchen across the way, into living rooms, bedrooms, across slate rooftops. "Tell me what I want," I called. Cars pulled in and out of the parking lot. Big rigs rushed by on the interstate. The air around me was as cool as water, the lighted swimming pools like pieces of the daytime sky. An important moment seemed to be rushing up. "Tell me what I want," I said again.

Then I heard my father open the window and come out onto the roof. He walked down and stood next to me, the bald spot on top of his head reflecting the streetlight. He took out a cigarette, smoked it for a while, pinched off the end. A bird fluttered around the light pole across the street. A car crossed below us with the words JUST MARRIED on the roof.

"Look," he said, "your mother's tried to make me understand this." He paused to put the unsmoked butt back in the pack. "And maybe I can. You think the gal's a little down and out; you don't want to kick her when she's down. Okay, I can understand that. So I've decided something, and you want to know what?"

He shifted his hands in his pockets and took a few steps torward the edge of the roof.

"You want to know what?"

"What?"

"I'm taking you off the hook. Your mother says you've got a few thoughts, that maybe you're on the verge of something, so I decided it's okay if you let the lady go if she comes in again."

"What?"

"I said it's okay if you let the gal go. You don't have to chase her."

"You're going to let her steal?"

"No," he said. "I hired a guard."

He was there the next morning in clothes that were all dark blue. Pants, shirt, cap, socks. He was only two or three years older than I was. My father introduced him to me as Mr. Sellers. "Mr. Sellers," he said, "this is Dade." He had a badge on his chest and a ring of keys the size of a doughnut on his belt. At the door he sat jingling them.

I didn't say much to him, and when I did my father came out from the back and counted register receipts or stocked impulse items near where he sat. We weren't saying anything important, though. Mr. Sellers didn't carry a gun, only the doughnut-size key ring, so I asked him if he wished he did.

"Sure," he said.

"Would you use it?"

"If I had to."

I thought of him using his gun if he had to. His hands were thick and their backs were covered with hair. This seemed to go along with shooting somebody if he had to. My hands were thin and white and the hair on them was like the hair on a girl's cheek.

During the days he stayed by the front. He smiled at customers and held the door for them, and my father brought him sodas every hour or so. Whenever the guard smiled at a customer I thought of him trying to decide whether he was looking at the shoplifter.

And then one evening everything changed.

I was on the roof. The sun was low, throwing slanted light. From beyond the New Jerusalem and behind the hills, four air force jets appeared. They disappeared, then appeared again, silver dots trailing white tails. They climbed and cut and looped back, showing dark and light like a school of fish. When they turned against the sun their wings flashed. Between the hills and the river they dipped low onto the plain, then shot upward and toward me. One dipped, the others followed. Across the New Jerusalem they turned back and made two great circles, one inside the other, then dipped again and leveled off in my direction. The sky seemed small enough for them to fall through. I could see the double tails, then the wings and the jets. From across the river they shot straight toward the store, angling up so I could see the V-wings and camouflage and rounded bomb bays, and I covered my ears, and in a moment they were across the water and then they were above me, and as they passed over they barrel-rolled and flew upside down and showed me their black cockpit glass so that my heart came up into my mouth.

I stood there while they turned again behind me and lifted back toward the hills, trailing threads of vapor, and by the time their booms subsided I knew I wanted the woman to be caught. I had seen a sign. Suddenly the sky was water-clear. Distances moved in, houses stood out against the hills, and it seemed to me that I had turned a corner and now looked over a rain-washed street. The woman was a thief. This was a simple fact and it presented itself to me simply. I felt the world dictating its course.

I went downstairs and told my father I was ready to catch her. He looked at me, rolled the chewing gum in his cheek. "I'll be damned."

"My life is making sense," I said.

When I unloaded potato chips that night I laid the bags in the aluminum racks as if I were putting children to sleep in their beds. Dust had gathered under the lip of the vegetable bins, so I swept and mopped there and ran a wet cloth over the stalls. My father slapped me on the back a couple of times. In school once I had looked through a microscope at the tip of my own finger, and now as I looked around the store everything seemed to have been magnified in the same way. I saw cracks in the linoleum floor, speckles of color in the walls.

This kept up for a couple of days, and all the time I waited for the woman to come in. After a while it was more than just waiting; I looked forward to the day when she would return. In my eyes she would find nothing but resolve. How bright the store seemed to me then when I swept, how velvety the skins of the melons beneath the sprayer bottle. When I went up to the roof I scrubbed the star with the wet cloth and came back down. I didn't stare into the clouds and I didn't think about the woman except with the thought of catching her. I described her perfectly for the guard. Her gray eyes. Her plaid dress.

After I started working like this my mother began to go to the back room in the afternoons and listen to music. When I swept the rear I heard the melodies of operas. They came from behind the stockroom door while I waited for the woman to return, and when my mother came out she had a look about her of disappointment. Her skin was pale and smooth, as if the blood had run to deeper parts.

"Dade," she said one afternoon as I stacked tomatoes in a pyramid, "it's easy to lose your dreams."

"I'm just stacking tomatoes."

She went back to the register. I went back to stacking, and my father, who'd been patting me on the back, winking at me from behind the butcher counter, came over and helped me.

"I notice your mother's been talking to you."

"A little."

We finished the tomatoes and moved on to the lettuce.

"Look," he said, "it's better to do what you have to do, so I wouldn't spend your time worrying frontwards and backwards about everything. Your life's not so long as you think it's going to be."

We stood there rolling heads of butterball lettuce up the shallow incline of the display cart. Next to me he smelled like Aqua Velva.

"The lettuce is looking good," I said.

Then I went up to the front of the store. "I'm not sure what my dreams are," I said to my mother. "And I'm never going to discover anything. All I've ever done on the roof is look at the clouds."

Then the door opened and the woman came in. I was standing in front of the counter, hands in my pockets, my mother's eyes watering over, the guard looking out the window at a couple of girls, everything revolving around the point of calm that, in retrospect, precedes surprises. I'd been waiting for her for a week, and now she came in. I realized I never expected her. She stood looking at me, and for a few moments I looked back. Then she realized what I was up to. She turned around to leave, and when her back was to me I stepped over and grabbed her.

I've never liked fishing much, even though I used to go with my father, because the moment a fish jumps on my line a tree's length away in the water I feel as if I've suddenly lost something. I'm always disappointed and sad, but now as I held the woman beneath the shoulder I felt none of this disappointment. I felt strong and good. She was thin, and I could make out the bones and tendons in her arm. As I led her back toward the stockroom, through the bread aisle, then the potato chips that were puffed and stacked like a row of pillows, I heard my mother begin to weep behind the register. Then my father came up behind me. I didn't turn around, but I knew he was there and I knew the deliberately calm way he was walking. "I'll be back as soon as I dust the melons," he said.

I held the woman tightly under her arm but despite this she moved in a light way, and suddenly, as we paused before the stockroom door, I felt as if I were leading her onto the dance floor. This flushed me with remorse. Don't spend your whole life looking backwards and forwards, I said to myself. Know what you want. I pushed the door open and we went in. The room was dark. It smelled of my whole life. I turned on the light and sat her down in the straight-back chair, then crossed the room and stood against the door. I had spoken to many children as they sat in this chair. I had frightened them, collected the candy they had tried to hide between the cushions, presented it to my father when he came in. Now I looked at the blue card. DO YOU KNOW WHAT YOU HAVE DONE? it said. DO YOU KNOW WHAT IT IS TO STEAL? I tried to think of what to say to the woman. She sat trembling slightly. I approached the chair and stood in front of her. She looked up at me. Her hair was gray around the roots.

"Do you want to go out the back?" I said.

She stood up and I took the key from under the silver samovar. My father would be there in a moment, so after I let her out I took my coat from the hook and followed. The evening was misty. She crossed the lot, and I hurried and came up next to her. We walked fast and stayed behind cars, and when we had gone a distance I turned and looked back. The stockroom door was closed. On the roof the star cast a pale light that whitened the aluminum-sided eaves.

It seemed we would be capable of a great communication now, but as we walked I realized I didn't know what to say to her. We went down the street without talking. The traffic was light, evening was approaching, and as we passed below some trees the streetlights suddenly came on. This moment has always amazed me. I knew the woman had seen it too, but it is always a disappointment to mention a thing like this. The streets and buildings took on their night shapes. Still we didn't say anything to each other. We kept walking beneath the pale violet of the lamps, and after a few more blocks I just stopped at one corner. She went on, crossed the street, and I lost sight of her.

I stood there until the world had rotated fully into the night, and for a while I tried to make myself aware of the spinning of the earth. Then I walked back toward the store. When they slept that night, my mother would dream of discovery and my father would dream of low-grade crooks. When I thought of this and the woman I was sad. It seemed you could never really know another person. I felt alone in the world, in the way that makes me aware of sound and temperature, as if I had just left a movie theater and stepped into an alley where a light rain was falling, and the wind was cool, and, from somewhere, other people's voices could be heard.

---

1. Exploring Meaning
a. At what moment in the story does the narrator, Dade, feel that his life is "making sense"? What causes him to feel this way?
b. In what ways is Dade like both his father and his mother? How is he different?
c. What does Dade do that disappoints both of his parents?
d. Were you satisfied with the ending of this story? Why or why not? How would you have ended it?

2. Drama *Role Play* With a partner, role-play a conversation between Dade and one of the following characters: his mother, his father, or the shoplifter. Your role play should be set some time after the events at the end of the story. Remember to consider the qualities and personality of the character you are portraying.
Self-Assessment: Briefly list the skills you used to develop and present your role play. Which of these skills do you think are most necessary in the workplace? How would you rate your command of these skills?

3. Technique and Style *Point of View* Rewrite the first three paragraphs of the story using the objective (third-person) point of view. Compare the original point of view to the rewritten version. Which do you find more effective and readable? Why? Who does Ethan Canin want the reader to focus on? In your opinion, could he have achieved this by using the third-person point of view? Explain.

4. Film Study Assume that a film director wants to make a movie of this story. Choose your favourite scene, and consider how it could be recreated as a movie scene. Create a storyboard with at least ten frames to represent your chosen scene. Remember that each frame should include instructions for lighting, sound effects, music, camera angles and shots, and other technical details. Use computer software or draw your storyboard by hand. Present your work to your classmates, explaining what you were trying to accomplish in your scene.

5. Visual Communication *Illustrating Characters* Examine the image on page 17 and consider how effectively it represents the story or the main character. Use a style similar to Alberto Ruggieri's to develop an image for another character in the story. Present your work to your classmates.

What can you learn about people from watching them on the job? Do the facial expressions, gestures, and body language of the people in these photos suggest how they feel about their work?

A Photographer at Work

Photo Essay by Vincenzo Pietropaolo, with text by Andrew Gorham

Photographer Vincenzo Pietropaolo wanted to use his camera to reclaim workers from their historical anonymity. His shots of men and women—on the factory floor and in nursing homes—capture the varied lives of working people across the country.

Painter Dougald Westhaven puts the final touches on a Norwegian liner built at Halifax Shipyard Ltd., in Halifax, Nova Scotia. Pietropaolo saw this shot from across the shipyard and ran to catch Westhaven before he moved on.

Sue Carly examines a steering column at Mackie Automotive Systems in Whitby, Ontario. "The sheer concentration she had really struck me. There was all this machinery and people around, but she was completely focused."

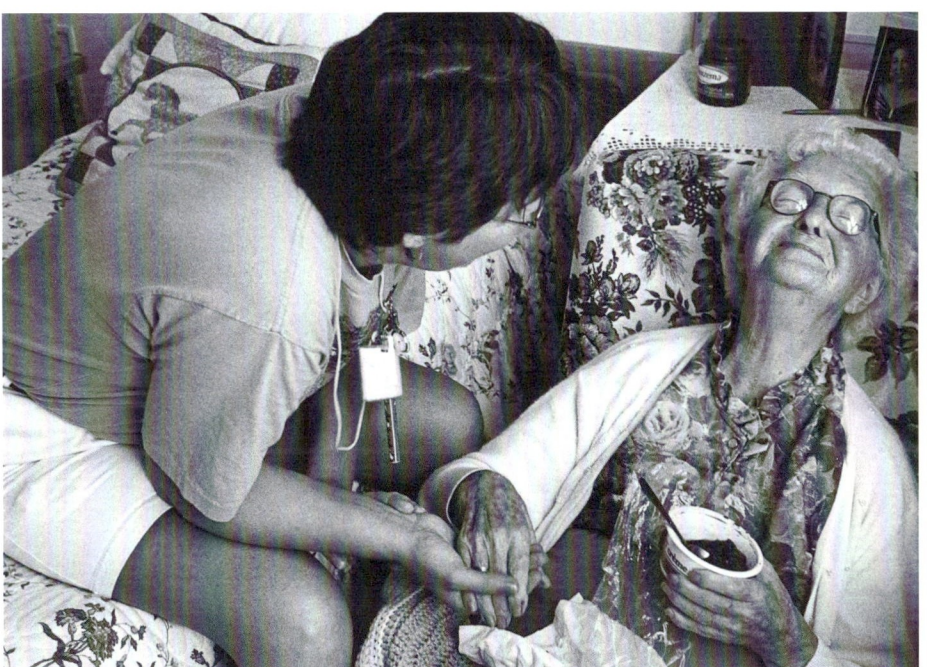

Pam Moisman, a health-care worker at Mahone Bay Nursing Home in Mahone Bay, Nova Scotia, shares some time with Ella Hints, 100. "Ella was so pleased to be in a photo with the woman who takes care of her. She was very proud of her."

Jagdev Singh Bal adjusts the hatch to a light armoured vehicle at the General Motors, Diesel Division plant in London, Ontario. Pietropaolo says the repetition in most work allows him to identify a photo opportunity and then get into the best position for the shot.

1. Exploring Meaning
a. Examine each photo. Write a sentence or two describing each scene.
b. What is the mood in each photo?
c. Does this photo essay present a realistic portrayal of people at work? Explain.

2. Visual Communication *Analyse Images* Which of the images in this photo essay communicates most strongly to you? Why? Examine this photo closely. Write a paragraph describing what the photo communicates, and your personal reaction to the image. Explain how its composition (choice of image, type of shot, angle, and so on) creates this response. Write your own caption for the photo.

3. Media *Collage* Create a collage about the varied lives of people at work. Make sure to include a range of textures, images, and words or phrases to convey your message.

Self-Assessment: Examine your collage. Does the layout help express your message? Is the message clear? Have you used a variety of images and words? Is your collage visually appealing?

Do you think the use of computer technology is causing a decrease or an increase in reading, writing, speaking, and listening skills? Debate this with a partner.

Hard Edges, Soft Skills

Expository Essay by Ann Coombs

Technological advances have indeed been a fantastic boon to business in terms of speed and scope. Time has been compressed into femtoseconds.[1] Geography is irrelevant. But what corporations—and the people who work in them—sometimes forget is that what makes a message important is the content, not the means of sending it.

As Mark Starowicz, project director and executive director of the Canadian Broadcasting Corporation's "The Canadian History Project," said, "What we are seeing may be occasioned by one piece of technology—the microchip—but it is not one revolution; it is a cluster of revolutions. Sometimes—I find this interesting—we are actually seeing the return of old media that we thought were dead or static. The digital age has, for example, resurrected telegraphy in the form of e-mail, restoring an almost Victorian level of letter-writing. It is a revolution in telephony, a century-old medium where we weren't expecting much excitement."

When workers send e-mails, they are sending letters, reports, proposals or responses. When they leave voice-mail messages, they are exchanging notes of information. Yet the prevailing view is to downgrade the need to learn how to develop and present thoughtful, well-crafted, clear content. The definition of technological literacy rarely, if ever, appears to include writing and speaking skills.

When workers use real-time video, video conferencing and other highly sophisticated technological tools, they are still sitting in isolation in front of

---

[1] **femtosecond:** a quadrillionth of a second.

a monitor. Even if they can see the person with whom they are linked, they will be blocked by a barrier that does not let them see or hear, for example, a foot tapping impatiently. Nor will they have the opportunity to build a friendship bit by bit by sharing moments of understanding over an informal lunch.

The day will come when 21st-century workers finally begin to understand that they need and want something more. The tools, however sophisticated, will lose their luster, as workers realize they are not truly connecting to their workplaces or to each other. That is when the demand for a new language characterized by honesty, energy and clarity will become a clamor—the day workers become aware of their hunger for true, full circle, say–listen–hear communication. They will be as hungry for it as they are for respect, regard and a spiritually supportive workplace.

This realization will also dawn on employers as they wage the war for talent. The first effects in the marketplace of knowledge workers being fought over are already being felt. But the shortcomings of these workers are also becoming apparent. As reported in *Stepping Up: Skills and Opportunities in the Knowledge Economy,* a study done in 2000 by the Conference Board of Canada, these workers are technically skilled but they generally do not have the "soft" skills, such as teamwork and oral and written communications. They are valuable for their technical talents and skill for moving messages across time and space. But they have not developed the discerning and intuitive skills of human discourse. They are not equipped to say, listen and hear beyond tightly defined boundaries. They are clumsy in social environments. These workers will become liabilities that corporations cannot tolerate if they are to compete successfully in the global marketplace.

Joseph F. Coates, president of Coates & Jarratt Inc., a Washington, D.C. company engaged in futures research, lays some of the responsibility at the door of the educational system. "The most important skills for the worker . . . are skills in communication—not just reading and writing, but in computation, and perhaps most importantly of all, in listening. Other skill needs will emphasize human interaction, sensitivity to people, ability to work in teams—the sorts of things that are reflected in a number of interesting books and reports on 'emotional intelligence.'"

1. Exploring Meaning

a. What is the **thesis** of this essay?

b. In your opinion, has technology promoted efficiency in the workplace? Explain.

c. What will workers in the twenty-first century need and want in their workplaces?

d. What do you think is meant by the words *emotional intelligence* at the end of this essay? Why is emotional intelligence important in the workplace?

e. Recall a time when you felt isolated by technology. Share this incident with a partner.

The **thesis** is the main idea, position, or view of the essay writer; it is the hypothesis of the writer's work.

2. Career Connections What do you believe are the top ten skills required by employers today? Develop a list of employability skills for one of the following occupations: biologist, sales clerk, construction worker, kindergarten teacher, or another career of your choice. Compare your list with the lists of other classmates. How many of these skills do you possess? Do a personal inventory of your employability skills.

3. Writing *Letter to the Editor* Write a letter to your local newspaper to present the point of view that today's workers *do* have the "soft skills" needed to function effectively. Justify your position with personal anecdotes, facts, and information from articles you have read.

Peer Assessment: Ask a classmate to read your letter and assess its clarity, language, voice, and use of language conventions.

Mud Woman's First Encounter with the World of Money and Business

Narrative Poem by Nora Naranjo-Morse

She unwrapped her clay figures,
    unfolding the cloth each was nestled in,
    carefully, almost with ceremony.
    Concerning herself with the specific curves, bends and
    idiosyncrasies, that made each piece her own.
Standing these forms upright, displaying them from
    one side to the next, Mud Woman
    could feel her pride surging upward
    from a secret part within her,
    translating into a smile that passed her lips.
    All of this in front of the gallery owner.
After all the creations were unveiled, Mud Woman held her
    breath.
    The gallery owner, peering
    from behind fashionably designed
    bifocals, examined each piece
    with an awareness Mud Woman
    knew very little of.
    The owner cleared her throat, asking:
    "First of all dear, do you have a résumé? You know,
    something written that would identify you to the public.
    Who is your family?
    Are any of them well known in the Indian art world?"

Pearlene by Nora Naranjo-Morse. Heard Museum.

Mud Woman hesitated, trying desperately to connect
    this business woman's voice with her questions,
    like a foreigner trying to comprehend
    the innuendos of a new language, unexpected
    and somewhat intimidating.
The center of what Mud Woman knew to be real
    was shifting with each moment in the gallery.
    The format of this exchange was a new dimension
    from what was taken for granted at home,
    where the clay, moist and smooth,
    waited to be rounded and coiled
    into sensuous shapes, in a workroom
    Mud Woman and her man had built
    of earth too.
    All this struggled against a blaring radio
    with poor reception and noon hour
    traffic bustling beyond the frame walls.

Handling each piece, the merchant quickly judged
        whether or not Mud Woman's work would be a profitable
            venture.
        "Well," she began, "your work is
        strangely different, certainly not traditional
        Santa Clara pottery and I'm not
        sure there is a market for
        your particular style, especially
        since no one knows who you are.
        However, if for some reason you make it big,
        I can be the first to say, 'I discovered you.'
        So, I'll buy a few pieces and we'll see how it goes."
        Without looking up, she opened a large, black checkbook,
        quickly scribbling the needed information to make
        the gallery's check valuable.
        Hesitantly, Mud Woman exchanged her work for the
        unexpectedly smaller sum that wholesale prices dictated.
After a few polite, but obviously strained pleasantries
        Mud Woman left, leaving behind her
        shaped pieces of earth.
        Walking against the honks of a harried
        lunch crowd, Nan chu Kweejo[1] spoke:
        "Navi ayu, ti gin nau na muu,
        nai sa aweh kucha?"
        "My daughter, is this the way it goes,
        this pottery business?"
        Hearing this, Mud Woman lowered her head,
        walking against the crowd of workers
        returning from lunch.
Nan chu Kweejo's question,
clouded Mud Woman's vision with a mist
of lost innocence,
        as she left the city
            and the world of
                money and business behind.

---

[1] **Nan chu Kweejo:** Clay mother.

1. Exploring Meaning

a. How does Mud Woman's personality differ from that of the gallery owner?

b. Why is there conflict between Mud Woman and the gallery owner?

c. Why are Mud Woman's pieces of pottery so special?

d. Why does Nan chu Kweejo's question cloud "Mud Woman's vision with a mist/of lost innocence"?

e. Do you think Mud Woman's first encounter with the world of money and business will be her last? Discuss your answer with a partner.

2. Genre Study *Narrative Poetry* Narrative poetry contains many of the elements found in fiction such as character, setting, **conflict**, and theme. With a partner, identify these elements as they appear in the poem. Discuss their effectiveness in telling Mud Woman's story.

> **Conflict** is the problem or struggle in a story that the main character has to solve or face.

3. Writing *Script* Reread this poem and compose a dialogue, in script form, of what takes place. Before you begin, look for examples of scripts to use as models. Make sure that your conversation is consistent with the poet's original presentation of Mud Woman and the gallery owner.

4. Film Study Assume that a producer has decided to use this poem to develop a feature film. Create a movie poster to advertise and promote this movie, incorporating details from the poem. What type of audience would you expect this movie to attract? Consider your audience and purpose as you design your poster. Be sure to include suitable images, names of actors, a title, capsule reviews, and so on. Examine real movie posters for ideas before you start.

Self-Assessment: Examine your poster and assess how accurately you have portrayed the poem and how effectively you have used the features of movie posters. How effectively does the poster match your purpose and audience?

List five adjectives that could describe how you might behave in a work environment.

THE WORK FARCE

Cartoons by Dušan Petričić

It takes all types to make a corporate community.

1. The Socialite
2. The Climber
3. The Social Convenor

4. **The Gatekeeper**
5. **The Hard Worker**
6. **The Grump**
7. **The Class Clown**

8. The Gossip
9. The Neurotic
10. The Ruthlessly Ambitious

1. Exploring Meaning

a. Describe the **tone** of these cartoons.

b. Discuss the meaning of, and wordplay in, the title "The Work Farce." Is it an effective title? Explain.

c. What is a *gatekeeper*? Look up this word in a dictionary and then discuss its meaning in a small group.

d. What is your opinion of the range of personalities illustrated in "The Work Farce"? Would you add or delete any? If so, which ones?

2. Oral Communication *Opinion Poll* Survey others to determine which personality type in the cartoons they would find most difficult to work with. Ask them for reasons to support their opinions. Share this information in a class discussion.

3. Critical Thinking Discuss in small groups how the cartoons in "The Work Farce" reflect a classroom community. What other personality types would you add to a classroom version of "The Work Farce"? What would you call that classroom community?

Self-Assessment: Did you contribute ideas to the group discussion? Did you listen and respond appropriately to the contributions of others?

Shoe Store

Poem by Raymond Souster

A good thirty years since I stood in this store,
shy boy of fifteen become forty-five.
Nothing's changed much, except the front
is a shoe store complete with fancy mirrors,
theatre folding seats, usual boxes piled
rack after rack to the ceiling.

The shoe repair's well to the rear,
separately walled off: in the old days
it was all shoe-making—whirling belts,
gleaming stitchers.
                  One thing that hasn't changed
is the shoemaker, no more bald
than he was then, stooped a little more
in the shoulders perhaps as he bends
over a buffer, working a pair of pumps
back and forth with complete absorption,
all the long years of skill centred
at the ends of his fingers, while I stand here quietly
(not wanting to break the spell I've somehow started)
for minutes before he notices me and nods.

Polish immigrant before the War, hardly able
to mouth an English word, he felt alien and lost
among us. All the strength in his body,
all his cunning, put to the service of his child,
beautiful girl I can scarcely remember,
early a piano virtuoso.
                Well, he's prospered,
no longer lives above the store. I wonder

if his wife's still alive, if all goes well
with his daughter.
                        But he wouldn't remember me,
so why bother? Why not leave it all
mercifully unknown?
                              I ask him simply,
"Can you stitch this up for tomorrow?"
and he answers, "Sure."
                        I don't ask for a ticket
and he doesn't offer one. I walk out slowly
between his mirrors, his shoe boxes,
close the door on thirty years gone forever.

---

1. Exploring Meaning

a. Does the shoemaker enjoy success? Support your answer with examples from the poem.

b. In your opinion, does the shoemaker remember the narrator? Explain your answer.

c. What do you think motivates the shoemaker to work so hard?

d. What words suggest his craft is a dying art?

e. Why does the narrator decide to leave the shoemaker's life "mercifully unknown"?

2. Writing *Character Profile* Write a paragraph describing the shoemaker. Use effective adjectives in your description so that a vivid image is created for your reader. Think of a person that you know who is in some way similar to the shoemaker. This may help make your description come alive.

Peer Assessment: Ask a classmate to read your character profile. From your profile, does your classmate get an accurate impression of the shoemaker? Are his personality and visual appearance made clear in your description?

3. Film Study "Shoe Store" is a poem about achieving success; about the North American dream. List films you have seen that relate to the theme of Raymond Souster's poem. How do their messages about success compare with the one presented in "Shoe Store"?

Spare a dime?.com

Cartoon by David Sipress

1. Exploring Meaning

a. List three physical differences between the two main characters in this cartoon.

b. Explain the message of this cartoon to a partner.

c. Brainstorm a list of jobs and how these jobs have been affected by computer technology. Can you think of an occupation or a type of work that has not been influenced by technology?

2. Media *Cartoons* Collect a variety of cartoons from local newspapers and examine those that seem to be about the workplace. What common messages or themes about the workplace or technology are portrayed?

With a small group, discuss three ideas for a cartoon about workplace communications or workplace survival. What workplace setting would your cartoon have? What types of characters would the cartoon include?

Summer Job

Poem by Nellie P. Strowbridge

By the time the call came,
she'd done a day's work.
Now it was mid-afternoon,
and she was on her way
to fish wharves in Harbour Grace
to stand in fish guts 'til late at night,
her fingers like frozen caplin[1]
inside her rubber gloves,
gory colours splashing her barbel[2]
in the abstract confusion of
an artist's palette.
"It was," she said,
"gettin' out of the 'ouse."

She smiled through blue lips
as the suit- and tie-clad plant owner
stopped for a word or two.

She took a break
to feed the family cold drinks and snacks.
Soon she was back to cold cod,
and easterly winds knifing her back,
and sweeping around to lash her face.

---

[1] **caplin:** a small fish of the smelt family.
[2] **barbel:** a long, thin growth hanging from the mouth of some fishes or any
of several large freshwater fish that have such a growth.

She gutted as fast as she could
to keep up with her man,
who slashed fish throats
and laid their bellies open
at the blink of an eye,
before they slid to her.

By the time the work was done,
the hands of the clock
had often climbed to midnight.
She went home and,
as if she hadn't moved all day,
prepared a hot meal for her family.
Those summers,
sleep alone meant rest.

My mother was liberated:
She worked outside the home,
once in awhile.

Summer Fish by Mary Pratt. Oil on panel.

1. Exploring Meaning
a. What work does the woman in this poem do?
b. How is it suggested that this job is a family affair?
c. Who is the speaker in the poem?
d. What message is the reader left with?

2. Technique and Style *Imagery* Read "Summer Job" aloud and concentrate on its **imagery**. List examples of the following: a visual image, a thermal image (temperature), and a kinesthetic image (movement). What effect do these images have on the poem and the reader? Discuss the effectiveness of these images.

   Generate a list of these three types of images for a job you've had. You can organize these images into a chart.

> **Imagery** is the pictures that writers create in the readers' minds. They use descriptive techniques such as figures of speech (personification, metaphor, simile, oxymoron), alliteration, and allusions.

3. Language Conventions *Specialized Language* "Summer Job" uses idiom and dialect to help establish the setting. Find examples of both of these and identify the poem's setting. How do idiom and dialect contribute to the poem's effectiveness? What other words help the reader identify where the events in this poem take place?

4. Oral Communication *Interview* Interview a family member who works outside the home *and* takes care of a family. Find out how this person copes with the workload. How does he or she balance a job, family responsibilities, domestic work, and personal time? What is the biggest stress element? Present your interview to others using a format of your choice—a written transcript of the interview, an oral recording of the interview, or a profile that includes quotations, facts, and conclusions.

5. Visual Communication *Representing the Poem* With a partner, discuss the image that accompanies "Summer Job." Why do you think this image was chosen? What mood and message does the image convey? In your opinion, is it an appropriate image to accompany this poem? Why or why not? With your partner, create or find another image to represent this poem. Explain your choice to another group.

Self-Assessment: When analysing the effectiveness of images that accompany selections, do you consider the mood and message of both the selection and the image? Do you consider your personal response to both the selection and the image?

As you read this scene, think about the personal sacrifices needed to achieve fame, especially on the big screen.

Screen Test

Script by Sally Clark from *Saint Frances of Hollywood,* a two-act play

ACT 1, Scene 5

Film crew bustling about. FRANCES sees the MALE ACTOR she is to do the scene with.

FRANCES: (*goes up to him*) Hi, I'm Frances Farmer. Do you want to rehearse our lines together?

ACTOR: You don't have lines, do you?

FRANCES: I have a few.

ACTOR: Not enough to waste my time on. It's not your screen test.

FRANCES: I was under the impression that we were both being tested.

ACTOR: Oh la de da, "I was under the impression—" you're a real little lady, aren't you. They aren't interested in you, doll. It's me they're after. I'm gonna be playing the lead in some jungle movie.

FRANCES: Really?

ACTOR: Yeah. (*moves away*) Now, I gotta get into character. I'll do what I do best and you do what you do best. Just stand there and look beautiful. (*leaves*)

DIRECTOR: OKAY EVERYONE! TAKE YOUR PLACES!

The MALE ACTOR stands in front of the camera. FRANCES stands off to one side.

DIRECTOR: ACTION!

ACTOR: (*turns and looks*) My God! It's you!

FRANCES: Yes.

Camera turns briefly to FRANCES, then focuses back on the man.

ACTOR: Get away from me! I can't bear to be near you! (*turns away from FRANCES*)

FRANCES: (*enters his "Frame" by grabbing him and spinning him around*) Look at me, you fool!

ACTOR: What? Hey! She's not supposed to—

FRANCES: Do you think I've come all the way from New York to stand here and do nothing?

ACTOR: What? Now, wait a minute. THIS IS MY SCREEN TEST!

FRANCES: You killed your wife, Tom!

ACTOR: What!

DIRECTOR: Keep rolling.

ACTOR: I did not! (*acting*) HOW DARE YOU ACCUSE ME OF SUCH THINGS!

FRANCES: I was afraid you might hate me. Every night I dream that you are looking at me and don't recognize me. If only you knew! Ever since I arrived I've been walking here . . . by the lake.

ACTOR: GET THE HELL OUT OF MY SCREEN TEST!

DIRECTOR: CUT! (*to FRANCES*) What's that last part from?

FRANCES: A play. *The Seagull.*

DIRECTOR: Do you know any more?

FRANCES: Oh yes.

ACTOR: What about me!

DIRECTOR: Oh, sorry. Thanks for coming, Tom.

ACTOR: Robert! My name's Robert!

DIRECTOR: We'll call you. (*to FRANCES*) Can you do a little more?

FRANCES: (*nods*)

DIRECTOR: Roll it!

FRANCES: (*waits for camera to frame her face*) "For the happiness of being a writer or an actress, I would endure poverty and disillusionment; I would live in a garret and eat black bread, suffer dissatisfactions with myself and the recognition of my own imperfections, but in return, I should demand fame . . . real, resounding fame . . ."

1. Exploring Meaning

a. Who is Frances? What do you learn about her in this scene?

b. What do you find out about the male actor? Which character do you like more? Which character do you think the author wants you to like?

c. What is a *screen test*?

d. Explain the **irony** in the male actor speaking the words "just stand there and look beautiful."

e. In your opinion, will the male actor ever achieve fame? What about Frances? Discuss.

Irony occurs when a statement or situation means something different from (or even the opposite of) what is expected.

2. Language Conventions *Exclamation Marks* An exclamation mark is used by a writer to emphasize a word, point, or idea. Skim this scene, noting how the exclamation mark has been used. Read these lines aloud with a partner, paying particular attention to what the author wishes to emphasize.

3. Drama *Performance* In a small group, perform the scene you have just read. Discuss the tone of voice, volume, tempo, gestures, and body language an effective portrayal of your character requires. Try to convey the mood that you think Sally Clark was trying to achieve. If you wish, you can use props and costumes to make your presentation more realistic. Once you have memorized the lines and rehearsed, present the scene to your whole class.

Peer Assessment: Ask your classmates what they thought of your dramatic presentation. Did they find it consistent with their own interpretations of the scene? Did they enjoy it? What suggestions would they make to improve future performances?

4. Writing *Scene* Reread "Screen Test" and compose the next scene. Begin where this scene ends. Consider your audience and purpose before you start to write. Be consistent with the original scene in terms of voice, style, and character portrayal. Format your scene as a script. When you have a final draft, ask a classmate for feedback on your scene's clarity and effectiveness.

Genre Focus: Survival

The Butterfly

Poem by Pavel Friedmann

The last, the very last,
So richly, brightly, dazzlingly yellow.
Perhaps if the sun's tears would sing
    against a white stone . . .

Such, such a yellow
Is carried lightly 'way up high.
It went away I'm sure because it wished to
    kiss the world good-bye.

For seven weeks I've lived in here,
Penned up inside this ghetto.
But I have found what I love here.
The dandelions call to me
And the white chestnut branches in the court.
Only I never saw another butterfly.

That butterfly was the last one.
Butterflies don't live in here,
    in the ghetto.

1. Exploring Meaning

a. In the poem, the butterfly is a **symbol**. What does it symbolize?

b. What are the similarities between the speaker in the poem and the butterfly?

c. What is a *ghetto*? What is the importance of the ghetto in this poem? What connotations does the word *ghetto* have for you?

d. What is the impact of the final line: "Butterflies don't live in here,/in the ghetto"?

e. Explain to a partner why this poem belongs in a Survival unit.

> A **symbol** is an object or person that represents a quality, idea, or condition.

2. Visual Communication *Representing Poetry*

Focus on one nature image from the poem and illustrate it. Choose colours that enhance the mood you want to convey. Try to be consistent with the mood or feeling of the poem.

3. Making Connections

Find and read the book *The Diary of Anne Frank* or another selection about the Holocaust. How are the selection you read and this poem similar? How are they different? Create a comparison chart using headings such as *characters, setting, main idea, point of view, sequence of events,* and *striking images.*

Self-Assessment: Assess the clarity with which you have presented your ideas. How effectively, in your opinion, have you compared the selections? What skills and strategies have you used to help you make comparisons between the selections?

4. Genre Study *Poetry*

With a small group, discuss the structure and poetic devices in "The Butterfly." Compare this poem with other poems you have read recently and reflect on what makes a poem a poem. Are there any rules for writing poems? Are there any rules for the subject or content of poems? Discuss.

In a small group, discuss what you know about World War II.

Quint Tells His Story

An Excerpt from *Jaws*, Script by Peter Benchley and Carl Gottlieb

Hooper (Richard Dreyfuss): You were on the *Indianapolis*?

Brody (Roy Scheider): What happened?

Quint (Robert Shaw): Japanese submarine slammed two torpedoes into our side, chief. It was comin' back, from the island of Tinian Delady, just delivered the bomb. The Hiroshima bomb. Eleven hundred men went into the water. Vessel went down in twelve minutes. Didn't see the first shark for about a half an hour. Tiger. Thirteen footer. You know how you know that when you're in the water, chief? You tell by lookin' from the dorsal to the tail. Well, we didn't know. 'Cause our bomb mission had been so secret, no distress signal had been sent. Huh huh. They didn't even list us overdue for a week. Very first light, chief. The sharks come cruisin'. So we formed ourselves into tight groups. You know it's . . . kinda like ol' squares in battle like a, you see on a calendar, like the battle of Waterloo. And the idea was, the shark comes to the nearest man and then he'd start poundin' and hollerin' and screamin' and sometimes the shark would go away. Sometimes he wouldn't go away. Sometimes that shark, he looks right into you. Right into your eyes. You know the thing about a shark, he's got . . . lifeless eyes, black eyes, like a doll's eye. When he comes at ya, doesn't seem to be livin'. Until he bites ya and those black eyes roll over white. And then, ah then you hear that terrible high pitch screamin' and the ocean turns red and in spite of all the poundin' and the hollerin' they all come in and they rip you to pieces.

Y'know by the end of that first dawn, lost a hundred men! I don't know how many sharks, maybe a thousand! I don't know how many men, they averaged six an hour. On Thursday mornin' chief, I bumped into a friend of mine,

The terrifying motion picture from the terrifying No. 1 best seller.

JAWS

ROY SCHEIDER ROBERT SHAW RICHARD DREYFUSS

JAWS

Co-starring LORRAINE GARY · MURRAY HAMILTON · A ZANUCK/BROWN PRODUCTION
Screenplay by PETER BENCHLEY and CARL GOTTLIEB · Based on the novel by PETER BENCHLEY · Music by JOHN WILLIAMS
Directed by STEVEN SPIELBERG · Produced by RICHARD D. ZANUCK and DAVID BROWN · A UNIVERSAL PICTURE ·
TECHNICOLOR® PANAVISION®

A poster from the movie *Jaws*.

Herbie Robinson from Cleveland. Baseball player, bosun's mate. I thought he was asleep, reached over to wake him up. Bobbed up and down in the water, just like a kinda top. Up ended. Well . . . he'd been bitten in half below the waist. Noon the fifth day, Mr. Hooper, a Lockheed Ventura saw us, he swung in low and he saw us. He'd a young pilot, a lot younger than Mr. Hooper, anyway he saw us and come in low. And three hours later a big fat PBY[1] comes down and starts to pick us up. You know that was the time I was most frightened? Waitin' for my turn. I'll never put on a lifejacket again. So, eleven hundred men went in the water, three hundred and sixteen men come out, the sharks took the rest, June the 29, 1945. Anyway, we delivered the bomb.

1. Exploring Meaning

a. What was Quint's mission aboard the USS *Indianapolis*? How is that mission significant to the impact of this script?

b. Why doesn't the Lockheed Ventura rescue the men when its pilot sees them?

c. Why do you think Quint ends his story by saying, "Anyway, we delivered the bomb"?

d. Quint's monologue contains graphic descriptions to help the reader visualize this scene. Give two examples of this.

e. Do you think the crew of the *Indianapolis* could have done anything differently to increase their chances of survival? Explain.

---

[1] **PBY:** a flying boat used to patrol the Pacific during World War II.

2. Writing *Newspaper Article* Rewrite the script as a newspaper article describing the event. Provide all the facts, and answer *who, what, where, when, why,* and *how.* If you choose to write your article as an **editorial**, incorporate personal opinion and share commentary on the event with the reader.

Peer Assessment: Ask at least two classmates for feedback on your article. Ask whether the information seems complete. If you've shared your opinion on the event, do they feel you have supported it adequately? Do they agree with your assessment? Have them check your grammar and sentence structure.

3. Language Conventions *Apostrophe* An apostrophe can be used to indicate a contraction (you've), to show possession (Laura's job), to replace missing letters in casual speech (what 'bout me?), or to replace missing numbers in a date (the meeting of Jan. '03).

Find examples of the use of apostrophes in "Quint Tells His Story." What are the apostrophes used for? How do they contribute to the script?

4. Film Study View at least two movies that focus on World War II. List three specific incidents that deal with survival in a war setting. Compare these situations with the situation in "Quint Tells His Story." What survival strategies do these movie characters use? Are there any lessons to be learned from these movies?

Alternatively, view the movie *Jaws*, and discuss its script with a partner. How is it a suitable movie for a Survival unit? What other movies have you enjoyed that could also represent the theme of this unit?

5. Drama *Performance* In groups of three, prepare a presentation of "Quint Tells His Story." Discuss how each line should be read—volume, emotion, pacing—and where emphasis should be placed. Consider what gestures, facial expressions, or body language would work most effectively. Once you have rehearsed and memorized your lines, present the script to your classmates.

Facing
Extinction

Newspaper Article by Kevin Hall

For many centuries, the Kawesqars (Kah-WESH-cars) endured in the harsh land at the bottom of South America where the bitter wind is sometimes strong enough to knock down a child, but they have not fared so well against their fellow man. Today, fewer than 20 pureblooded Kawesqars survive.

Most pureblooded Kawesqars and another 100 people of mixed-race live in Punta Arenas, Chile's southernmost city; in Puerto Williams, on the Chilean coast of Tierra del Fuego Island near the southern tip of South America; or in Puerto Eden, on Wellington Island.

Diseases brought by European sheep farmers and seal hunters at the end of the 19th century killed many Kawesqars. So did alcoholism. The settlers' bounty on the heads of Kawesqars who hunted their sheep was a factor, too, but so was the simple act of switching to Western clothing.

Discarded clothing carried Western diseases, and because the stormy Patagonia region of South America often experiences all four seasons in a day, paddling in wet clothing soon brought pulmonary diseases for which the Kawesqars had no immunity. Tuberculosis reached epidemic proportions.

Today, the Kawesqars are nearly extinct, pursued by social scientists on "cultural salvage" operations to learn as much as possible about them before they disappear.

With the deaths of the last surviving elders "goes all our ancestral knowledge," said Oscar Aguilera, an ethnolinguist (a student of the languages of societies) at the University of Chile in Santiago who has spent two decades among the Kawesqars.

The nomadic Kawesqars had neither a tribal structure nor leaders, living instead in extended families headed by the oldest male. To the surprise of anthropologists, they also had no god or gods.

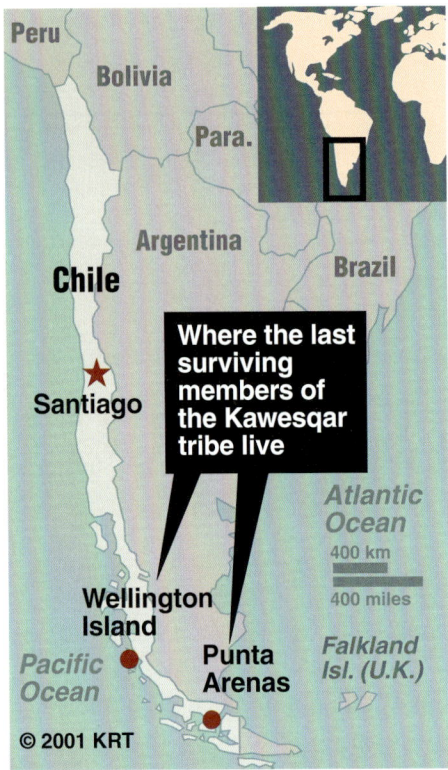

The Kawesqars live in Punta Arenas, Chile, in Puerto Williams on the Chilean coast of Tierra del Fuego Island, or in Puerto Eden, on Wellington Island.

"They believe in a force that gives balance to all things," said Nelson Aguilera Aguila, an anthropologist who heads the Punta Arenas office of the National Indigenous Development Corp. (Conadi), a quasi-governmental aid agency for native Chileans. When the balance is upset, Kawesqars blame a spirit called Ayayema.

Alberto Achacaz Walakial, whose family guesses he is between 70 and 80, is one of the surviving elders. He lives in a shack with a car seat as his couch. To put food on the table, he carves sea lion bones into makeshift harpoon tips and sews tiny toy canoes out of sea lion skins, souvenirs for the tourist trade.

"We used to navigate these straits in canoes. But that was when we were children," he recalled in Spanish. He is short and stocky, round-faced, with oriental eyes, coarse hair, a dark complexion and a halting speech rhythm. Kawesqars resemble Alaskan Inuit, who also are believed to have come to the Americas from Asia, and who live in a similarly unforgiving environment.

Achacaz became animated—and hard to understand—as he recalled fishing and hunting expeditions in his childhood.

That was before 1936 when Chile built an air force base on Wellington Island. The last Kawesqars abandoned their wigwams in favour of ramshackle subsidized housing. Instead of fishing, they began taking odd jobs. Cheap jackets replaced the wraps of sea lion skin that had helped them fend off the cold for generations.

Only one of Achacaz's three daughters, Veronica, speaks Kawesqar. There are almost no Kawesqars left to marry who are not blood relatives.

"It would be really nice, because we understand things among ourselves that no one else does," said Veronica, 40, who married a mixed-race man.

Their daughter, Susan, 4, soon will begin learning Kawesqar from elders. It won't be easy, because of the way their language reflects the Kawesqars' unique experience. For example, the Kawesqars have words for the immediate future, but not for the indefinite future—basically, for tonight's dinner but not for next Friday's meal.

"For them, this is a concept that just doesn't exist," said Paz Errazuriz, a Chilean artist who brought the Kawesqars national attention in 1996 with an acclaimed photography exhibit called Nomads of the Sea, which has since travelled the globe.

She contends the Kawesqars' lack of the concept of a future helps explain their inability to escape poverty.

On the other hand, Kawesqars have at least 32 variants of the word "here," one each for the principal places or kinds of places they used to visit as nomads.

Their ancestors are believed to have wandered across the Bering Strait from Siberia to Alaska thousands of years ago. They lived in isolation until 1520, when Ferdinand Magellan, a Portuguese captain sailing under the Spanish flag, discovered the southern strait that links the Atlantic and Pacific oceans.

"They were always people with great mobility," said Conadi's Aguilera. "Land means nothing to them. They view the sea as land."

Offered land, a few Kawesqars accepted small parcels in southern-most Chile, but most did not. Some, such as Patricio Tonko Paterito, 30, want exclusive fishing rights in certain Patagonian channels and government aid to buy commercial fishing boats.

But their dwindling numbers make it hard to win attention from Santiago, the Chilean capital 2,500 kilometres to the north.

Alberto Achacaz Walakial (back right), his daughters Veronica (back left) and Anita (front right), and his granddaughter Susan Vargas.

"There is nobody who represents us. All the indigenous power is in the north," where another more numerous native group lives, the Mapuches, said Tonko, a full-blooded Kawesqar who was adopted and raised in Punta Arenas in a Spanish-speaking household.

Among the Kawesqars' biggest challenges is escaping the impression they're already extinct. Tourist haunts in Patagonia sell postcards and buttons made from grainy, sepia-coloured photographs of Kawesqars at the end of the 19th century.

"The impression left is that Chile had an indigenous past but that it's over," said Mario Barrientos Martinez, one of the first activists to help the Kawesqars.

"Everything there points to an end: An end of the race and the culture," photographer Errazuriz said in an interview in Santiago. "They are at the end of their lineage and live at the end of the world . . . It is evident in everything that they are the last."

1. Exploring Meaning

a. Referring to both the map and the article, explain to a partner exactly where the Kawesqars live.

b. How do the Kawesqars live today? How did they live in the past?

c. List two reasons why this people's survival is threatened. What solutions do you think are needed for the problem of Kawesqar survival?

d. What do you think the future will be like for the family featured in this article?

2. Language Conventions *Sentence Structure* Kevin Hall uses various sentence types in this article. There are *simple sentences* that contain one main clause:

> Only one of Achacaz's three daughters, Veronica, speaks Kawesqar.

There are *compound sentences* that contain two or more main clauses connected by a co-ordinating conjunction (*and, but, or, nor*):

> The settlers' bounty on the heads of Kawesqars who hunted their sheep was a factor, too, *but* so was the simple act of switching to Western clothing.

There are *complex sentences* that contain one main clause and one or more dependent clauses:

> Kawesqars resemble Alaskan Inuit, who also are believed to have come to the Americas from Asia . . .

Reread "Facing Extinction," looking at how the author structures his sentences. What types of sentences are used most often? Draw a conclusion about the author's writing style.

Revise an article you have written, considering how you can most effectively use a variety of sentence types.

3. Media *Comparing Formats* Do you think the print format can do justice to an issue such as this—the survival of a people? Find examples of documentary films, radio interviews, or TV information programs on the topic of cultural survival. How are these formats similar to "Facing Extinction"? Do these other formats illustrate the problem more effectively? Create a chart listing the examples you find as well as their specific forms, features, advantages, and disadvantages. Assess the strengths and limitations of each example.

4. Language Focus *Biassed Language* What does the phrase "their fellow man" suggest to you? Reread the first paragraph of this selection and discuss this sentence and its impact on the reader. Would you change this line to be more inclusive? If so, how would you change it? If not, why not? **Self-Assessment:** How aware are you of language issues such as gender bias as you read? What effect does such language have on you as a reader?

5. Genre Study *Newspaper Article* With a small group, list the features of newspaper articles including format and structure. Collect national newspapers for a week and read at least ten different articles from various sections. In what section of the newspaper do you think "Facing Extinction" would have appeared? What makes you think so? How do articles within the various sections of the newspaper vary? Using the newspapers you have collected, pick three articles by the same reporter, and analyse his or her style, language, and use of literary or rhetorical devices.

Suitcase Lady

Newspaper Article by Christie McLaren

Night after night, the woman with the red hair and the purple dress sits in the harsh light of a 24-hour doughnut shop on Queen Street West.

Somewhere in her bleary eyes and in the deep lines of her face is a story that probably no one will ever really know. She is taking pains to write something on a notepad and crying steadily.

She calls herself Vicomtesse Antonia The Linds'ays. She's the suitcase lady of Queen Street.

No one knows how many women there are like her in Toronto. They carry their belongings in shopping bags and spend their days and nights scrounging for food. They have no one and nowhere to go.

This night, in a warm corner with a pot of tea and a pack of Player's, the Vicomtesse is in a mood to talk.

Out of her past come a few scraps: a mother named Savaria; the child of a poor family in Montreal; a brief marriage when she was 20; a son in Toronto who is now 40. "We never got along well because I didn't bring him up. I was too poor. He never call me mama."

She looks out the window. She's 60 years old.

With her words she spins herself a cocoon. She talks about drapes and carpets, castles and kings. She often lapses into French. She lets her tea get cold. Her hands are big, rough, farmer's hands. How she ended up in the doughnut shop remains a mystery, maybe even to her.

"Before, I had a kitchen and a room and my own furniture. I had to leave everything and go."

It's two years that she's been on the go, since the rooming houses stopped taking her. "I don't have no place to stay."

So she walks. A sturdy coat covers her dress and worn leather boots are on her feet. But her big legs are bare and chapped and she has a ragged cough.

Yes, she says, her legs get tired. She has swollen ankles and, with no socks in her boots, she has blisters. She says she has socks—in the suitcase—but they make her feet itch.

As for money, "I bum on the street. I don't like it, but I have to. I have to survive. The only pleasure I got is my cigaret." She lights another one. "It's not a life."

She recalls the Saturday, a long time ago, when she made $27, and laughs when she tells about how she had to make the money last through Sunday, too. Now she gets "maybe $7 or $8," and eats "very poor."

When she is asked how people treat her, the answer is very matter-of-fact: "Some give money. Some are very polite and some are rude."

In warm weather, she passes her time at the big square in front of City Hall. When it's cold she takes her suitcase west to the doughnut shop.

The waitresses who bring food to the woman look upon her with compassion. They persuaded their boss that her sitting does no harm.

Where does she sleep? "Any place I can find a place to sleep. In the park, in stores—like here I stay and sit, on Yonge Street." She shrugs. Sometimes she goes into an underground parking garage.

She doesn't look like she knows what sleep is. "This week I sleep three hours in four days. I feel tired but I wash my face with cold water and I feel okay." Some questions make her eyes turn from the window and stare hard. Then they well over with tears. Like the one about loneliness. "I don't talk much to people," she answers. "Just the elderly, sometimes, in the park."

Her suitcase is full of dreams.

Carefully, she unzips it and pulls out a sheaf of papers—"my concertos."

Each page is crammed with neatly written musical notes—the careful writing she does on the doughnut shop table—but the bar lines are missing. Questions about missing bar lines she tosses aside. Each "concerto" has a French name—*Trésor, La Tempête, Le Retour*—and each one bears the signature of the Vicomtesse. She smiles and points to one. "A very lovely piece of music. I like it."

She digs in her suitcase again, almost shyly, and produces a round plastic box. Out of it emerges a tiara. Like a little girl, she smooths back her dirty hair and proudly puts it on. No one in the doughnut shop seems to notice.

She cares passionately about the young, the old and the ones who suffer. So who takes care of the suitcase lady?

"God takes care of me, that's for sure," she says, nodding thoughtfully. "But I'm not what you call crazy about religion. I believe always try to do the best to help people—the elderly, and kids, and my country, and my city of Toronto, Ontario." ◆

1. Exploring Meaning

a. What does the "suitcase lady of Queen Street" call herself? In your opinion, what does this name reveal about her?

b. What else did you learn from the article about this woman and her situation?

c. Describe the cherished items in her suitcase. In what sense is the suitcase "full of dreams"?

d. What does the final sentence tell you about this woman?

e. Do you think this woman is content with her life? Why or why not?

2. Technique and Style *Tone* Reread "Suitcase Lady" and select five phrases or sentences that you find effective. Consider the facts and opinions presented, the images created by specific words, and the use of direct quotations. Based on your choices, come up with a conclusion about Christie McLaren's tone. How does the tone help to convey McLaren's message? How does it reveal her attitude towards her subject?

3. Writing *A Poem* Reread the article and jot down words or phrases that describe the suitcase lady and her situation. Now rewrite "Suitcase Lady" as a poem using the words and phrases you've chosen and any others you think necessary. Decide whether to use the first- or third-person point of view. Use free verse if you wish, or try adding rhythm and/or rhyme.

Self-Assessment: What is your message or theme? Is it evident? Evaluate the language you used. Does it evoke images that will help present your theme? Do you provide a clear picture of the woman?

Discuss with a partner what you might do if you were camping or hiking and came face-to-face with a bear.

THE CABIN
DOOR

Short Story by Charles G. D. Roberts

What was known as the County Line Road, though in winter a highway of some importance for the sleds and sleighs of the lumbermen, was in summer little more than a broad, straight trail, with grass and wild flowers growing undisturbed between the ruts. Just now, in the late and sodden northern spring, it was a disheartening stretch of hummocks and bog-holes, the bog-holes emphasized by a leg-breaking array of half rotten poles laid crossways. It was beautiful, however, in its lonesome, pallid, wistful fashion, for its hummocks, where dry enough, were already bluing tenderly with the first violets, its fringes were sparsely adorned with the shy blooms of wind-flower, dog-tooth, and hepatica, and scattered through the dark ranks of the fir trees on either side were little colonies of white birch or silver poplar, just filming with the first ineffable green.

To the slim girl who, bundle in hand and with skirts tucked up half-way to the knee, was picking her steps along this exasperating path, the wildness of the scene—its mingled harshness and delicacy—brought a pang which she could but dimly understand. The pale purpling of the violets, the aerial greening of the birch tops against the misty sky, the solemnity of the dark, massed fir trees—it was all beautiful in her eyes beyond anything words could suggest, but it made her heart ache with something like an intolerable home-sickness. This was incomprehensible to her, since she was already, in a sense, at home. This was her native wilderness, this was the kind of chill, ethereal, lonesome spring which thrilled through the memories of her childhood. And she was nearing—she could not now be more than twelve miles from—the actual home of her childhood, that grey cabin on the outskirts of the remote and windswept settlement of Stony Brook.

Gothic Tree by Cecil Day. Etching.

For the past three years—going on for four now, indeed—Sissy Bembridge had been away from this wild home, working hard, and saving her wages, in the big shoe factory at K——, down by the sea. Called home suddenly by word that her mother was ill, she had come by train to the end of the branch, and tried to get a rig to take her around by the main road to Stony Brook. There was no rig to be had for love or money. Too anxious to wait, and confident in her young vigour, she had left her luggage, tied up a few necessaries and eatables in a handy bundle, and set out by the short cut of the old Line Road. Deaf to all dissuasions, she had counted on making Stony Brook before nightfall. Moreover—though she would never have acknowledged to herself that such a consideration could count for anything when all her thoughts were on her mother's illness—she was aware of the fact that Connor's gang was stream-driving on the Ottanoonsis, and would be by now just about the point where the Line Road touches the river. Mike Farrell would be on the drive, and if she should chance to pass the time o' day with him, and let him know she was at home—why, there'd be no harm done to anybody.

For hours the girl trudged on, picking her way laboriously from side to side of the trail, and often compelled to stop and mend a bit of the corduroy roadway before she could get across some particularly bad stretch of bog. Her stout shoes and heavy woollen stockings were drenched with the icy water, but she was strong and full of abounding health, and she felt neither cold nor fatigue. In spite of her anxiety about her mother, her attention was absorbed by the old familiar atmosphere of the wilderness, the haunting colours, the chill, elusive, poignant smells. It was not till fairly well along in the afternoon, therefore, that she awoke to the fact that she had not covered more than half the distance which she had to travel. The heavy going, the abominable state of the road, had utterly upset her calculations. The knowledge came to her with such a shock that she stopped short in consternation, almost dropping her bundle. At this rate, she would be in the forest all night, for it would be impossible to traverse the bog-holes in the dark. Child of the backwoods though she was, she had never slept out alone with the great trees and the mysterious night stillness. For the first time she cast a look of dread into the vistaed shadows of the fir trees. Forgetting the violets, the greening birches, the delicate spring smells, she hurried on at a reckless pace which soon forced her to stop and recover her breath. The best she could hope was to reach the river shore before dark, and perhaps find the camp of the stream-drivers. She felt cold, and tired, and small, and terribly alone.

Yet, as a matter of fact, she was by no means so alone as she imagined. For the past half hour or more she had been strangely companioned.

Keeping parallel with the road, but at a distance, and hidden in the shadows, went an immense and gaunt black bear. For all his bulk, he went noiselessly as a wild-cat, skirting the open spaces, and stopping from time to time to sit up, motionless as a stump, and listen intently, and sniff the air with sensitive nostrils. But his little, red-rimmed savage eyes never lost sight of the figure of the girl for more than a few seconds at a time.

For bears this was the hungry season, the season of few roots and no fruits, few grubs and little honey. The black bear loves sweets and berries far better than any flesh food, however dainty. And human flesh he either fears or dislikes so heartily that only under special stress can he bring himself to contemplate it as a possible article of diet. But this bear considered himself under special stress. His lean flanks were fairly clinging together from emptiness. To his eyes, thus prejudiced, the fresh young form of Sissy Bembridge, picking its way down the trail, looked appetizing. Girl was something he had never tried, and it *might* be edible. At the same time, this inoffensive and defenceless-looking creature undoubtedly belonged to the species Man, as his nostrils well assured him. Therefore, small as she was, she was apt to be very dangerous, even to go off at times with flame and a terrifying noise. He was afraid to show himself to her, but his hunger, coupled with curiosity, led him to track her, perhaps in hope that she might fall dead in the trail and so make it safe for him to approach and taste.

The girl, meanwhile, under the influence of her uncertainty and fatigue, was growing more and more apprehensive. She assured herself that there was nothing to fear, that none of the wild inhabitants of these New Brunswick woods would dare to interfere with a human being. At the same time she found herself glancing nervously over her shoulder, as the shadows lengthened and deepened, and all the wilderness turned to dusky violet. From the wet pools began the cold and melancholy fluting of the frogs, the voice of solitude, and under the plangency[1] of it she found the tears running down her cheeks. At this she shook herself indignantly, squared her shoulders, stamped her foot, and plunged ahead with a firm resolution that the approach of dark should *not* make her a fool. And away in the shadows of the firs the bear drew a little nearer, encouraged by the fading of daylight.

Just as it was growing so dark that she found it hard to choose her path between the pools and the bog-holes, to her infinite relief she caught sight of a cabin roof crowning a little rise of ground by the roadside. She broke into a run in her eagerness, reached the door, and pounded upon it breathlessly. But there was no light in the window. With a sinking heart she realized that it was empty—that it was nothing more than a deserted lumber camp. Then, as if in answer to her vehement knocking, the door swung slowly open, showing the black darkness within. It had been merely closed, not latched. With a startled cry she sprang back, her skin creeping at the emptiness. Her first impulse was to turn and run. But she recovered herself, remembering that, after all, here was shelter and security for the night, infinitely preferable to a wet bivouac[2] beneath some dripping fir tree.

She could not bring herself, however, to grope her way into the thick darkness of the interior. Stepping some paces back from the threshold, she nervously untied her bundle and got out a box of matches. Lighting one, she shaded it with her hand, crept forward, and cautiously peered inside. In the spurt of light the place looked warm and snug. She returned for her bundle, went in and shut the door. Then she drew a long breath and felt better. The camp was small, but dry and in good repair. It was quite empty, except for the tier of bunks along one wall, a rough-hewn log bench, a broken stove before the rude chimney, and several lengths of rust-eaten stove-pipe scattered on the floor. Lighting match after match, she hunted about for something to serve as fuel, for she craved the comfort, as well as the warmth of a fire.

There was nothing, however, but a few handfuls of dry, fine spruce tips, left in one of the bunks. This stuff, she knew, would flare up at once and die in a couple of minutes. She made up her mind to go out and grope about in the wet gloom for a supply of dead branches, though she was now conscious of a childish reluctance to face again the outer solitude. Almost furtively she

---

[1] **plangency:** resounding mournfulness.
[2] **bivouac:** a temporary camp outdoors without tents.

lifted the heavy latch and opened the door half-way. Instantly, with a gasp, she slammed it to again and leaned against it with quaking knees. Straight in front of her, not twenty feet away, black and huge against the grey glimmer of the open, she had seen the prowling bear.

Recovering herself after a few seconds, she felt her way stealthily to the bench and sat down upon it so as to face the two windows. The windows were small— so small that she was sure no monster such as the one which had just confronted her could by any possibility force its way through them. But she waited in a sort of horror, expecting momently that a dreadful shadowy face would darken one or the other of them and glare in upon her. She felt that the eyes of it would be visible by their own light, and she summoned up all her resolution that she might not scream when it appeared. For the time, however, nothing of the sort took place, and the two little squares continued to glimmer palely.

After what seemed to her an hour of breathless waiting, she heard a sound as of something rubbing softly along the logs of the back wall. She swung around on her seat to stare with straining eyes at the spot where the sound came from. But, of course, all was blackness there. And she could not keep her eyes for more than a few seconds from the baleful fascination of the window-squares.

The door of the camp was a heavy one and sturdily put together, but along its bottom was a crack some half an inch in width. Presently there came a loud sniffing at this crack, and then the door creaked, as if a heavy body were leaning against it. She shuddered and gathered herself together for a desperate spring, expecting the latch or the hinges to give way. But the honest New Brunswick workmanship held, and she took breath again with a sob.

After this respite, a thousand fantastic schemes of defence began to chase themselves through her brain. Out of them all she clung to just one, as possibly offering some hope in the last emergency. Noiselessly she gathered those few handfuls of withered spruce twigs and heaped them upon the top of the stove. If the bear should succeed in squeezing through the window or breaking down the door, she would light the dry stuff, and perhaps the sudden blaze and smoke might frighten him away. That it would daunt him for a moment, she felt sure, but she was equally sure that its efficacy would not last very long.

As she was working up the details of this scheme—more for the sake of keeping her terror in check than for any great faith she had in it—the thing she had been expecting happened. One of the glimmering grey-blue squares grew suddenly dark. She gave a burst of shrill, hysterical laughter and ran at it, as a trapped rat will jump at a hand approaching the wires. As she did so, she scratched a bunch of four or five matches and threw them, spluttering and hissing, in the face of the apparition. She had a glimpse of small, savage eyes and an open, white-fanged mouth. Then the great face withdrew itself.

Somewhat reassured to find that the monster could be disconcerted by the spurt of a match, she groped back to her seat, and fell to counting, by touch, the number of these feeble weapons still left in the box. She had only six more, and she began to repent of having used the others so recklessly. After all, as she told herself, *that* bear could not possibly squeeze himself through the window, so why should he not amuse himself by looking in at her if he wanted to? It might keep him occupied. It occurred to her that she ought to be glad that the bear was such a big one. His face alone had fairly filled the window. She would save the remaining matches.

For a good ten minutes nothing more happened, though from time to time her intent ears caught the sound of cautious sniffing on the other side of the log walls, as if the enemy were reconnoitring to find a weak point in her fortress. She smiled scornfully there in the dark, knowing well the strength of those log walls. Then, all at once her face stiffened and she sat rigid, clutching the edge of the bench with both hands. The door had once more begun to creak and groan under the weight of a heavy body surging against it.

There was a sound of scratching, a rattle of iron claws, which told her that the beast was rearing itself upright against the door. The massive paws seemed to fumble inquisitively. Then her blood froze. She heard the heavy latch lift with a click.

The door swung open.

She felt as if she were struggling in a nightmare. With a choked scream she leaped straight at the door. She had a mad impulse to slam it in the monster's face and brace herself, however impotently, against it. As she sprang, however, her foot caught in one of the pieces of stove-pipe. She fell headlong, and the pipe flew half-way across the floor, clattering over its fellows as it went, and raising a prodigious noise.

Through a long, long moment of horror she lay flat on her face, expecting a gigantic paw to fall upon her neck as a cat's paw falls upon a mouse. Nothing happened. She ventured to raise her head. The door was wide open and the doorway quite clear. A dozen feet away from it, at the edge of the road, stood the bear, staring irresolutely. He had been rather taken aback by the suddenness with which the door had flown open, and had hesitated to enter, fearing a trap. The wild clatter of the stove-pipes had further disturbed him, and he had withdrawn to consider the situation. In one bound the girl was at the door and had shut it with a bang.

The problem was now to fix the latch so that it could not again be lifted from the outside. She lit one more precious match, examined the mechanism, and hunted frantically for a splinter of wood with which to jam it down. There was nothing in sight that would serve. She tried to tear off a strip of her petticoat to bind it down with, but all her underwear was of a most serviceable sturdiness, and would not tear. She heard his breathing close to the door. Desperately she thrust a couple of fingers into the space above the latch, so that it would not lift. Then with the other hand she whipped off one shoe and stocking. The stocking was just the thing, and in a minute she had the latch secure.

It was no more secure, however, before the weight of the bear once more came against the door. From the heavy, scratchy fumblings the girl could perceive that her enemy was trying to repeat his former manoeuvre. On this point, at least, she had no anxiety. She knew the door could not now be unlatched from the outside. She could almost afford to laugh in her satisfaction as she groped her way back to the seat.

But her satisfaction was of brief life. The door began to creak more and more violently. It was evident that the bear, having once learned that this was a possible way in, was determined to test it to the utmost. The girl sprang up. She heard the screws of a hinge begin to draw with an ominous grating sound. Now at last the crisis was truly and inevitably upon her. And, to her amazement, she was less terrified than before. The panic horror had all gone. She had small hope of escape, but her brain worked calmly and clearly. She moved over beside the broken stove, and stood, match in hand, ready to set fire to the pile of dry spruce tips.

The door groaned and creaked. Then the upper hinge gave way, and the door leaned inward, admitting a wide streak of glimmer. For some moments thereafter all sounds ceased, as if the bear had drawn back cautiously to consider the result of his efforts. Then he came on again with more confidence. Under his weight the door came crashing down, but slowly, with the noise of yielding latch and snapping iron. As it fell, the girl scratched the match and set it to the dry stuff.

In the doorway the bear paused, eyeing suspiciously the tiny blue spurt of the struggling match. After a second or two, however, he came forward with a savage rush, furious at having been so long balked. The girl slipped around the stove. And just as the bear reached the place where she had been standing, the spruce tips sparked sharply and flared up in his face. With a loud *woo-oof* of indignation and alarm, he recoiled, turned tail, scurried out into the road, and disappeared.

In a couple of minutes the cabin was full of sparks and smoky light. The girl ran to the door and peered out. Her heart sank once more. There was the bear, a few paces up the road, calmly sitting on his haunches, waiting. He had seen camp fires before, and he was waiting for this one to die down.

Sissy Bembridge knew that it would die down at once, and then—well, her last card would have been played. She wrung her hands, but in the new self-possession which had come to her, she could not believe that the end had really arrived. It was unbelievable that within some half a dozen minutes she could become a lifeless, hideous, shapeless thing beneath those mangling claws. No, there must be—there was—something to do, if she could only think of it.

And then it came to her.

At first thought the idea was so audacious, so startling, so fantastic, that she shrank from it as absurd. But on second thought she convinced herself not only that it was the one thing to be done, but also that it was practical and would almost certainly prove effective. But there was not a moment to be lost.

Snatching up one of the fragments of stove-pipe, she used the edge as a shovel, and carried a portion of the blazing stuff to the open doorway. Here she deliberately set fire to the dry woodwork, nursing with hand and breath the tiny uplicking flames. She fed them with a few more scraps of spruce scraped up from another bunk, till she saw that they would surely catch. Then, with her stove-pipe shovel, she started another fire in the further corner of the camp, and yet another in the uppermost bunk. When satisfied that all were fairly going, she retrieved her stocking from the broken latch, reclothed her naked foot and set her bundle safely outside. Then she looked at the bear, still sitting on his haunches a little way up the road, and she laughed at him. At least she had him worsted. She darted in through the doorway—now blazing cheerfully all up one side—and dragged forth the heavy bench, that she might have something dry to sit on while she watched the approaching conflagration.

Her calculation—and she knew it was a sound one—was that the cabin, a solid structure of logs, would burn vigorously the whole night through, and terrify the bear to final flight. If it should by any chance die down before full daylight, she would be able to build a circle of small fires with the burning remnants. And she felt sure that in daylight her enemy would not dare to renew the attack.

In another ten minutes the roof was ablaze, and soon the flames were shooting up riotously. The woods were lighted redly for hundreds of yards around, the pools in the road were like polished copper, and the bear was nowhere to be seen. Sissy dragged her bench and bundle still further away, and sat philosophically warming her wet feet. The reaction from her terror, and her sense of triumph, made her so excited that fatigue and anxiety were all forgotten. She grew warm and comfortable, and finally, opening her bundle, she got out a package of neglected sandwiches and made a contented meal.

As she was shaking the crumbs from her lap, she heard voices and pounding, splashing hoofs from up the trail. She sprang to her feet. Three lumbermen came riding into the circle of light and drew rein before her in astonishment. "Sissy—Bembridge—*you!*" cried the foremost, springing from saddleless mount.

The girl ran to him. "Oh, Mike," she exclaimed, crying and laughing at the same time, and clutching him by the arm, "I *had* to do it! The bear nigh got me! Take me to mother, quick, I'm *that* tired."

1. Exploring Meaning

a. Describe the setting of this short story. What clues reveal the setting? In what way is setting significant to the plot?

b. What three words best describe Sissy Bembridge? Give examples from the story to support your choices.

c. Why is Sissy in so much of a hurry that she chooses to walk to Stony Brook rather than wait for a ride?

d. What two things happen as a result of the fire?

e. Do you think Sissy does the right thing given her situation? Would you have done anything differently? Explain.

2. Focus on Context

Rewrite "The Cabin Door" from the point of view of the bear. Write as if you, the mother or father bear, are telling this story to your bear cub. Consider your audience and purpose before you begin. Choose vivid, suspenseful language to make the characters, conflict, and setting come alive. Remember to use a variety of sentences and check that you have used apostrophes and dashes correctly and effectively.

Self-Assessment: Assess how effectively you've reflected the new context in your writing. What else might you have done to make the new context more evident?

3. Language Conventions

Dashes Writers sometimes use the **dash** for emphasis or for adding information and detail. Jot down examples of how dashes are used in "The Cabin Door." Could some of these stand on their own as complete sentences? Would parentheses or commas be more effective alternatives? How does the use of dashes contribute to the author's style? As you proofread your story in Activity 2, check for the effective use of dashes, commas, and parentheses.

A **dash** [—] makes a strong break and can be used to separate an interjection from the rest of the sentence.

4. Film Study

With a small group, discuss how bears and other wild animals are commonly portrayed in movies. Is their portrayal similar to how animals are portrayed in this story? Do you enjoy watching movies with wild animals as central "characters"? Why or why not?

Crying
Totem Pole

Oil Painting by Emily Carr

Survivor Drifting

Etching by David Blackwood

Visual Communication *Analyse Paintings* Discuss these paintings with a partner. Describe what you see in each one. What do you think these images represent? What types of survival do these paintings represent? What is the mood of each painting? How do the colours the artists used contribute to these moods? What techniques have they used? How would you describe their styles?

What Stays in the Family

Memoir by Lorna Crozier

"It's too late," my mother said when my father wanted her by his side when he fell ill. For the first time in forty years, he stayed home in the evenings. They ate their supper together, and then he sat in the La-Z-Boy beside her smaller chair to watch TV. Sometimes he was well enough to sip a beer, sometimes not. Even before he was hospitalized in the palliative ward, the tumours in his throat from lymphatic cancer made swallowing a chore. Often what he tried to drink dribbled from his nose.

It was difficult to watch him try to satiate his hunger or walk the few steps from the kitchen to the bathroom; difficult to watch him sit so small behind the wheel of his car and drive around the block just for the sake of getting out. But my mother's distress went beyond these things. His sudden need of her company, his new-found domesticity, didn't sit well with her. At seventy, she had spent the best part of their marriage making a life of her own, one that didn't depend on him for companionship or money. In the past, he'd spent his nights at the Legion or in the Imperial and Healy hotels, drinking beer and playing shuffleboard or pool. He'd had no problem paying for his games, his gambling and his drinks, but when Mom would ask for grocery money, he'd hand her a one-dollar bill with the attitude of a patron bestowing great gifts—and for that, she'd almost have to beg.

When I was eight Mom found a job at the outdoor swimming pool, lifting heavy baskets stuffed with shoes and clothing to their numbered places on the four-tiered shelves, lifting them down again when the swimmers plunked their metal tags on the counter and claimed their belongings to get dressed. It was hard and menial work, but it was a paying job, and she finally had money of her own. She also did "day work," the name then given to cleaning other people's houses, and in the winter she sold tickets at the Bronco hockey games. After her first paycheque, I don't think she ever asked my father for grocery money again.

In her social life, she developed the same independence. I can't remember her getting together with women friends for a night on the town, but she curled and bowled in afternoon ladies' leagues, and she met her neighbours for coffee once a week. If she wasn't working, she'd be home with me, keeping Dad's supper warm on the back of the stove, knitting, reading, watching television. After my older brother left home when I was eleven, she and I spent Christmas Eves alone, Dad finding somewhere else to go after the bars shut down. Who can blame her for not welcoming him with open arms when he wanted to cling to her the last months of his life? It was too damn late.

My father was a drunk. It brings me great relief to say that now because his drinking was the biggest secret of my childhood. My mother never spoke about it to anyone but me, and I was warned not to tell my friends. His drinking was our skeleton in the closet, our mad child hidden in the attic. The bones rattled, the feet banged on the floor above our heads, but if someone else was around, we pretended not to hear.

Mom's attitude was small-town and pragmatic. What went on in the family stayed in the family and was no one else's business. It wasn't that she was hiding any kind of physical or sexual violence—no matter how much my father drank, he never hit her or me or my brother. He never abused us. She was simply covering up embarrassing behaviour, like the time he woke up in the middle of the night and peed in his shoe. Why tell anyone about that? Or the time he tripped on an imaginary branch on the sidewalk and came home with his nose scraped and bleeding and his glasses broken. Or the nights he spent in jail. Or the summer evening we caught the train to Winnipeg for my brother's wedding and he kept everyone in the car awake with his shouting and singing, my mother and I hunched mortified in our seats as the porter threatened to throw him off. Her insistence on privacy had something to do with pride. She was honest and hardworking and she wanted, in spite of our family's poverty and her husband's bad behaviour, to hold her head up high. Although I respect and love her and understand her need to conceal our family troubles, I suffered terribly from our silence.

What our secret meant in small and practical terms was that I couldn't ask a girlfriend to sleep over if Mom thought Dad was on a toot. I couldn't tell anyone the real reason that Mom and I walked everywhere—Dad was too inebriated to drive, or he'd already lost his licence and then his job operating heavy machinery in the oil patch. I couldn't tell my high-school boyfriend why I didn't ask him to spend Christmas with my family when he was left alone, his parents responding to a distant relative's emergency. When Dad didn't come home the night before my grade twelve graduation, Mom sent me to tell the teacher advisor that he'd been called out of town for work. I had to let the teacher know of Dad's absence because I was the valedictorian, and my parents were to sit at the head table beside the principal. As the gymnasium doors at the school banged shut behind me, I walked towards the teacher who stood at the far end by the stage, the distance I had to cross seemingly endless, the crepe-paper graduation streamers and balloons swaying above me. A few steps away, I stammered the excuse I had been rehearsing. I'll never forget the look of pity in his eyes. I turned around and walked back across that long shining floor, the soles of my runners squeaking with every step, the back of my neck burning. Later, when I was dressed in my first long gown and Mom and I were about to leave the house, Dad showed up. He couldn't even tie his shoes. I walked ahead of my parents to the gym, told the same teacher that the job had ended early, my father would sit at the head table after all. Beside the principal he took his place. Soon his head was nodding over the jellied salad and slices of ham, his mouth drooping open as I stood up to speak.

Perhaps the worst effect of our secret was that it forced me to hide my sadness. I buried it beneath an exterior that had little to do with what was going on at home and with how I saw myself. My cheerful, outgoing double sang in the operettas, captained the cheerleading team, served on the executive of Teen Town, taught swimming lessons, acted in drama nights, went steady with boys, worried about how far a good girl should go, delivered the valedictorian address and never spoke of anything that mattered. On the surface I was well-adjusted, popular, optimistic. Inside I burned with shame. My father's drinking was such a disgraceful thing that it couldn't be talked about. It had to be carried invisibly like a terrible disease that had no name.

By the time I went to university, the only one in my extended family to do so, the shame over my father's drinking went hand in hand with the fear that I, as well as he, would be found out. It would be discovered that I was the daughter of the town drunk, and that I came from the kind of working-class poverty where not one good book, not one piece of art graced the shelves or walls of our run-down rented house. The fear that I have been tricking people has been with me almost all my life. One day someone will rise from an audience and say, "You're not good enough to read, publish, teach, write, pass those exams, get those promotions, win those awards. I'm going to tell everyone how dumb and bad you really are. I'm going to tell everyone where you come from."

When I went back to my home town at twenty-four to teach in the high school, I returned with my husband's name, not my father's, which had felt like such a burden. Most of my colleagues didn't know who my father was. One Friday night I joined a group of fellow teachers at the Legion for a beer. An older man came to our table and asked me to dance. I rose to his outstretched hand and he whirled me around to a country tune. A few songs later he returned and I danced with him again. He slurred his words, but he moved with grace across the floor, his arm around my waist guiding me through a two-step. The teacher beside me when I sat down the second time said, "That old drunk really likes you." I paused. I was tempted to say "Yes" and laugh it off, but instead I replied, "That old drunk is my father." As I hesitated before replying, I had to muster some courage. It would have been

Photo by Jane Sapinsky.

so easy to deny him. That moment of honesty loosened something inside as if my breath had been held in a fist that was slowly beginning to open.

It took ten years before I dropped my married name and reclaimed my father's. In 1983, "Crozier" appeared for the first time on a book of my poetry. Not until 1990, when I was over forty, did I write about my father's drinking in a poem. My mother still hadn't spoken of this area of her life with any of her friends. Since my poems would be the first public acknowledgement of it, I warned her they were coming and excused myself by insisting I had the right to my own version of my childhood. She wasn't pleased, but she didn't pressure me to stop. Some days I think I should be more concerned with privacy, or at least with my mother's sense of what should remain confidential in the past we shared. But the harm our silence caused continues to compel me to speak as openly as possible about those old family wounds.

At the same time I feel almost driven, now that my father has died, to put him on the page, to give him life in the music of my lines, not out of anger or shame but out of love, for the censorship of my childhood damaged him as well as me and my mother. It made him smaller because we let his drinking loom above everything else he brought to our lives. The shame I felt made me deny the other things he was—the young man who lost the farm, the hard worker, the one who believed things would always work out okay, the curler who won all the local bonspiels, the old-time fiddler who loved to dance, the man my mother loved and married. It's too late now for me to make amends to him, but it's not too late to tell our family secrets, to find words for what could not be spoken. My father was a drunk. What a relief to say that! And what a delight to know there is so much more I need to say.

---

1. Exploring Meaning

a. How does Lorna Crozier's mother cope with her husband's drinking prior to his illness?

b. How does his illness create additional problems for his wife?

c. How does her father's behaviour affect Crozier in her youth? Give specific examples.

d. Why do you think Crozier feels compelled to share her family secret? Does this present any additional problems for her?

e. What message does Crozier leave the reader with at the end of her memoir?

2. Making Connections
What qualities helped Lorna Crozier to survive her family situation? Find examples of other people who have accomplished great things in spite of a difficult childhood. Think of individuals you know, have heard or read about, or have seen in movies. Make a list of these people and share it in a class discussion. Are there similarities among these individuals?

3. Visual Communication
Analyse Photo With a partner, discuss the image on page 81—its mood and message, as well as the techniques the photographer has used and the effect they have on the viewer. Write a brief review of the image, including an explanation of how it works with the selection.

4. Genre Study
Memoir Use this memoir as a model to write about a significant event in your childhood or about an experience that tested your survival skills. You will need to describe the situation fully, and include notes about how you felt, and how those around you acted or felt. You should use the first-person point of view and the past tense (use present tense for any current reflections on the events of the past). If you wish, you can share your memoir with a partner.

Self-Assessment: Read your final draft and reflect on how effectively you presented events, emotions, and ideas. What would you change to improve your memoir? What did you like about writing in this format? What didn't you like?

"Surviving death is nature's way of challenging the human spirit." Discuss this statement with a partner, making reference to anything you have heard about, read, or seen to support or refute it.

EPIC OF SURVIVAL: *Shackleton*

Narrative Essay by Caroline Alexander

It is one of the very greatest survival stories in the annals of exploration. Sir Ernest Shackleton, his ship *Endurance* crushed by ice in Antarctica's Weddell Sea, led his men to safety through a series of impossible journeys over land and sea that, more than 80 years later, still leaves one gasping.

The Imperial Trans-Antarctic Expedition left Plymouth, England, on August 8, 1914, just at the outbreak of the First World War. Shackleton's ship was a three-masted wooden sailing vessel—a barkentine—specially designed to withstand ice. Called *Polaris*, the ship had been built by Norway's most renowned shipyard out of oak, Norwegian fir, and greenheart, a wood so dense that it has to be worked with special tools. Shackleton renamed her *Endurance*, after his family motto, "*Fortitudine vincimus*—By endurance we conquer."

In 1915 Ernest Shackleton lost his ship and his dream of crossing the Antarctic on foot. What began as a journey of exploration became a twenty-month battle to stay alive, demanding ingenuity, courage, and leadership.

Heading south, the expedition's last port of call was the island of South Georgia, a wild sub-antarctic outpost of the British Empire inhabited by a small community of Norwegian whalers. From here the *Endurance* set sail for the Weddell Sea, the dangerous ice-infested ocean abutting the Antarctic continent. Battling her way through one thousand miles of pack ice over a six-week period, the *Endurance* was about a hundred miles from her destination—one day's sail away—when on January 18, 1915, the ice closed in. A drastic drop in temperature caused the seawater to freeze, effectively cementing the compressed ice. The *Endurance* was trapped, "frozen," as the ship's storekeeper wrote, "like an almond in a piece of toffee."

Shackleton was by this time already a famous polar explorer. He had first been south with Captain Robert Falcon Scott in 1901, drawn to Antarctica by the ideal of heroic quest. But the expedition ended in failure for Shackleton when he was invalided home with scurvy after the first winter. Five years later, at the head of his own expedition, he won renown for marching to within one hundred miles of the South Pole, the farthest south anyone had been. In December 1911 Roald Amundsen claimed the South Pole for Norway, leaving only one prize remaining in polar exploration—the crossing on foot of the Antarctic continent. It was on this Shackleton had set his sights.

Now, with the entrapment in the ice, his most daring venture was thwarted. More important, he was responsible for the care of 27 men—as well as 60 sledging dogs, two pigs, and the ship's cat, Mrs. Chippy. For the next ten months the *Endurance* zigzagged more than a thousand miles with the north-west drift of the pack. As each day passed, Shackleton and his crew knew that the Antarctic continent was falling farther and farther away.

All hands on board knew that one of two things would eventually happen: Come spring, the pack would thaw and disperse, freeing them. Or, the pressure exerted by the grinding floes would take hold of the little ship and crush her like an eggshell. In October 1915 the signs were ominous.

In his diary, now in the State Library of New South Wales, Australia, Frank Hurley, expedition photographer, wrote on October 26: "At 6 p.m., the pressure develops an irresistible energy. The ship groans and quivers, windows splinter, whilst the deck timbers gape and twist. Amid these profound and overwhelming forces, we are the absolute embodiment of helpless futility. This frightful strain is observed to bend the entire hull some 10 inches along its length.

On the following day, Shackleton gave the order to abandon ship. The men spent their first night on the ice in linen tents so thin the moon shone through them. The temperature was minus 16° Fahrenheit.[1]

---

[1] **–16° Fahrenheit:** about –27° Celsius.

For two days in February 1915 the crew chopped a channel for the *Endurance* in hopes of reaching open water. But they gave up 400 yards short of the lead, thwarted by layered ice up to 18 feet thick.

Most of the expedition's food supplies were still trapped in the *Endurance*. Their warmest clothes were their woolen underwear and Burberry windbreakers, about the weight of umbrella fabric. They had no radio communication, and no one in the world knew where they were. To get to safety once the ice broke up, they had only three salvaged lifeboats—and Shackleton to lead them.

"I can't remember the matter being discussed or argued in any way," expedition physicist Reginald James would recall. "We were in a mess, and the Boss was the man who could get us out."

In London's Royal Geographical Society, a venerable institution that has sponsored innumerable expeditions of discovery, the archivist brought me a Bible. I turned to the 38th chapter of the Book of Job—or, more accurately, to where the 38th chapter of Job once was. The page, as I already knew, was missing.

The day after the abandonment of the *Endurance*, Shackleton gathered his men and quietly told them they were going to try to march over the ice to Paulet Island, nearly 400 miles to the northwest. Only the barest essentials could be carried, and personal gear had to be sacrificed. By way of example, Shackleton took the ship's Bible and, ripping out a page from Job, deposited the book on the ice. The verses he saved read:

> *Out of whose womb came the ice?*
> *And the hoary frost of Heaven*
>   *who hath gendered it?*
> *The waters are hid as with a stone,*
> *And the face of the deep is frozen.*

It was a dramatic gesture. What Shackleton never learned was that one of the sailors, a superstitious old salt named Tom McLeod, secretly carried the Bible away, believing that leaving it would invite bad luck.

The march to land was reluctantly abandoned: Dragging the loaded boats, each of which weighed at least a ton, over the colossal fragments of pressure ice and through deep snow proved impossible. The expedition now regrouped, and Shackleton determined there was nothing to do but pitch camp on the drifting ice and see where the current and winds would take them before conditions permitted the use of the boats.

Ocean Camp—the first of two camps pitched on the ice—was their new home. An eccentric supply of food was salvaged from the half sunk *Endurance*; the crates that first floated to the surface—soda carbonate, walnuts, onions—were not necessarily what the men would have chosen for starvation rations. Sledging rations originally intended for the transcontinental trek were put aside for use in the boats.

It was now summer in the Southern Hemisphere, and temperatures crept as high as 33° Fahrenheit.[2] The soft slush of snow made walking difficult, and the men's clothing was always wet; then the temperatures dropped each night, freezing the sodden tents and clothes. The principal diet was penguin and seal, and seal blubber provided the only fuel.

The men spent most of their time analyzing the direction of the ice drift. Their greatest hope was that the drift would continue north by northwest, carrying them within striking distance of Paulet Island, off the tip of the Antarctic Peninsula, where there was a hut with supplies from an earlier Swedish expedition.

---

[2] **33° Fahrenheit:** about 0° Celsius.

In mid-January four teams of sledging dogs were shot; the ice had become too treacherous for them to be safely used, and meat for their food was in increasingly short supply.

"This duty fell upon me & was the worst job I ever had in my life," reported Shackleton's loyal second-in-command, Frank Wild, in his memoir. "I have known men I would rather shoot than the worst of the dogs."

By March the northerly drift of the pack had carried them abreast of Paulet Island—but far to the east of it.

The last of the dogs were shot—and this time eaten. The men lay in the tents, huddled in their bags that had frozen as stiff as sheet iron, too cold to read or play cards.

In April, the ice cracked through their camp, and Shackleton knew that the long-awaited breakup was at hand. On April 9 he gave the order to launch the three boats, the *James Caird,* the *Dudley Docker,* and—barely seaworthy—the *Stancomb Wills,* all named after sponsors of the expedition. Twenty-eight men crammed aboard them with their basic camping gear and rations. The temperature dropped to minus 10° Fahrenheit,[3] and high seas poured over the open boats and men, who had no waterproof clothing.

Day and night, through the minefield of grinding ice, then through the crashing waves of the open sea, the helmsman of each boat tried to hold his course, while his shipmates bailed. The boats were too small to maneuver in gale force winds, and after several changes of direction, Shackleton gave the order to run due north, with the wind behind them, for a splinter of land called Elephant Island.

For seven sleepless, nightmarish days and terrifying black nights, the men endured cold that froze their clothing into solid plates of icy armor. Out of the night-dark sea, with explosive rhythmic exhalations, white-throated killer whales rose beside the boats, taking the measure of the men with their small, knowing eyes. Shackleton was exhausted.

"Practically ever since we had first started Sir Ernest had been standing erect day and night on the stern counter of the *Caird*," wrote Orde Lees. Shackleton knew it was important to his men that they see him in charge.

At last, on April 15, the boats hove under the forbidding cliffs of Elephant Island, and a landing was made.

"Many were suffering from temporary aberration," was Hurley's description of his shipmates' mental state. Many lay on the ground burying their faces in the stones or reeled down the small beach, laughing uproariously. It

---

[3] **–10° Fahrenheit:** about –23° Celsius.

had been 497 days since they had last set foot on land, but, as they soon discovered, a more godforsaken, blizzard-raked part of the Earth could scarcely exist. Howling 80-mile-an-hour winds off the glacial peaks shredded their tents and swept away precious remaining possessions—blankets, ground sheets, cooking utensils. The sailors crawled into the boats to take cover; others lay with the cold wet tent canvas collapsed about them, draped over their faces.

Shackleton knew that the outside world would never come to Elephant Island. There was only one remotely feasible course of action, and it was terrifying. He would take the largest lifeboat, the *James Caird,* and with a small crew sail 800 miles across some of the most dangerous water on the planet, the South Atlantic, in winter, to the whaling stations of South Georgia. They could expect to encounter waves as high as 50 feet from tip to trough, the notorious Cape Horn rollers. They would navigate by sextant and a chronometer whose accuracy was unknown, depending on sightings of the sun—but they knew that in these latitudes weeks of overcast weather could prevent a single sighting.

The *James Caird* was a $22^{1/2}$-foot-long wooden lifeboat, whose gunwales had been raised by the skill of Henry "Chippy" McNish, Shackleton's gifted Scottish carpenter. Working outside with frost-nipped hands as the blizzards raged on Elephant Island, McNish salvaged what timber he could from packing cases and old sledge runners. The "decking" was made of canvas, painfully thawed over a blubber flame and stitched with brittle needles. The nails were secondhand, extracted from packing cases. In lieu of hemp and tar for caulking, Chippy used lamp wicks, seal blood, and the oil paints of the ship's artist. The ballast was two tons of rough Elephant Island beach stone.

Shackleton chose five men whose seamanship and fortitude he felt he could trust; two of the men—McNish and John Vincent, a bullying sailor who had worked on trawlers—were also known to be "difficult" characters, and he wanted them on board under his watchful eye. His navigator would be Frank Worsley, a high-spirited, somewhat rambunctious New Zealander, whose talent for navigation under impossible conditions had already helped bring them safely to Elephant Island. Tim McCarthy was a cheerful young Irish sailor, well liked by the whole company. The sixth man, Tom Crean, was a powerful, apparently indestructible Irishman who had sailed both of Scott's expeditions; on the last he had been awarded the Albert Medal for bravery when he trekked 35 miles alone through snow, supplied only with three biscuits and two pieces of chocolate, to bring help to a stricken companion.

The *Caird* set out on April 24, 1916, on a rare afternoon of relative calm. "Bravo! Brave leader," Orde Lees exclaimed in his diary, now in the National Library of New Zealand, as they left. The men Shackleton left behind faced their own trials, surviving on penguins and seals and living in a makeshift shelter under the two remaining overturned boats. Frank Wild, Shackleton's lieutenant, was in charge of the demoralized and shaken men, some of whom were in grave need of medical attention.

The day after departure the *Caird*'s ordeal began in earnest. Of seventeen days sailing, there would be ten days of gales. Icy waves soused the men. Beneath the canvas decking, the off-duty watch lay for four hours on stone ballast in wet and putrefying reindeer-skin sleeping bags; the dark space beneath the thwarts was so narrow that it gave the men a sensation of being buried alive. One night they awoke to find the boat staggering in the water. Ice as much as 15 inches thick encased every sodden inch of wood and sail. Despite the dangerous pitching and rolling of the boat, the men had to crawl onto the glassy decking and hack the ice away.

If Shackleton noticed that any one of the men seemed to be suffering more than usual, he ordered hot drinks prepared for all hands on their little Primus stove.

"He never let the man know that it was on his account," Worsley recorded, "lest he become nervous about himself." Despite Shackleton's care, Vincent collapsed after the first few days, and McNish was in a bad way, although still soldiering on. All six found that their feet, which were constantly wet, were white and swollen and had lost all surface feeling, while their bodies were cruelly chafed by their salt-ridden, icy clothes. Yet grimly, mechanically, through all the upheaval of wind and surf, they kept their watches, prepared their meals, took their turns at the makeshift pump, worked the sails, and held their course.

As feared, Worsley was able to take few sightings with the sextant he had borrowed from Hudson. Drawing on experience and an uncanny instinct for assessing wind and tide, Worsley navigated mostly by dead reckoning, the sailor's calculation of courses and distance. Their proposed landfall, South Georgia, represented a mere speck in thousands of miles of ocean. Reluctantly the men decided to aim for the island's uninhabited southwest coast; if they overshot this landfall, prevailing winds would blow them east to other land. If they aimed for the inhabited northeast coast and missed—they would be blown into oblivion.

Near dusk on May 7, the 14th day, a piece of kelp floated by. With mounting excitement they sailed east-northeast through the night, and at dawn on the 15th day spotted seaweed. Land birds appeared in the thick fog, and when the fog cleared just after noon, McCarthy cried out that he saw land.

"There, right ahead, through a rift in the flying scud, our glad but salt-blurred eyes saw a towering black crag, with a lacework of snow around its flank," wrote Worsley. "One glimpse, and it was hidden again. We looked at each other with cheerful, foolish grins. The thoughts uppermost were: 'We've done it.'"

It was a triumph of navigation as much as seamanship and endurance; even the five sightings Worsley had been able to make had involved a degree of guesswork, as the boat had pitched too wildly for him to gain secure fixes of the sun. As if out of spite, a full-blown hurricane roared up to thwart any attempt at landing that day. On top of all else, the men had discovered that their remaining water supply was brackish, and they were tormented with thirst. But on the evening of May 10, with Shackleton and his men at their very limits, the *Caird* ground onto a gravelly beach on South Georgia.

The nearest whaling stations lay about 150 miles distant by sea, too far for the battered boat and debilitated crew. Instead, Shackleton determined that he and two companions—Worsley and Crean—would cross overland to the stations at Stromness Bay. The distance was only 22 miles as the crow flies, but over a confusion of jagged rocky upthrusts and treacherous crevasses. While the coasts of the island had been charted, the interior had never been crossed, and their map depicted it as a blank.

Shackleton's main concern was the weather, as a blizzard in the mountains could finish them. But at 3 a.m. on May 19 the conditions were right, and—by a gift of providence—there was a full, guiding moon.

"We decided to . . . make the journey in very light marching order," wrote Shackleton. "We would take three days' provisions for each man in the form of sledging ration and biscuit. The food was to be packed in three socks, so that each member of the party could carry his own supply." They also carried matches, a cooking pot, two compasses, a pair of binoculars, 50 feet of rope, a Primus stove filled with enough fuel for six hot meals, and McNish's adze in lieu of an ice ax. They were dressed in threadbare long woolen underwear worn under ordinary clothing that had not been changed for seven months. For traction on the ice McNish had also put screws from the *James Caird* in their boot soles. Their frostbitten feet had not regained feeling in the nine days since their landing.

With moonlight glinting off the glaciers, Shackleton, Worsley, and Crean left their companions and set out from the head of King Haakon Bay into the mountains. Guided only by common sense, they made three failed attempts to pass through the rocky crags that lay athwart their path. The fourth pass took them over just as daylight was failing. After an initial precipitous drop, the land on the other side merged into a long, declining snow slope, the bottom of which lay hidden in mist.

"I don't like our position at all," Worsley quotes Shackleton as saying. With night coming, they were in danger of freezing at that elevation.

Shackleton remained silent for some minutes. "We'll slide," he said at last. Coiling the length of rope beneath them, the three men sat down, one behind the other, each locking his arms around the man in front. With Shackleton in the lead and Crean bringing up the rear, they pushed off toward the pool of darkness below.

"We seemed to shoot into space," wrote Worsley. "For a moment my hair fairly stood on end. Then quite suddenly I felt a glow, and knew I was grinning! I was actually enjoying it. I yelled with excitement, and found that Shackleton and Crean were yelling too."

Their speed slackened, and they came to a gentle halt in a snowbank. Rising to their feet, they solemnly shook hands all round. In only minutes they had descended 1,500 feet.

They tramped on through the night, half asleep. More blunders were made as they became too tired to calculate the lay of the land. But as dawn was breaking, they passed over a ridge and saw below the distinctive, twisted rock formation that identified Stromness Bay. They stood in silence, then for the second time turned and shook each other's hands.

At 6:30 a.m. Shackleton thought he heard the sound of a steam whistle. He knew that about this time the men at the whaling stations would be roused from bed: If he had heard correctly, another whistle should sound at seven o'clock, summoning the men to work. With intense excitement, Shackleton, Worsley, and Crean waited, watching as the hands moved round Worsley's chronometer. At seven o'clock to the minute, they heard the whistle again. Now they knew they had succeeded.

At three o'clock on the afternoon of May 20, after 36 hours without rest, they walked into the outskirts of Stromness station. Filthy, their faces black with blubber smoke, their matted, salt-clogged hair hanging almost to their shoulders, they presented a fearsome sight, and two small children—their first human contact—ran from them in fright.

Eventually they came upon the station foreman, and Shackleton asked to be taken to the manager. Tactfully unquestioning, the foreman led the trio to the home of Thoralf Sørlle, whom they had met when the *Endurance* came to South Georgia, nearly two years before.

"Mr. Sørlle came out to the door and said, 'Well?'" Shackleton recorded.

"'Don't you know me?' I said.

"'I know your voice,' he replied doubtfully. 'You're the mate of the *Daisy*.'

"'My name is Shackleton,' I said."

Aghast at their story, the Norwegian whalers received the castaways with admiration and open hearts. A ship was sent to collect the other three members of the *James Caird* crew—and the *James Caird* itself, which was carried into the station on the shoulders of the whalers like a sacred relic.

Dawn came clear and cold on Elephant Island. It was August 30, 1916, nearly five months since the *Caird* had departed, and Frank Wild had privately begun preparations to mount his own rescue.

At one in the afternoon, Wild was just serving a "hoosh," stew of limpets scavenged from tidal pools, when George Marston, the expedition's artist, excitedly poked his head inside the shelter they had made under the two remaining boats.

"Wild, there's a ship," he said. "Shall we light a fire?"

"Before there was time for a reply there was a rush of members tumbling over one another," Orde Lees reported, "all mixed up with mugs of seal hoosh making a simultaneous dive for the door-hole which was immediately torn to shreds."

Outside, the mystery ship drew closer, and the men were puzzled to see it raise the Chilean ensign. Within 500 feet from shore the ship lowered a boat, and as she did so, the men recognized the sturdy, square-set figure of Shackleton, and then of Tom Crean.

"Then there was some real live cheers given," recalled William Bakewell, one of the sailors. This was Shackleton's fourth attempt to reach Elephant Island; pack ice around the island had thwarted three earlier efforts.

For the fourth journey the Chilean government had given Shackleton the use of the *Yelcho*, a small steel-hulled tug that had last served as a lighthouse tender, and her crew. In this eminently unsuitable vessel, he, Worsley, and Crean had set forth.

In one hour, the entire company of Elephant Island and their few possessions were aboard the *Yelcho*, Hurley bringing along his canisters of photographic plates and film that he had cached in the snow.

"2.10 All Well!" Worsley recorded in his log. He had been watching from the bridge. "At last! 2.15 full speed ahead."

Through all the long months of their terrible ordeal, Shackleton had lost—not a man.

1. Exploring Meaning

a. What did Ernest Shackleton rename his ship? In your opinion, is this a suitable name? Why or why not?

b. Why do you think Shackleton saved only one page from the Bible? What happened to the rest of it?

c. What food did the crew eat after they abandoned ship?

d. Why were the crew of the *James Caird* so excited to see a piece of kelp on their fourteenth day at sea?

2. Technique and Style *Narrative Detail* Real stories can be just as gripping as fiction. In both, good storytelling incorporates vivid description as well as a strong impression of action. Find five examples of effective narrative writing in "Epic of Survival: Shackleton." How do these examples contribute to the storytelling? How do they make you feel?

3. Vocabulary Every occupation has its own specialized words or **jargon**. Reread "Epic of Survival: Shackleton" to find five examples of specialized nautical jargon such as *sextant*, *chronometer*, and *ensign*. Define each word, using a dictionary to help you. How does your knowledge of these words increase your understanding of the article?

> **Jargon** is language that does not communicate clearly. It is usually particularly complex or obscure and the language of a particular group or profession.

4. Film Study Numerous movies have been made about surviving physical ordeals. Sometimes these are biographical accounts of a situation; often they are fictionalized versions of an original story and sometimes they are just pure fiction. Make a list of movies dealing with physical survival. Are they fact or fiction, or a mixture of both? Decide on at least two you want to see and view them. Does it make any difference to you whether survival stories are based on real events? Why?

Imagine not being able to read or write. How would this affect your day-to-day life? Share your thoughts with a partner.

Why Canada Has to Beat Its Literacy Problem

Essay by June Callwood

Carole Boudrias shudders when she remembers the time she almost swallowed Drano because she thought it was Bromo. Even more painful to recall is the time she mistook adult pain-killers for the child-size dose and made her feverish child much sicker.

"When you can't read," she explains, "it's like being in prison. You can't travel very far from where you live because you can't read street signs. You have to shop for food but you don't know what's in most of the packages. You stick to the ones in a glass jar or with a picture on the label. You can't look for bargains because you can't understand a sign that says 'Reduced.' I would ask the clerk where is something and the clerk would say, aisle five. Only I couldn't read aisle five. I'd pretend that I was confused so they'd lead me right to the shelf."

Carole Boudrias is able to read now, at last. She's a thirty-three-year-old single parent who lives with her five children in a handsome townhouse on Toronto's harbourfront and holds a steady job. But her struggle with illiteracy is all too vivid in her memory. "You can't get a job," she says earnestly. "You can't open a bank account. You have to depend on other people. You feel you don't belong. You can't help your children. You can't help yourself."

Six years ago when her oldest child started school, the boy floundered. Because he had been raised in a household without books, print was strange to him. He would point to a word in his reader, that classic, endearingly silly *Dick and Jane,* and ask his mother what it was. She was as baffled as he, so he'd check with his teacher the next day and that evening would proudly read the new word to his mother. She began to absorb the shape of the words he identified. She found she could recognize them even days later.

That was astonishing. As a child she had been labelled mentally retarded and confined to "opportunity classes" where reading wasn't taught. She grew up believing that she wasn't intelligent enough to learn. Nevertheless, she *was* learning. The vocabulary of words she could read in her son's reader was growing. She began to think maybe the experts were wrong. Then, one miraculous day, she realized she was learning to read even faster than her son was.

"My son was my first teacher," she grins. She had never allowed herself to believe that it was possible that she could learn to read. She hadn't even tried: no one whose life is made up of poverty and failed relationships is ready to take on, voluntarily, the potential for another defeat, another kick in the self-esteem. She hesitated a long time but the evidence was persuasive—she was beginning to read. Her welfare worker had always been kind, so she summoned the nerve to ask her where she could find help.

That led her to Beat the Street, a program that helps people who are illiterate for all the reasons that befall sad children: unrecognized learning disabilities, emotional stress, too many schools, scorn and belittling, terror, bad teachers. She was linked with a volunteer tutor, and they came to admire each other deeply.

"Now I can read. I can read books, anything. I can write. In English *and* French."

Carole Boudrias has written a book, *The Struggle for Survival,* which tells of her tortured childhood and her triumphant recovery from illiteracy.

"Learning to read," Carole Boudrias says quietly, "was like a second birth, this time with my eyes open. Before I could read, I was a blind person."

Canada has nearly five million adult citizens who are described as functionally illiterate, which means that they can recognize a few words, such as washroom signs and exits, but they can't read dense print at all. They can't decipher directions, for instance, or application forms, or warnings on labels. The world of newspapers, posters, advertising, books, menus, banking, recipes, and instructions-for-assembly that literate people take for granted is barred to them; they live a life of bluff, anxiety, embarrassment, and isolation.

A good many Canadians are as profoundly illiterate as Carole Boudrias was. People who meet illiterate adults are struck by the similarity of their textural experience. All of them liken the inability to read and write with being disabled or chained in a prison.

The sense of being caged and blinded is not morbid fantasy. People who can't read may be able to walk freely but then can't go far. Subway stops rarely have pictures to guide them and the destinations bannered across the front of buses and streetcars are meaningless. If they ask for directions, well-intentioned people tell them, "Go along Main Street to Elm and turn left." Consequently, they must travel by taxi or stay home, though they usually are the poorest of the poor.

Almost every job, even simple manual labour such as streetcleaning, requires an ability to read. Personnel managers don't take kindly to people who can't fill out an application, or when asked, can't spell their own addresses.

The divide between the literate and illiterate has never been wider. In this half of the century North America has become a world of forms and documents and instructions, written warnings, posted rules, leaflets, and vital information circulated in brochures. Two generations ago, illiteracy was prevalent but not such a great disadvantage. Someone functionally illiterate could fake it through an entire lifetime and still hold a good job. Employment skills were acquired by watching someone else; apprenticeship was the accepted teacher, not two years in a community college.

Today inability to read is a ticket to social segregation and economic oblivion. A poignant example is the skilled housepainter who turned up one day in the crowded quarters of the East End Literacy Program in Toronto. He said he wanted to read. The counsellor asked him, as all applicants are asked, what he wanted to read. "Directions on paint cans," he answered promptly. "I'm losing jobs. I can't read how to mix the colours."

Many who are illiterate can't read numbers. When they are paid, they don't know if they are being cheated. Because she couldn't fill out bank deposit slips, Carole Boudrias used to cash her welfare cheque in a storefront outlet which clips poor people sharply for no-frills service. To pay for goods, she would hold out a handful of money and let the cashier take what was needed—and perhaps more, she never knew. Once she would have been short-changed $50 she could ill afford if a stranger who witnessed the transaction hadn't protested.

The common emotional characteristic of people who can't read is depression and self-dislike. All feel at fault for their situation; with few exceptions, they went through school with bright little girls exactly their age who leaped to their feet to recite and smart little boys who did multiplication in their heads. Everyone else in the world, it seemed, could learn with ease; for them, even C-A-T looked a meaningless scribble.

People who can't read come readily to view themselves as worthless junk, and many feel they must grab what they can out of life and run. Canada's prisons are full of young people who can't read.

Because Canada has five million people who can't read, the political shape of the country and the priorities of governments are not influenced greatly by the needs of the poor. Candidates rarely find it advantageous to uphold the causes that matter most to Canada's illiterates—an end to homelessness and the need for food banks, welfare payments that meet the poverty line, and better educational and job-training opportunities. Few votes would follow any politician with such a crusade. The electorate that can't read won't be there to ruffle the complacent on election day.

Their silence costs this country severely. Education is free in Canada because it was recognized that democracy isn't healthy unless all citizens understand current events and issues. Five million Canadians can't do that. Voters, most of them literate, choose candidates who help their interests; those who don't vote, many of them illiterate, by default get a government that does not need to know they exist.

The result is a kind of apartheid. The government has lopsided represen-tation which results in decisions which further alienate and discourage the unrepresented.

Carole Boudrias is working on a project, Moms in Motion, to help young mothers to get off welfare rolls. She says to them, "What do you want?" They reply, "To go back to school."

Another chance. Five million Canadians need another chance. Maybe they can become literate, maybe they can become healed and whole. What a lovely goal.

---

1. Exploring Meaning

a. What two memories of illiteracy does Carole Boudrias share at the start of this essay? How does her recounting of these memories affect you?

b. Why didn't Boudrias learn to read as a child? Do you think her experi-ences are unusual or typical? Explain.

c. Why do you think Boudrias wrote a book called *The Struggle for Survival*?

d. What reason does June Callwood give for why eradicating illiteracy is not a major cause for politicians? Would you agree with Callwood's assessment of the situation? Why or why not?

2. Critical Thinking

In this essay, June Callwood makes the point that "two generations ago, illiteracy was prevalent but not such a great disad-vantage. Someone functionally illiterate could fake it through an entire life-time and still hold a good job." Are there still jobs available today in which literacy is not needed? Brainstorm any jobs you can think of that involve very little reading and writing. Would they be considered "bad" jobs to have? Discuss this in small groups.

3. Genre Study *Essay* Consider the following questions as you discuss this essay with a partner: What is the thesis of this essay? How does the title support the thesis? How is the thesis introduced? How is it supported? What conclusions does the author make? Where are these conclusions placed? Does this essay follow a traditional essay format? How would you describe this essay more specifically? That is, is it persuasive, argumentative, personal, narrative, or another kind of essay? Analyse how Callwood uses language and rhetorical devices to communicate to her reader.

4. Researching Using a range of sources such as books, magazines, newspapers, or Web sites, prepare a short report on the current state of illiteracy in Canada. What are the various levels of government doing to improve literacy rates? Find statistics that reflect trends and changes. What programs are available to help people learn to read? Remember to keep track of your sources so that you can cite them in your report.
Self-Assessment: Assess how effectively you gathered and organized your information. Did you check the accuracy of your sources? Did you delete irrelevant information from your report? Did you provide source information?

Personal Focus: People in Profile

HOW WE LIVED:
Canada's Century of Change

Photo Essay by Mary Vincent

1900

Peek back at the daily lives of Canadians at the turn of the 20th century, and you'll find a young nation wrestling with the transition from a rural culture of farming, logging and hunting to an urban society of industry and commerce. Most people remain close to the land, but 37 percent, and counting, reside in cities and towns. Drawn from the countryside and from overseas to toil in the burgeoning factories, Canada's city dwellers enter a period of explosive growth in the early 1900s.

This allows for great contrasts in how we live, work and play: country and city; 60-hour workweek and leisurely Victorian lifestyle; destitute slums and affluent enclaves; mass production and conspicuous consumption. The 1900s bring dramatic changes to the character of Canadian society and, in turn, the daily lives of individual Canadians.

New waves: From 1901 to 1911, some 1.6 million immigrants—including this German family on a Québec railway platform—start new lives, new households and new traditions in Canada, flocking to industrializing cities and prairie farmlands.

The factory factor: In sprawling cities, industrial workers produce clothing, furniture and other goods once made exclusively by craftspeople. Factories, such as this one in Montréal (right), provide an expanding new realm of employment, albeit monotonous and even dangerous, with poor ventilation, oppressive heat and ear-damaging noise. Most workers remain poor— taking home less than $500 a year— and struggle to survive.

Housing boom and bust: Fashionable homes, such as this Victorian on Winnipeg's Home Street (left), boast large verandas and leaded glass. But even with 400,000 new houses built nationwide from 1901 to 1911, affordable housing remains in short supply.

Frontier Town, Canada: Schoolgirls span Bernard Avenue in Kelowna, B.C., in 1908 (above), while sawmills, orchards and fruit canneries spring up nearby, nourishing one of the West's many regional centres. The cost of relentless westward settlement is the further displacement of native groups: numerous reserves are abolished, and valuable land is sold off by the federal government. Aboriginal Peoples also face increasing government control over their lives.

1950

After a decade of depression and six years of war, Canadians are bursting with optimism in the 1950s. It is a time of prosperity and mass consumerism for most—products Canadians want are readily available, and we have the money to buy them. And do we ever: during the 1950s, we buy 3.5 million cars and more than a million new homes. The baby boom brings a massive flight to suburbia in search of a peacetime Utopia. Within the space of eight years, 250,000 families become suburbanites. But this new affluence doesn't reach everyone. While only three other cities in the world buy more Cadillacs per capita than Toronto, one in five Canadian households still lacks indoor plumbing. All in all, though, the fifties are fabulous, and Canadians are living large.

State of education: In 1951, half of the adults in Canada have not completed grade nine. Teachers' salaries are so low that many must moonlight; in Ottawa, they are paid more to mow school lawns in the summer than to teach.

Cityscapes: Three in five Canadians live in cities or towns by the 1950s. Streets, such as Edmonton's Jasper Avenue (left), take on a decidedly cosmopolitan feel yet still retain some small-town charms. As streetcars give way to buses to move the growing masses, public transit becomes a vital issue. Downtown traffic flow slows to a crawl, while urban planners struggle to catch up with the automotive revolution.

The baby boom and a middle-class desire to escape the congestion and grime of the city spur an explosion of suburbs across the country. New dream homes are typically 1,200-square-foot bungalows with large front lawns, picture windows and a sedan parked out front for the daily commute.

Career choice: Leaving the kitchen and entering the workforce as never before, women, including this Montréal teletype operator (above), buy into mass consumption and struggle to raise their families' standard of living.

For Inuit residents in Arctic communities (above), a can of powdered milk symbolizes the incursion of Southern commodities into a culture with deep ties to the bounty of the land.

2001

The 21st century was supposed to bring us a life of post-industrial leisure, with all kinds of high-tech, time-saving gadgets to make life a little easier. Turns out, we do have a dizzying choice of gadgets, but less free time than ever. Technology has accelerated the pace and volume of work to the point where one-third of Canadians between the ages of 25 and 44 identify themselves as workaholics, and more than half worry about not having enough leisure time to spend with family and friends.

Statisticians in the 1950s projected our population at the end of the 20th century would reach 15 million. In 2001, we were at 30 million and counting. And as the cost of raising children creeps upward—more than $150,000 from birth to age 18—poverty becomes an increasingly critical concern: 57,000 Canadian families have children who go hungry on a regular basis.

A day's work: Many of us are working longer hours and feeling trapped in a daily routine, whether it's in a pharmaceutical plant (above) or a downtown office. According to the 1996 census, truck driving is the most common occupation for men, while more women work in retail sales than any other occupation.

We are family: Averaging three people per household, Canadian families are about half the size they were a century ago. Increased divorce rates among other factors have brought a new look to many families. Regardless, Canada's families still share the common purpose—love, support and a place to go for Sunday dinner.

Home front: Whether it's a glass tower with hundreds of neighbours overhead and beneath or a suburban home with hundreds of neighbours all around (above), today's housing options seem limitless. Yet we still haven't figured out how to ensure that all Canadians have a safe and affordable place to call home.

Protest culture: Canadians are social activists (above), fighting for causes ranging from the environment and health care to global trade practices and poverty.

Vidkids: Many nine-year-olds spend more time on the Internet than do their folks. And when these students graduate from high school, they will have spent 11,000 hours in the classroom, but 15,000 hours watching television, including 350,000 commercials.

1. Exploring Meaning

a. A photo essay develops a thesis or point of view through a combination of photos and text. Identify the thesis of this essay. Consider the accuracy of any predictions you made before reading the selection.

b. What is Mary Vincent's purpose in creating this photo essay? How effectively does she use text and photos to meet her purpose?

c. Compare how Canadians lived at the turn of the twentieth century to how they lived in the 1950s.

d. Discuss the following statement from the photo essay: "The 21st century was supposed to bring us a life of post-industrial leisure, with all kinds of high-tech, time-saving gadgets to make life a little easier." Do you agree or disagree with this statement? Explain.

2. Visual Communication *Photos* Choose one of the photos and examine the composition of the image. With a partner, discuss elements such as shape, texture, balance, framing, lighting, motion, and juxtaposition. Explain what this photo communicates to you about how people lived in that time period.

Self-Assessment: Assess the process you used to view the image. Did you view the photo from different angles? Did you think about the photographer's purpose, or about how the subjects and colours made you feel?

Think about your family stories and what they mean to you. Read "My Father's Escapes" and consider the realization Joseph Pivato comes to about family tales and their connection to identity.

My Father's Escapes

Memoir by Joseph Pivato

The film *Seven Beauties* opens with two Italian soldiers running through the woods in central Europe to escape pursuing German soldiers. One of the Italian soldiers, played by Giancarlo Giannini, is caught after stealing some food and survives a labour camp to return home to his family in Italy. The scene of soldiers escaping into the woods is vivid in my mind because it recreates an incident in my father's life. As a young man he was drafted into the Italian army to fight in Mussolini's wars in Greece, Albania, and southern France. My father was in the Alpini artillery and survived these fronts: enduring night bombardments, guiding mules along narrow ledges, climbing cliffs, fighting artillery battles from mountain ridges, sleeping in rain and mud. One month his regiment received orders to go to the Russian Front and were issued winter gear, only to have the order changed as they were boarding the train. Many of the Alpini from his region never returned from Russia. The whole of the Julia division disappeared. My father was lucky to escape that fate.

When Italy surrendered to the Allies on the 8th of September, 1943, Italian soldiers in German-occupied northern Italy became German prisoners. My father's regiment of Alpini was stationed in southern France near Grenoble. They woke up one morning to find themselves surrounded by German soldiers. My father and his companions were taken to Modane, on the French-Italian border, and used by their German captors to do dangerous bomb disposal work. One day during a detonation of a bomb, my father and two other soldiers ran into the woods and never looked back. Much like the characters in *Seven Beauties*, they ran blindly through those wet October woods.

Later they climbed across narrow mountain passes, crawled, and hid to avoid being captured. Their alpine training in Albania and Greece was useful. From Bardonecchia they walked all day and all night to get to Susa. There was more hiding and walking to reach Rocciamelone, then north to Biella, then around to Cattinara and then Novara. They had to avoid the cities of Torino and Milano, where there were concentrations of German soldiers. Any Italian soldiers found there were taken into Germany to work in labour camps. From Novara my father travelled alone across northern Italy to reach his village of Tezze sul Brenta, east of Vicenza and west of Treviso. The distance he travelled was about 420 km. That he escaped and managed to avoid German patrols is a feat he often told us about. He would list the place names of his journey as if they were stations of the cross: Modane, Bardonecchia, Biella, and Cattinara. He had help from several people along the way: one woman hid him and gave him potatoes to eat. Later in his journey another gave him a change of clothes, and he was able to get a ride on a train. He managed somehow to send word home and his younger sister, Bianca, was able to come to get him at Fontaniva, a few kilometres from their farm. He got home half-starved and so full of fleas that they had to burn the clothes he wore.

After he got home he had to remain hidden for weeks. German soldiers were active in the area, as were partisans. In the nearby town of Bassano del Grappa the Germans hung twenty-one men one Sunday morning as a retribution for the killing of one German soldier by the local partisans. Then the Germans retreated north across the border. And for a time there were bands of outlaws roaming the countryside. Slowly my father recovered his health. He used a local remedy, *ovo col vino*, a tonic of raw eggs mixed with sugar and red wine. As children we were often given this tonic.

To my father, even after fifty years, these memories were so vivid that he could tell these stories in minute detail. He recalled the smell of the stable he slept in one night, the feel of the hay on wet clothes, the taste of those boiled potatoes, the cold water from a mountain spring in Piemonte. At other times he seemed reluctant to recall these sad events, as if the suffering and death of companions and neighbours were too painful to relive, even in Canada. He never had much use for the depiction of heroics in war movies. We must remember that for many Italians the war did not begin in 1939, but years before in 1926 when Mussolini invaded parts of North Africa to meet Italy's colonial ambitions. By the 1930s young Italian men started coming home in wooden boxes. My aunt showed me my mother's class picture from grade school and pointed out the nine boys who had died in the war, some having disappeared on the Russian Front.

My father, from the generation of 1917, was lucky to be alive at the end of the war. He was alive and in love. He enjoyed telling us the story of how he met my mother in a dentist office in Citadella. They then conducted a courtship between Tezze sul Brenta in Veneto and Nogaredo del Corno (her village) in Friuli, a distance of 100 km. In that part of Italy there were no trains running in the last months of the war, and my future parents had to travel back and forth by bicycle and by rowboat across rivers where all the bridges had been blown up either by aerial bombs or the retreating Germans. When we drove the distance years later it was hard to believe that they were able to bicycle back and forth. Besides the bad roads and wide rivers there were soldiers, partisans, and outlaw bands.

This region was a battle front in the First World War. Towns were devastated. It is the area romanticized in Hemingway's novel *A Farewell to Arms*. My family does not share this romantic view of these years. My grandfather, my mother's father, fought in this first war. He returned from Canada, where he was working as a stone mason, to defend his home territory. He was in the retreat at Caporetto and saw first-hand friends and neighbours die. My father had uncles who died in the white trenches and limestone caves of Monte Grappa. And twenty years later my parents were tracing the steps of dead soldiers across this dangerous landscape of granite war memorials and military graveyards.

In 1991, a few kilometres from these war memorials, Europeans were killing each other in the wars of ethnic cleansing of the former Yugoslavia. When I visited Friuli in 1992 I met Slovenian and Croatian refugees. Did these people escape into wet October woods to save their lives and their families?

Just after the second war my parents got married in a poverty so severe that there are no pictures to record the wedding. To escape the poverty my father went to work in a coal mine in Belgium for a while. He did not stay because of the danger of the work. He would ask, "Did I survive the war and escape the Germans to die in a coal mine?"

Then in 1951 he emigrated to Canada. My mother, my sister, and I followed him a year later. I grew up in Canada. I learned the language and the culture of North America. We forgot the Italy we left and my father put the war far behind. And Italy too forgot about us as it neglected millions of other emigrants. When I read the English history books in school there was little mention of Italy, Italian soldiers, or Italian immigrants. Yes, we would read about the great men of the Renaissance, but this seemed far removed from the simple immigrant culture we lived day-to-day. Was I aware that there was something missing?

Like many Italian immigrants my father worked in construction. In the 1950s there were few safety measures in place for construction workers. In March of 1960 five Italian workers were killed in a tunnel cave-in at Hogg's Hollow in Toronto. At another location my father was also buried in a deep trench cave-in and survived. And even in the 1960s, after safety measures came into force, the work was still dangerous. In one high building a man working on my father's floor fell to his death. On another site my father was crushed when a tall scaffolding tipped over on him. He was pinned for some time in this trap, and was only saved from mutilation and death by the chance occurrence that the falling scaffolding came to rest on some building materials behind him. He shrugged off this narrow escape like many others in his life. It was just fate.

We grew up in Canada. We became Canadian, but somewhere I was also aware that my family was different. The Veneto dialect that my parents spoke, the Italian regional dishes that we ate, and the Italian people we socialized with reminded us that there was another aspect to our identity. For us the backyard garden was an extension of our kitchen. Every vegetable and fruit had a meaning and a link back to Italy. One Christmas my father came to stay with us in Edmonton and brought some cuttings from a fruit tree in the backyard. It was a fig tree that Italians had developed to survive the Canadian winter. In Edmonton we planted it in a big flowerpot inside our sun room and it has flourished ever since and produced figs. Italians have always transplanted their culture. We were not conscious of it at the time, but my father's stories, my stone mason grandfather's migrations, and other family tales were part of this identity.

When I began to read the stories by other Italian-Canadian writers I became conscious of these family stories of escapes and migrations. There was often a dead grandfather in the background; an almost forgotten mother or an old uncle who had survived to retell some old family story. These younger writers, the sons and daughters of immigrants, were trying to reconcile their lives in Canada with their roots in Italy, migrations to Argentina or Australia or New York. Beyond the summer trips to Italy, the search for lost family recipes, the home-made pasta, and the home-made wine, we wonder if there is an Italian culture outside of Italy? Can we capture it in a poem or song?

My father lived for eighty years, and he was always physically active. Two days after I said goodbye to him in front of our old family house in Toronto he died in his garden. It was a cool morning on the 23rd of October, the anniversary of his escape from Modane, and he was getting his garden ready for winter. He made one last escape. He quietly slipped away before anybody could notice. And he is probably still hurrying through those cool October woods with the other Alpini.

1. Exploring Meaning

a. Summarize the various escapes referred to in "My Father's Escapes." Explain what Joseph Pivato means when he refers to his father's "one last escape."

b. What five words would you use to describe Joseph Pivato's father? For each description, provide evidence from the memoir to support your choice.

c. Explain the connections Pivato sees among the film *Seven Beauties*, Ernest Hemingway's novel *A Farewell to Arms*, and his father's life.

d. What does Pivato mean when he says, "Italians have always transplanted their culture"? Do you think this is true of all cultures? Explain.

e. The author uses specific appeals to the senses to create vivid pictures in the minds of the readers. Find and record two images that appeal to each of the five senses.

f. In your opinion, is it important to hand down family stories? Why or why not?

2. Technique and Style *Circular Structure* Reread the first two paragraphs and the last paragraph of the profile, noting the use of **circular structure**. What event or idea does the author repeat? Why do you think the author uses this type of repetition? How does the repetition reinforce the message of the memoir?

> **Circular structure** occurs when a phrase, line, or idea at the beginning of a text is repeated at the end.

3. Film Study Joseph Pivato states that his father "never had much use for the depiction of heroics in war movies." Why do you think his father felt this way? In your opinion, do the media present a glorified picture of war? Select a war movie to view and review. Write a short movie review addressing this question.

Peer Assessment: Ask a classmate to assess your review. Is your opinion clearly stated? Does the review include evidence from the movie to support your viewpoint? Does the review end with a clear statement of your conclusions?

4. Writing *Poem* In "My Father's Escapes" the author suggests his sense of Italian-Canadian identity is connected with family stories told by relatives—a father, a mother, a grandfather, or an uncle. The memoir, in a sense, is used to honour his father's life. Write a narrative poem to honour one of your older family members. Include the person's name and relationship to you and describe him or her and what he or she has done.

Self-Assessment: Evaluate the main image in your poem. What central picture is created in the reader's mind? Does it help to convey your message? Does your message connect to your purpose?

Another story altogether

Poem by Anne Le Dressay

Not my story, but the other one
that was there all along, tangled with mine
and utterly separate, breathing at night
in the bed across the room, while I lived
my own story. My own. Small, centred,
mine, that talked my words and saw
through my eyes.

This other story sees it through her eyes,
and they are 3 years younger and a different
colour. It's not the same family and not the same
traumas. The family is 3 years older when she
starts remembering, and there are more people in it.

Two stories, two worlds barely touching,
the light hitting the same things at such
different angles they are not the same things
at all. To her, I am part of the world outside of
her, in which she must find or make a place.
To me, she is outside.

You'd think it would be the same house at least,
the same bedroom. But she was afraid of the dark
and I wasn't. We had a fair and equal arrangement:
one night, the door closed tightly for me, the next
night, left open a crack for her.

Only now does it occur to me to wonder
if, every second night when the door was closed
to spare me the small distraction of that
shaft of light, she lay awake, facing alone
the terrors of the dark,
while I slept.

1. Exploring Meaning

a. Whose stories are referred to in the poem?

b. With a partner, take turns reading the stanzas and explaining the meaning of each line.

c. In later years, what does the speaker wonder about the "fair and equal arrangement" mentioned in stanza four? Do you think it was a fair and equal arrangement? Do you think the speaker feels guilty about the past?

d. What is the theme of the poem? What is the author saying about the nature of memory?

2. Writing *Changing Point of View* "Another story altogether" is told in the first person from the point of view of the older sister. Using the poem as a model, write a poem in which you relate the younger sister's story. Consider whether you will use the first person (*I, me, we*) or the more objective third person (*he, she, they*). How will your choice of person affect the **style** of the poem?

Style is the overall texture of a piece of writing; the particular way in which ideas are expressed. Style is made up of many elements including diction, figurative language, sentences, and tone.

As you edit the poem, examine the pronouns you've used for consistency of person and gender, and ensure that you've maintained a consistent verb tense.

Self-Assessment: Assess the process you used to develop your poem. Did you brainstorm for ideas and images? Did you choose a central image to focus your message? What advice would you offer to someone writing a poem?

Remember?

Poem by Alice Walker

Remember me?
I am the girl
with the dark skin
whose shoes are thin
I am the girl
with rotted teeth
I am the dark
rotten-toothed girl
with the wounded eye
and the melted ear.

I am the girl
holding their babies
cooking their meals
sweeping their yards
washing their clothes
Dark and rotting
and wounded, wounded.

I would give
to the human race
only hope.

I am the woman
with the blessed
dark skin
I am the woman
with teeth repaired
I am the woman
with the healing eye
the ear that hears.

Untitled by Christopher Myers. Mixed media.

I am the woman: Dark,
repaired, healed
Listening to you.

I would give
to the human race
only hope.

I am the woman
offering two flowers
whose roots
are twin

Justice and Hope

Let us begin.

1. Exploring Meaning

a. What is the significance of the title "Remember?" Do you think the title is effective? Why or why not?

b. Briefly describe the girl and the woman. How are they different?

c. What do the rotten teeth, wounded eye, and melted ear say about the girl?

d. Explain who "their" might refer to in the second stanza.

2. Literature Studies *Analyse Poem* With a partner, read and analyse the poem. Use the following prompts to get you started:

• What metaphors are used in the poem?

• What other poetic techniques does Alice Walker use?

• What is the poem's message? What techniques reinforce the message?

• Discuss the shift in tone in the fourth stanza. Explain how this shift relates to Alice Walker's message.

3. Language Conventions *Parallel Structure* To emphasize ideas, writers often repeat phrases, sentences, or grammatical patterns. This technique is called *parallel structure*. Alice Walker uses this form of repetition in the phrases "I am the girl" and "I am the woman." Find other examples of parallel structure in the poem. Why do you think the poet uses it? Is this technique effective in the poem, or is it overused?

4. Oral Communication *Dramatic Reading* Prepare a dramatized oral reading of "Remember?" Before your performance, decide what techniques you can use to develop an effective reading that conveys the tone and meaning of the poem.

Self-Assessment: Tape your reading and then listen to it. Are you satisfied with your presentation? What can you do to improve future readings?

5. Visual Communication *Analyse Image* Examine the image accompanying the poem. Do you think the image represents the speaker of the poem? What aspect of everyday life does it show? What mood does it convey?

Draw or find a visual that you think represents the speaker of the poem. Discuss your visual with a classmate, explaining your choice.

Think about any acts of kindness you have experienced or have heard about that have significantly changed a life. Share these stories with a partner.

THE GIFT: How One Act of Kindness Changed a Life

Anecdote by Monty Hall as told to Robert Kiener

Although I haven't appeared on television as emcee of "Let's Make a Deal" since 1991, not a day goes by that someone doesn't recognize me. "Hey, Monty!" a stranger will invariably yell at me. "What's behind Door Number One?" While I appreciate the recognition, I sometimes wish that I were known more for what I do today—charity work.

I make more than 50 charity appearances a year and must have raised nearly a billion dollars for worthwhile causes. In 1988 I received the Order of Canada for my humanitarian work.

Countless times I have seen that if you cast your bread upon the waters, it will come back a hundredfold. But there is one story in particular that, for me, illustrates the point. To this day it can still move me to tears.

On a crisp spring day in 1942, Max Freed, the owner of a Winnipeg shirt-making company, Hercules Manufacturing, was returning to his factory with a bundle of orders tucked neatly beneath his arm. Business was good and Max, although only 30, was carving out a niche as a successful businessman.

As he walked to his office, he noticed a young man across the street, on his hands and knees, scrubbing the front steps of Churchill's, a clothing wholesaler. The young man looked familiar. Freed crossed the street and asked him, "What are you doing here?"

The 20-year-old answered: "I work for Churchill's. My boss told me to scrub these steps."

"What's your name?" asked Freed. The young man told him.

"Is your father my butcher?" Yes, the youth replied.

Freed went to his office and phoned the butcher. "I just saw your son washing the steps at the company across the street from mine. He seems like an intelligent young man—is that the kind of work he's chosen to do?"

"He wants to go back to college," the soft-spoken butcher told Freed, "but I can't afford to send him." He explained that his son had worked for two years after graduating from high school, saving for college. But after a year and a half at the University of Manitoba, his money had run out. Business was poor, and even though the butcher's wife worked two jobs, the family barely scraped by. The young man's weekly salary of nine dollars helped out tremendously.

"Tell your son to come see me tomorrow," Freed told the butcher.

The next night, after finishing his work as a delivery boy and cleaner at Churchill's, the wiry 20-year-old met with Freed in his factory office.

"Do you want to go back to college?" Freed asked.

"More than anything!" the young man replied.

Freed looked him straight in the eye. "I'll put you through college. Write down how much money you need and bring it back to me—tuition, books, everything."

A smile broadened across the youth's face; he could not believe this was happening. Where had this guardian angel come from?

The next day when the young man showed Freed his figures, the shirt-maker looked them over and said: "Don't you want something for yourself? Don't you eat lunch or get the occasional haircut? You'll also need some new clothes. Add all that in."

Before handing over a cheque, Freed told the young man, "There are several conditions I insist upon."

The youth sat silently, eyes wide with expectation.

"First, you must tell no one where this money came from." The young man nodded. "Second, you must maintain top grades; I'm not sending you to college to be a playboy.

"Third, this is a loan. You have to pay me back every penny when you can afford to. And lastly, you must promise to do this for someone else in your lifetime."

"Thank you, Mr. Freed," the 20-year-old replied. "I won't disappoint you."

Each month he visited Freed to report on his progress. At the University of Manitoba, he earned high grades, was near the top of his class and was elected president of the student body.

Over three years, Max Freed lent the butcher's son $990. The young graduate began repaying the debt as soon as he landed his first job after college. He sent Freed $100 the first year, $100 the next and the rest the third year after he graduated.

Throughout his life, he never forgot the day he'd been given the opportunity he needed to succeed. He also remembered the vow he'd made to do the same for someone else and has since helped several young people through college.

There was one promise the young man made to Max Freed that he couldn't keep. For nearly 30 years, he told no one the identity of his mysterious benefactor. But he finally decided to tell his story because he felt it would inspire others to help someone, and because he felt that Max Freed deserved the recognition despite wanting to be anonymous.

I often tell this story. It reminds me that no matter what we do in life, no matter how high we climb the ladder of success, we will ultimately be remembered for how we helped others less fortunate than ourselves.

There's another reason I love telling this story: I am the butcher's son.

---

1. Exploring Meaning

a. Who is the butcher's son? Describe him and support your descriptions with examples from the anecdote.

b. Which of the promises he made to Max Freed couldn't the young man keep? Why did the young man break his promise?

c. The author states, ". . . I have seen that if you cast your bread upon the waters, it will come back a hundredfold." In your own words, explain the meaning of this sentence. How does the story of Max Freed and the butcher's son illustrate this point?

d. What is the **allusion** in the quotation in question c? What is the source of the allusion?

> An **allusion** is a brief reference within a literary work to another literary work, or a person, place, event, or object from history, literature, or mythology.

2. Writing *Anecdote* Think about one story you shared with a partner in the pre-reading activity. What life lesson or message can be drawn from the incident? Recount this event in a short anecdote. Before you develop the anecdote, jot down a list of the features of this format. Consider how you can incorporate these features as you write. Share your anecdote with your classmates.

Self-Assessment: Read over your anecdote. Have you used the features of the format? Have you painted a clear picture of the subject? Revise your work with these questions in mind.

Think back to your childhood and pinpoint one moment in which you moved into adulthood. Describe the event in your notebook.

To Everything There Is a Season

Short Story by Alistair MacLeod

I am speaking here of a time when I was eleven and lived with my family on our small farm on the west coast of Cape Breton. My family had been there for a long, long time and so it seemed had I. And much of that time seems like the proverbial yesterday. Yet when I speak on this Christmas 1977, I am not sure how much I speak with the voice of that time or how much in the voice of what I have since become. And I am not sure how many liberties I may be taking with the boy I think I was. For Christmas is a time of both past and present and often the two are imperfectly blended. As we step into its nowness we often look behind.

We have been waiting now, it seems, forever. Actually, it has been most intense since Halloween when the first snow fell upon us as we moved like muffled mummers upon darkened country roads. The large flakes were soft and new then and almost generous and the earth to which they fell was still warm and as yet unfrozen. They fell in silence into the puddles and into the sea where they disappeared at the moment of contact. They disappeared, too, upon touching the heated redness of our necks and hands or the faces of those who did not wear masks. We carried our pillowcases from house to house, knocking on doors to become silhouettes in the light thrown out from kitchens (white pillowcases held out by whitened forms). The snow fell between us and the doors and was transformed in shimmering golden beams. When we turned to leave, it fell upon our footprints and as the night wore on obliterated them and all the records of our movements. In the morning everything was soft and still and November had come upon us.

My brother Kenneth, who is two and a half, is unsure of his last Christmas. It is Halloween that looms largest in his memory as an exceptional time of being up late in magic darkness and falling snow. "Who are you going to dress up as at Christmas?" he asks. "I think I'll be a snowman." All of us laugh at that and tell him Santa Claus will find him if he is good and that he need not dress up at all. We go about our appointed tasks waiting for it to happen.

I am troubled myself about the nature of Santa Claus and I am trying to hang on to him in any way that I can. It is true that at my age I no longer *really* believe in him yet I have hoped in all his possibilities as fiercely as I can; much in the same way, I think, that the drowning man waves desperately to the lights of the passing ship on the high sea's darkness. For without him, as without the man's ship, it seems our fragile lives would be so much more desperate.

My mother has been fairly tolerant of my attempted perpetuation. Perhaps because she has encountered it before. Once I overheard her speaking about my sister Anne to one of her neighbours. "I thought Anne would *believe* forever," she said. "I practically had to tell her." I have somehow always wished I had not heard her say that as I seek sanctuary and reinforcement even in an ignorance I know I dare not trust.

Kenneth, however, believes with an unadulterated fervour, and so do Bruce and Barry who are six-year-old twins. Beyond me there is Anne who is thirteen and Mary who is fifteen, both of whom seem to be leaving childhood at an alarming rate. My mother has told us that she was already married when she was seventeen, which is only two years older than Mary is now. That too seems strange to contemplate and perhaps childhood is shorter for some than it is for others. I think of this sometimes in the evenings when we have finished our chores and the supper dishes have been cleared away and we are supposed to be doing our homework. I glance sideways at my mother, who is always knitting or mending, and at my father, who mostly sits by the stove coughing quietly with his handkerchief at his mouth. He has "not been well" for over two years and has difficulty breathing whenever he moves at more than the slowest pace. He is most sympathetic of all concerning my extended hopes and says we should hang on to the good things in our lives as long as we are able. As I look at him out of the corner of my eye, it does not seem that he has many of them left. He is old, we think, at forty-two.

Yet Christmas, in spite of all the doubts of our different ages, is a fine and splendid time, and now as we pass the midpoint of December our expectations are heightened by the increasing coldness that has settled down upon us. The ocean is flat and calm and along the coast, in the scooped-out coves, has turned to an icy slush. The brook that flows past our house is almost totally frozen and there is only a small channel of rushing water that flows openly at its very centre. When we let the cattle out to drink, we chop holes with the axe at the brook's edge so that they can drink without venturing onto the ice.

The sheep move in and out of their lean-to shelter, restlessly stamping their feet or huddling together in tightly packed groups. A conspiracy of wool against the cold. The hens perch high on their roosts with their feathers fluffed out about them, hardly feeling it worthwhile to descend to the floor for their few scant kernels of grain. The pig, who has little time before his butchering, squeals his displeasure to the cold and with his snout tosses his wooden trough high in the icy air. The splendid young horse paws the planking of his stall and gnaws the wooden cribwork of his manger.

We have put a protective barricade of spruce boughs about our kitchen door and banked our house with additional boughs and billows of eel grass. Still, the pail of water we leave standing in the porch is solid in the morning and has to be broken with the hammer. The clothes my mother hangs on the line are frozen almost instantly and sway and creak from their suspending clothespins like sections of dismantled robots: the stiff-legged rasping trousers and the shirts and sweaters with unyielding arms outstretched. In the morning we race from our frigid upstairs bedrooms to finish dressing around the kitchen stove.

We would extend our coldness half a continent away to the Great Lakes of Ontario so that it might hasten the Christmas coming of my oldest brother, Neil. He is nineteen and employed on the "lake boats," the long flat carriers of grain and iron ore whose season ends any day after December 10, depending on the ice conditions. We wish it to be cold, cold on the Great Lakes of Ontario, so that he may come home to us as soon as possible. Already his cartons have arrived. They come from different places: Cobourg, Toronto, St. Catharines, Welland, Windsor, Sarnia, Sault Ste. Marie. Places that we, with the exception of my father, have never been. We locate them excitedly on the map, tracing their outlines with eager fingers. The cartons bear the lettering of Canada Steamship Lines, and are bound with rope knotted intricately in the fashion of sailors. My mother says they contain his "clothes" and we are not allowed to open them.

For us it is impossible to know the time or manner of his coming. If the lakes freeze early, he may come by train because it is cheaper. If the lakes stay open until December 20, he will have to fly because his time will be more precious than his money. He will hitchhike the last sixty or hundred miles from either station or airport. On our part, we can do nothing but listen with straining ears to radio reports of distant ice formations. His coming

Bringing Home the Christmas Tree by Eric Sloane. Oil on masonite.

seems to depend on so many factors which are out there far beyond us and over which we lack control.

The days go by in fevered slowness until finally on the morning of December 23 the strange car rolls into our yard. My mother touches her hand to her lips and whispers "Thank God." My father gets up unsteadily from his chair to look through the window. Their longed-for son and our golden older brother is here at last. He is here with his reddish hair and beard and we can hear his hearty laugh. He will be happy and strong and confident for us all.

There are three other young men with him who look much the same as he. They too are from the boats and are trying to get home to Newfoundland. They must still drive a hundred miles to reach the ferry at North Sydney. The car seems very old. They purchased it in Thorold for two hundred dollars because they were too late to make any reservations, and they have driven steadily since they began. In northern New Brunswick their windshield wipers failed, but instead of stopping they tied lengths of cord to the wipers' arms and passed them through the front window vents. Since that time, in whatever precipitation, one of them has pulled the cords back and forth to make the wipers function. This information falls tiredly but excitedly from their lips and we greedily gather it in. My father pours them drinks of rum and my mother takes out her mincemeat and the fruitcakes she has been carefully hoarding. We lean on the furniture or look from the safety of sheltered doorways. We would like to hug our brother but are too shy with strangers present. In the kitchen's warmth, the young men begin to nod and doze, their heads dropping suddenly to their chests. They nudge each other with their feet in an attempt to keep awake. They will not stay and rest because they have come so far and tomorrow is Christmas Eve and stretches of mountains and water still lie between them and those they love.

After they leave we pounce upon our brother physically and verbally. He laughs and shouts and lifts us over his head and swings us in his muscular arms. Yet in spite of his happiness he seems surprised at the appearance of his father, whom he has not seen since March. My father merely smiles at him, while my mother bites her lip.

Now that he is here there is a great flurry of activity. We have left everything we could until the time he might be with us. Eagerly I show him the fir tree on the hill which I have been watching for months and marvel at how easily he fells it and carries it down the hill. We fall over one another in the excitement of decoration.

He promises that on Christmas Eve he will take us to church in the sleigh behind the splendid horse that until his coming we are all afraid to handle. And on the afternoon of Christmas Eve he shoes the horse, lifting each hoof and rasping it fine and hammering the cherry-red horseshoes into shape upon the anvil. Later he drops them hissingly into the steaming tub of water. My father sits beside him on an overturned pail and tells him what to do. Sometimes we argue with our father, but our brother does everything he says.

That night, bundled in hay and voluminous coats, and with heated stones at our feet, we start upon our journey. Our parents and Kenneth remain at home but all the rest of us go. Before we leave we feed the cattle and sheep and even the pig all that they can possibly eat so that they will be contented on Christmas Eve. Our parents wave to us from the doorway. We go four miles across the mountain road. It is a primitive logging trail and there will be no cars or other vehicles upon it. At first the horse is wild with excitement and lack of exercise and my brother has to stand at the front of the sleigh and lean backwards on the reins. Later he settles down to a trot and still later to a walk as the mountain rises before him. We sing all the Christmas songs we know and watch for the rabbits and foxes scudding across the open patches of snow and listen to the drumming of partridge wings. We are never cold.

When we descend to the country church we tie the horse in a grove of trees where he will be sheltered and not frightened by the many cars. We put a blanket over him and give him oats. At the church door the neighbours shake hands with my brother. "Hello, Neil," they say. "How is your father?"

"Oh," he says, just "Oh."

The church is very beautiful at night with its festooned branches and glowing candles and the booming, joyous sounds that come from the choir loft. We go through the service as if we are mesmerized.

On the way home, although the stones have cooled, we remain happy and warm. We listen to the creak of the leather harness and the hiss of runners on the snow and begin to think of the potentiality of presents. When we are about a mile from home the horse senses his destination and breaks into a trot and then into a confident lope. My brother lets him go and we move across the winter landscape like figures freed from a Christmas card. The snow from the horse's hooves falls about our heads like the whiteness of the stars.

After we have stabled the horse we talk with our parents and eat the meal our mother has prepared. And then I am sleepy and it is time for the younger children to be in bed. But tonight my father says to me, "We would like you to stay up with us a while," and so I stay quietly with the older members of my family.

When all is silent upstairs Neil brings in the cartons that contain his "clothes" and begins to open them. He unties the intricate knots quickly, their whorls falling away before his agile fingers. The boxes are filled with gifts neatly wrapped and bearing tags. The ones for my younger brothers say "from Santa Claus" but mine are not among them anymore, as I know with certainty they will never be again. Yet I am not so much surprised as touched by a pang of loss at being here on the adult side of the world. It is as if I have suddenly moved into another room and heard a door click lastingly behind me. I am jabbed by my own small wound.

But then I look at those before me. I look at my parents drawn together before the Christmas tree. My mother has her hand upon my father's shoulder and he is holding his everpresent handkerchief. I look at my sisters who have crossed this threshold ahead of me and now each day journey farther from the lives they knew as girls. I look at my magic older brother who has come to us this Christmas from half a continent away, bringing everything he has and is. All of them are captured in the tableau of their care.

"Every man moves on," says my father quietly, and I think he speaks of Santa Claus, "but there is no need to grieve. He leaves good things behind." ◆

1. Exploring Meaning

a. Why does Alistair MacLeod tell the story from the point of view of a first-person narrator reflecting back to a time when he was eleven years old?

b. What does the narrator mean when he says, "I am not sure how much I speak with the voice of that time or how much in the voice of what I have since become"?

c. What change is the narrator referring to when he says, "It is as if I have suddenly moved into another room and heard a door click lastingly behind me. I am jabbed by my own small wound"? How does he feel about this change? Can you think of a similar event or feeling you've experienced in your life?

d. The narrator states, "All of them are captured in the tableau of their care." What does he mean? Describe what the tableau reveals to you about his family and their relationships.

e. To what degree do you believe this story to be autobiographical? Is there any evidence to support your viewpoint?

2. Technique and Style *Allusion* The title, "To Everything There Is a Season" is a Biblical allusion. With a partner, read the following quotation from the Bible and discuss the appropriateness of the allusion. How does knowledge of the Biblical passage help you to understand the theme of the short story? Discuss your viewpoint in a small group.

> There is a time for everything, and a season for every activity under heaven: a time to be born and a time to die, a time to plant and a time to uproot, a time to kill and a time to heal, a time to tear down and a time to build, a time to weep and a time to laugh, a time to mourn and a time to dance, a time to scatter stones and a time to gather them, a time to embrace and a time to refrain, a time to search and a time to give up, a time to keep and a time to throw away, a time to tear and a time to mend, a time to be silent and a time to speak, a time to love and a time to hate, a time for war and a time for peace.
>
> *Ecclesiastes 3:1–8*

3. Language Conventions *Commas* The comma is a punctuation mark with many uses. These uses include separating items in a series, dividing subordinate clauses from main clauses, and creating compound and complex sentences. Reread "To Everything There Is a Season" to find examples of each of these uses of the comma and list them in your notebook. Use a grammar handbook to help you.

4. Visual Communication *Analyse Painting* Examine and discuss the image accompanying the story. What message does this image send? How does it support the story? Discuss its use of colour, texture, space, light, depth, and any visual elements you find appealing.

With a partner, search the Internet or other sources to discover three facts about Sherpas. For example, you could explore the training, skills, or aptitudes they need to become mountaineers.

Babu Chhiri

Obituary from *The Times, London*

Among the tough and tireless Sherpa people who serve the international expeditions to the world's highest mountains, Babu Chhiri Sherpa was a national hero and icon. Everest became his speciality and he reached the 29,028-foot summit 10 times, holding the record for the fastest ascent and becoming the first man to survive a night "camping" on the summit.

He died on the mountain he had helped so many clients climb in what first reports suggest was an elementary accident.

While taking photographs alone above the notorious Khumbu ice-fall, he fell more than 100 feet into a crevasse.

Climbers on the Kathmandu Metropolitan Everest expedition, which he was leading, retrieved his body.

Babu Chhiri did much to improve the status of the Sherpas who cheerfully carry loads for traditionally small reward, supporting the attempts on the giant peaks that are the natural backdrop to their villages. There is a stark distinction between locals simply doing a tough job for which they are naturally equipped and mountaineers whose motives for risking their lives on Everest and its lofty neighbours are more elusive.

Mountaineers pay handsomely for the privilege of facing the physical and objective dangers the Himalayas present. George Mallory famously attempted Everest "because it is there," and while western mountaineers today reach for

Babu Chhiri, a Nepalese professional mountain guide, waves to supporters in Kathmandu in May 2000. Photo by Binod Joshi.

some intellectual justification for exploring this tilted wilderness, the Sherpas have more pragmatic reasons. Babu Chhiri climbed to provide for his six daughters, to give them a better life than, as he put it, "having to carry someone else's gear up Everest."

He built his formidable reputation in the hope of being able to provide a school for his daughters to attend in their home village, to ensure that they could enjoy the education he never had.

He concentrated on Everest because the biggest reputations are forged on the biggest mountains.

But he was not the epitome of a mountain athlete, being short and even plumply built. His father, Llakpa Sherpa, was one of the porters hired by the British expedition led by Colonel John Hunt which first conquered Everest in 1953; in the early 1980s Babu Chhiri was set to follow his career as a load carrier in the trekking business. When he was 17, he worked as a porter carrying 60-pound loads for trekking groups for 30 pence a day.

Having "never seen the door of a school," he taught himself to read and picked up a smattering of English from trekking clients.

Over the next few years, he worked as a cook for trekking and climbing parties, helping to finance a small tea house run by Puti, his wife. But it was not until 1989, when a Soviet expedition engaged him on an expedition to traverse Kanchenjunga, that he first showed exceptional talent as a high-altitude mountaineer. The climbers spent 100 days on the mountain, which allowed him a crash course in climbing techniques and revealed his remarkable tolerance for surviving at altitudes mountaineers regard as a "death zone." Ten climbers completed the traverse and two of them, accompanied by Babu Chhiri, reached the 28,208-foot summit of Kanchenjunga. Unlike Soviet climbers, he got there without the added boost from bottled oxygen that only a few years earlier many had regarded as essential for survival in the thin air above 26,000 feet. Throughout his mountaineering career he never resorted to what the Sherpas once called "English air."

From this springboard, Babu Chhiri gained a leading position among the Sherpa guides catering for the 24,000 trekkers and climbers who explore the Solo Khumbu region each year. In the spring of 1990, he climbed 26,795-foot Dhaulagiri with a French expedition, and in the autumn of the same year, again with a French expedition, he reached the summit of Everest for the first of 10 times. Thereafter, he accompanied New Zealand, British, South African and Nepalese expeditions, and added Shisha Pangma (26,397 feet), Cho Oyu (26,906 feet) and Ama Dablam (22,494 feet) to his list of conquests.

As his reputation increased, Babu Chhiri turned to even more impressive feats of endurance which, he said, "gives me power." In May 1999 he climbed Everest by the south-west ridge with Dawa, his older brother, and another

Sherpa. Together they dug a platform on the summit and anchored down a small tent, shaped to withstand the howling winds. Babu Chhiri crawled into its protection wearing a down suit and cocooned in a sleeping bag designed to withstand extreme cold. After singing the Nepalese national anthem, he lay there for 21 hours before returning home.

Last spring, he set out to beat the speed record up and down the mountain. Starting from base camp, an acclimatized mountaineer may expect to take four days to reach the top. The previous fastest time to the top and back, set by Kaji Sherpa in 1998, was 20 hours. Babu Chhiri jogged into base camp from the summit in less than 17 hours. In Kathmandu he was given a hero's welcome.

Sherpas in general have the lungs, stamina and a natural in-built resistance to the effects of thin air; to these qualities Babu Chhiri added a shrewd professionalism. He was an executive director and major shareholder in Nomad Expeditions and was devoted to winning for the local community more of the hard currency earned by the trekking and mountaineering industry in Nepal. His next ambition had been to make two ascents of Everest in 2001, which would have established him as having climbed the mountain more times than any other person. Sadly instead, he has joined the 167 climbers and Sherpas who have died on Everest.

Babu Chhiri Sherpa leaves a widow, Puti, and six daughters.

1. Exploring Meaning

a. The obituary describes Babu Chhiri as a national hero and icon. How does the obituary prove this description?

b. According to the author, there is a distinction between local Sherpas doing a job and the mountaineers who hire them. What is this distinction? Why did Babu Chhiri become a mountaineer?

c. List Babu Chhiri's accomplishments in both his professional life and his personal life. Do you think he is a hero? Explain.

d. Do you think it is appropriate to include an obituary in a Biography unit? Explain.

2. Writing *Choose a Format* Decide on a Canadian hero you wish to honour and praise. This hero may be a friend, a family member, a local hero, or a national hero, alive or dead. Choose a writing format that you feel will best express your praise (for example, an essay, a letter to the editor, an obituary, or a poem) and develop your text.

Revise your draft to ensure an effective style. Examine your sentence construction, word choice or diction, tone, and figurative language.

Self-Assessment: Read your work aloud to check that the style is appropriate to the topic and the audience.

Where I Come From

Poem by Elizabeth Brewster

People are made of places. They carry with them
hints of jungles or mountains, a tropic grace
or the cool eyes of sea-gazers. Atmosphere of cities
how different drops from them, like the smell of smog
or the almost-not-smell of tulips in the spring,
nature tidily plotted in little squares
with a fountain in the centre; museum smell,
art also tidily plotted with a guidebook;
or the smell of work, glue factories maybe,
chromium-plated offices; smell of subways
crowded at rush hours.

Where I come from, people
carry woods in their minds, acres of pine woods;
blueberry patches in the burned-out bush;
wooden farmhouses, old, in need of paint,
with yards where hens and chickens circle about,
clucking aimlessly; battered schoolhouses
behind which violets grow. Spring and winter
are the mind's chief seasons: ice and the breaking of ice.

A door in the mind blows open, and there blows
a frosty wind from fields of snow.

1. Exploring Meaning

a. Describe the structure of the poem and discuss its effectiveness.

b. What two types of places does Elizabeth Brewster compare? Does she show a preference for one place over the other? Explain.

c. Where do you think Brewster comes from? What descriptions in the poem provide you with clues?

d. What is the strongest image in the poem?

e. Explain Brewster's theme or message using references from the poem.

2. Focus on Context Use your research skills to compile background information about Elizabeth Brewster. You could give an overview of her career, list her major poetic works, and summarize any themes common to her poetry. Include any other information that you believe would help a reader to discover the context for her work.

Self-Assessment: Assess the process you used to complete your research. Did you develop a research plan before beginning? Did you develop a list of questions about the author to focus your research? How would you change the process the next time you conduct research?

3. Language Conventions *Vivid Language* One of the keys to good poetry is the use of description to create mental images for the reader. Create a four-column chart with the headings *strong verbs, specific nouns, vivid adjectives,* and *strong adverbs*. Find examples from the poem to complete the chart.

Choose one of these descriptions and describe in your own words the image that comes to mind.

Fulfillment

Oil Painting by Ruth Pawson

Fulfillment by Ruth Pawson, S.O.M., 1952. Oil on canvas board.

Visual Communication *Examine Painting* With a partner, discuss how the artist uses elements of colour, line, shape, texture, and size to create an impact. What mood or feeling does the painting evoke? How does this painting evoke feelings similar to those expressed in the poem "Where I Come From"?

In a small group, speculate about why someone famous and successful would want to disappear from the spotlight.

The Reluctant Black Hawk

Profile by Brenda Zeman

So you want to find the Indian guy who walked out thirty years ago on the Chicago Black Hawks? Good luck. Freddie Sasakamoose has no phone. Nor does he return a phone message passed on to him by his friend, Ray Ahenakew. Maybe, you think, he's had his fill of strangers asking him why he gave up a Canadian boy's dream to play in the National Hockey League. Yet, because you want to understand how it happened, you decide to jump in your car, go look for this Freddie Sasakamoose, track him down.

You head north from Saskatoon into Doukhobor country beyond the North Saskatchewan River. In the Lucky Dollar store at Blaine Lake, a fair-haired woman looks at you, then says "*Nyet*" to a baby fussing in a grocery cart.

North of town, past the Muskeg Lake Reserve sign, you veer northwest. The road is paved and bales of hay and swaths of wheat lie on golden hills set into the blue sky. To your relief you see people ahead, a road crew. You ask directions but even the road crew doesn't seem to know the road. About thirty miles, says one fellow. Sixty, for sure, says another. A third says, Better ask at the garage this side of Shell Lake.

Simonar's Repair Service and Café. The old garage man eyes you curiously when you say you want to go to Sandy Lake.

I'm looking for Freddie Sasakamoose, you add.

So am I, he says.

Why?

He owes me, he drawls, his face crinkling into a slow smile, no sign of malice in his tired blue eyes.

Three teenage girls stand hitchhiking on a reserve road. You stop and they pile in. They don't know much about Freddie Sasakamoose. One girl says, He used to be Chief of Sandy Lake and he used to play for the Sandy Lake Chiefs.

That's all you know? you ask. What about the slapshot? What about his ambidexterity? The rink-long rushes? His magic on the ice?

The girls are puzzled and they giggle, not knowing what to say. No, they've never heard about Freddie going to Chicago when the NHL only had six teams. Or about the time in 1974 when Freddie was in Edmonton making final preparations to take a young Saskatchewan Indian hockey team to Finland. Howie Meeker heard about it and invited Freddie to a Team Canada (World Hockey Association) practice. Later, in the dressing room, Bobby Hull greeted Freddie with, I know who you are! You're the Indian who played with Chicago. You're the beggar with the slapshot I had to live up to!

You drive on in the silence wondering what is beyond the next hill. From the top you see the centre of the reserve, a cluster of buildings just down the road. You breathe a sigh of relief.

The name "Atahkakoop" is everywhere. On the rink, on the school, finally at the entrance to the band office. After the hereditary chief, one girl says. You ask why the name "Sasakamoose" isn't on the rink, but the girls get out saying they don't know.

You go in the band office and ask for Freddie Sasakamoose, former elected chief of the Atahkakoop Indian Reserve. He's in there, a man points to a door three steps away. At an all-day meeting, he says, only happens once a month. He goes inside to get him. You notice a sign in the office, NO LONG DISTANCE TELEPHONE CALLS.

Councillor Freddie Sasakamoose emerges from the meeting room. Your eyes meet at the same level; he can't be more than five feet seven inches tall in his Texaco cap and he's stocky. He doesn't know you from Eve. You tell him you've come to find him, to ask him if he'll tell his story. His black eyes are amused. Oh yeah, he grins, I was gonna phone you sometime.

You find yourself grinning with Frederick George Sasakamoose.

Freddie

I was born December 25, 1933, over at Whitefish Reserve, now they call it Big River Reserve, just neighbourly out from here, about fifteen miles from this reserve, Sandy Lake. My mother's father, old Gaspar Morin, lived at Victoire. It used to be a Metis settlement near Whitefish. My grandmother Morin was an Indian from Sandy Lake who married out to a Metis. That made my mother Metis too, until she married in to a Sandy Lake Indian. My mother's name is Sugil.

Them days in the thirties it was tough. My father, Roderick Sasakamoose, was into loggin'. Very hardly did I see my old man trap. His father was Alexander Sasakamoose and he married a Favel, Julia was my grandmother. Old Alexander musta been into some farming. I remember the time he chased me for jumpin' on some haystacks. He was mute, he couldn't talk or hear, but he could run, that old man. Caught me too, and gave me a good lickin'.

I had a good childhood, real good.

When I was about eight years old my parents sent me to school at St. Michael's over at Duck Lake. Maybe they seen something ahead for me, I don't know. It wasn't too far, only about sixty miles, but it seemed like the other end of the world away.

Sugil

I really missed my kids when I had to send them so far away from home. I had eleven kids but only five lived. I've lost two sets of twins and another boy and another girl, they all died from illness. I knew Freddie and the others would be well taken care of at the residential school. It was better I send them because we didn't have no bus and I didn't want them to get sick. I've sent all my children away to school, including Clara[1] who was five when she left.

My husband was a great sportsman in his day, a really good soccer player for this reserve. He used to travel all around and he scored lots of goals, just like Freddie did in hockey. Anyway, my husband and I used to listen to the radio. I didn't understand many words but I used to hear "Chicago" and "Sasakamoose, Sasakamoose," so I knew Freddie was good. I don't know why he quit. He never talked about it. My husband and I were kind-hearted, we never spoke in anger to each other, we never asked him about it.

But I know one thing. The reason he played hockey so well is because his Indian name is *Ayahkokopawiwiym.* I know Freddie had strong legs for hockey because Bertha Starblanket named him according to the spirit of a young bull. His Indian name means "to stand firm."

Freddie

Maybe three times I tried to run away from St. Michael's School. Once there were three of us boys. In them days priests were tough. They shaved our heads and made us sit in the middle of the floor on the cement to embarrass us. All the kids would watch us sittin' there eatin', even the girls.

We were also punished for speakin' Cree at school. Whipped sometimes.

We didn't have no excuse for runnin' away. We were bein' fed good and were bein' treated right. In about seven or eight years after the priests and the sisters had offered me everything into my life, I didn't feel so bad about school. But I wouldn't go back to that kind of system. I guess when you're young like that you like to come back home. I was lonesome.

Come August I never wanted to go back to school but my parents were determined. They wanted me to be somebody education-wise. And then there was hockey, hockey was the main issue for me. And for the priests too.

---

[1] Clara Sasakamoose Ahenakew translated her mother's Cree to English for this story.

What would happen is that old Father Roussel had maybe fifty pucks in the middle of the bloody ice and if a guy was coastin', not movin' on the whistle, Father Roussel would fire a puck right at him. Of course, when it gets 20 or 30 below, these pucks freeze and in them days we didn't have no padding, everything was homemade, maybe just a few sticks here and there in your pants to stop you from getting hit on your charleyhorse.

Father Georges Roussel

I first met Frederick Sasakamoose in September, 1944. From the very beginning you noticed Frederick Sasakamoose. He played in the brass band, trombone or bass, something big to make a lot of noise! He was puffing all right, sometimes his notes were not correct but he seemed to enjoy it.

He showed more promise on the ice. Let's put it this way, let's acknowledge the gifts that God has given to us.

To make them move, I'd use my hockey stick, a little tap on the seat, not a big one, for the ones who were lagging behind. The boys used to enjoy that. They'd say, Look at him, slowpoke, go after him. Shoot the puck at them? No, well, maybe shoot towards them, on the side. I could shoot straight enough.

As for Frederick's shot, I believe in the wrist shot, quick and accurate. Frederick developed a good, excellent, I would say, wrist shot when he played at St. Michael's. He practised all the time, even taking practice with the younger boys when I was too busy. I would say Frederick lived for hockey.

Frederick knew what he was doing on the ice by the time he left St. Michael's. He had confidence. The exciting thing about watching Frederick was this: you knew he was going to score. You just didn't know his plan of attack. And that provided the suspense.

Freddie

In the spring of 1949 we beat Regina and won the midget championship of Saskatchewan, eh? That's when I thanked Father Roussel. That time was something I'll never forget. Of course, the team rode back to the school in one of those big damn grain trucks we used to use, squeezin' together to keep warm.

After that I came back home and I had no intention of goin' into junior hockey. None at all. Never had no dream.

I was back here in the fall, about this time of year. We were stookin'[2] over at Blue Heron, my Mum and Dad and me, it was thrashin' time. All of a sudden a car pulled into the field and I thought I seen Father Roussel comin'.

---

[2] **stookin':** the practice of setting sheaves of grain in an upright arrangement, intended to speed drying in the field.

I thought he was comin' to take me back to school and I said to my Dad, Oh, no, I'm not goin' back. I'm fifteen and I'll be sixteen in December and I don't have to go back.

Ends up it was Father Chevrier, he was gonna be boss at Duck Lake, and two other guys. He said, D'ya wanna go to trainin' camp in Moose Jaw? And I said, Where's that?

Phyllis Vogan Hendry

My Dad was general manager of the Moose Jaw Canucks. I was sixteen at the time. I came home late one night and I heard something in the living room. I went upstairs and asked my brother's girlfriend—she was visiting from Michigan where my brother was playing minor pro—I asked her who was in the living room. Phyllis, she said, your father brought home another hockey player and this time he's an Indian!

I got up the next morning and there was Freddie. He had on a pair of heavy plaid pants and a thick plaid shirt and a cap pulled down over his ears. Anyway, there he sat, looking terrified. About like Metro Prystai looked when he'd come to live with us about seven years before.

Freddie lived with us for four years, three years with Mum and Dad, and when my husband and I got married he moved in with us next door for a year. Freddie couldn't have lived with just anybody in those days. He needed to be looked after in lots of ways.

I remember after he went up to Chicago for a few games in the spring of '53. He came home with a big cheque and he wasn't supposed to cash it till he got to Saskatchewan.

Anyway, next day after Freddie got to Moose Jaw, he went out and bought a big car with the cash he had on him. I remember he used to correspond with an Indian girl named Rose, a nursing student I think, and an Isbister girl named Loretta from up north. He still had his cheque when he headed off to Humbolt to see Rose.

He didn't make it. I got a frantic call, well about as frantic as Freddie ever got. Phyl, he said, my tire went flat and when I was changing the tire the wind came along and blew my cheque away. What am I gonna do, Phyl? he says.

Dad phoned Chicago right away to put a stop payment on the cheque and I phoned "The Mailbag" on CHAB Moose Jaw to tell people to be on the look-out for a Chicago Black Hawk cheque made out to Frederick Sasakamoose. Wouldn't you know it? A farmer found it in his field and called up the radio station.

Haven't seen Freddie since he was on his way to see Rose. But I remember getting a Christmas card and him telling me he'd named his oldest daughter, Phyllis, after me and his older son, Elgin, after a friend of his in Moose Jaw.

Freddie

The year I went to Chicago we'd lost out in junior hockey to Regina or somebody. I was in the Canuck dressing room takin' my stuff off. Nobody was talkin'. We were sad about bein' taken out. I was thinkin' about goin' home.

First person I seen was George Vogan. That man and his family offered me everythin'. He was just like my Dad and my Dad was a good man.

All of a sudden the manager came up to me and said, Here's a telex. Here's your plane ticket. You're goin' to Chicago Black Hawks the remainder of the season.

So I didn't know what to do. I just stood there and I looked at the players. They were astonished, me bein' an Indian to be called and go play in the big leagues. Then people walked in there with a watch and my name engraved and a ring and two suitcases filled with clothes so I'd look respectable on my way in. It was a real joy.

I took the plane the next day. I met the team in Toronto.

Anyway, I got on the ice and I was skatin' around warmin' up. At that time I was just like a . . . I'm not braggin', but I could skate and skate and shoot, real good. I had my slapshot by then. I don't know where it come from. I don't know where I seen it. Nobody was usin' it much then. It just came natural to me. So I took a shot or two and a referee come up to me and says, Somebody wants to talk to you on the phone. I went over to the penalty box and some guy said over the phone, How the hell do you pronounce your damn name? Saskatchewan Moose? Sack-a-Moose? Sask-a-moose? I said, Who am I talkin' to? And the voice said, Foster Hewitt. My gosh, I said, Foster! You know, I heard so much about Foster. Back home and at the school we used to listen to Saturday-night hockey all the time. So I was talkin' to Foster and I gave him my name properly, Sa-sa-ka-moose, and I guess that's how he done it, bein' the professional he was. I was in the big time now.

Metro Prystai

I'd been traded to Detroit by the time Freddie went up to Chicago. Chicago wasn't doin' that well at the time and Freddie was supposed to be the saviour. And, of course, management made a big ballyhoo about him bein' the first treaty Indian to make the NHL.

Freddie had to contend with livin' at the Midwest Athletic Club. They had a place downstairs where gamblers used to hang out. It was a boxing club. And all these hoodlums used to sit at ringside in their white and black fedoras. The gangsters used to feel sorry for us poor hockey players. They used to tell us they could get us jobs payin' a lot more.

Freddie

I don't know how in hell I ever come to have a crest like that one, me bein' a treaty Indian and playin' for Chicago Black Hawks.

When I played my first game in Chicago I ended up on TV and they gave me a transistor radio and a box of cigars. That night about 19,000 people come and see the Indian play. And when I first walked in, the organist started playin' the *Indian Love Call*. He was kind of a comical fella.

I come back home that spring after I turned pro. I bought a car. I never owned no car, I used to take cabs. I bought a big DeSoto, a fluid drive, and everybody knew I was back.

It's something I have to thank the Creator for, my younger life. I was called from all over to play exhibition games, a hundred dollars a game. There was still ice in Saskatchewan and every place I went was filled. I was young and I was single and everyone wanted to see me play.

Loretta Sasakamoose

I thought it was pretty good of Freddie to come and see me, little Loretta Isbister from Bodmin, when he could have had almost anybody, eh? We kinda got together through my brothers. They had this thing about Freddie. Wherever he played hockey they wanted to see him because he was such a good player.

My mother died when I was fourteen which was tragic for all of us. From then on I raised my younger six brothers and sisters. There was no one else to do it. I was young but you grow up pretty fast when you have to.

I was sixteen when I met Freddie and he was eighteen. I think there was quite a bit of difference there. I was kinda tied up at home whereas he was from one city to another seeing all those places. But we hit it off real good as friends and he'd write letters to me and send me a Christmas present, a valentine card, this and that.

My brothers were really happy when I married Freddie four years later. But I don't know about my Dad. Well, you know, most dads have this thing about trying to hang on to their girl as long as they can. I had raised the family and probably they hated to see me go. Leaving them behind sorta felt like I was neglecting them and, finally, my Dad said, You did your share for this long and it's fine. But I still had that feeling.

The thought of going to Chicago was a bit much. I don't know much about cities and at that time I didn't know nothing about big cities! There's a lot of good things about people here. They tend to be a little backward, a little shy. You can't just say, I'll make a friend there. It just wasn't in me.

The only time I've ever been away was when I lived for three years with Freddie in Kamloops. I read and I read and I read when I was alone during the day. At night there were times we'd sit together and Freddie would say, It's so lonely Lorett, I'll be glad when hockey season's over.

Big Boys Playing Hockey by Allen Sapp. Acrylic on canvas.

Freddie

I was in the '55 Chicago training camp in Welland and I was expectin' some letters from Lorett, we'd just been married July 22, that summer. Every day I looked and there was nothin'.

About ten days before the thirty-day camp was over I got hold of my wife. I said, I'm gonna make the team, Loretta, now you come over here. I got a house all ready, I'm making good money. She held back, she didn't want to come. She told me no.

I moved to New Westminster, to Calgary, to Chicoutimi—Quebec league—bouncing all over the damn place. I guess maybe it was a little bit of control, that was the problem, not using alcohol, not using anything, just that I kinda fell apart because she wouldn't come with me. My wife was a beautiful girl and I loved her very much.

Muriel Gottfriedson Sasakamoose

I first met Freddie in 1957 when he came to Kamloops to play for the Kamloops Chiefs. Before the hockey season was over I married his brother Peter.

After Peter and I lived for a time at Sandy Lake I got to know Freddie as a person. He has a lot of self-confidence. He's a survivor. He's also a bit of a trend-setter, you should see his new log house. He's outgoing, he's musical, he plays guitar and sings and he can really dance. Freddie's a good person to have at a party. People crowd around him because he's energetic and he's a good storyteller. Freddie can take to down-and-outers, drunks, and he can also talk to the Prime Minister of Canada.

Now that I'm Band Administrator for Sandy Lake, I get the opportunity to see Freddie in a different light. I always thought in terms of women, children, and men, the total community, whereas the men tended to think more of what the men wanted to do. The women here are quite silent compared to me. The men often said, That Muriel, she's a women's libber, and a lot of the flak came from my brother-in-law Freddie!

Freddie and I realized our differences right away. Freddie tends to be a bleeding heart and he believes every sob story that comes his way. Freddie's a dreamer. I am most often a realist and I sort of say, Give them a swift kick in the ass, and that's the direction they should go. But Freddie and I both believe in the community and the betterment of Indian people and see that change has to take place.

I admire Freddie very much. I really think if he wasn't so tied to this family and his community, he would probably have stayed longer. But it doesn't matter. Freddie gave us all something to be very proud of. But he rarely talks about it. Freddie doesn't live in the past.

Freddie

If I was to die today, I wouldn't cry for my life. I've met a lot of good people, a lot of good Indians and a lot of good white people. The enemies I created through my hockey life, the fans that called me names, you know, every one of them came back, I know every one of them. I hear them when I'm on the ice, you know. You're an Indian and this and that, but, you know, I never looked. It never hurted me because I always had pride in me. Enemies from that time come up now and shake hands with me and say, Remember when I used to call you names? I don't know, I say, did you? Well, I say, that's gone.

The people on this reserve, they treated me real good when I came back. Not once had I leave this reserve since I come back. Although there's a brighter future on the outside, there's freedom here. A lot of time I sat down and asked myself what went wrong with my hockey life. Maybe there were just some things I could not adjust to.

Now I meet people who say, Any of your children as good as you were? I don't think so, I say. People look at me and think I should be able to produce all good hockey players. But I never did go out there with my kids and support them by trainin' them.

I lost my oldest daughter three years ago when I was chief. I knew that my daughter was killed in a car accident due to alcohol. At that time I too was drinkin', but not heavy; I was chief. I knew it hurt my life and hurt my family so I very, very seldom used alcohol. I was blessed with a good wife. She never drank, she's a beautiful woman, she took care of my children when I was not always there. I'm blessed. Funny thing, I didn't know till I was almost fifty. When I lost my daughter it changed me.

Now I'm fifty-two, almost fifty-three. I'm a community man. I was chief for four years, served my people well. I believe in the system of competition with the outside white society. When I was a kid I learned to compete with the outside and I had to be able to do things twice as good to continue to play hockey with them.

But the thing I remember is comin' home from school every summer, eh? It was wonderful when we come on top of that hill over there. We used to drive up in that big three-ton grain truck, you know, fifty or sixty of us piled in there. About six, seven miles south of here I could see the hill and at the top, oh boy, what a feeling, to see this reserve.

1. Exploring Meaning

a. Write a description of Freddie Sasakamoose. Include at least four descriptive adjectives.

b. On the ice, what abilities was Sasakamoose known for?

c. Which individual do you believe played the most important role in Sasakamoose's life? Support your answer with references to the selection.

d. What life lesson did Sasakamoose learn when he was almost fifty?

e. Reread the last paragraph of the selection. Do you feel that the paragraph accurately sums up Sasakamoose's reasons for giving up his hockey career? Explain.

2. Language Conventions

Language Level "The Reluctant Black Hawk" is written in an informal, conversational style. Identify the specific techniques Brenda Zeman uses to create this style. To begin, reread the introduction to Freddie Sasakamoose's story, paying attention to how Zeman creates a strong sense of the places she visits and people she meets in her quest to find him. Find examples of specific nouns and verbs and vivid adjectives and adverbs. Choose one or two sentences that present a vivid description and explain why they are appealing. Pay attention to aspects such as sentence structure, punctuation, diction (choice of words), and non-standard grammar.

3. Media *Documentary* Assume that you are responsible for creating a *Heritage Minute* about the moment that Freddie Sasakamoose steps out on the ice to play his first NHL game. To plan the *Heritage Minute*, develop a list of four to six frames for a storyboard. Create the storyboard and beneath each frame include notes about the shot, narration, lighting, sounds effects, and music.

Self-Assessment: Assess your storyboard. Does it contain helpful information about the shots, narration, sound effects, and music? Could you shoot your documentary using the storyboard as your guideline?

4. Researching Find out about another Canadian athlete who has had an impact on his or her sport. Develop a short profile of the person, including information about his or her most important contribution to sports. You could organize your profile using two or more voices as Brenda Zeman has done.

What motivates individuals to help others who are less fortunate? Read the selection to find out what motivates Naomi Segal-Bronstein.

Naomi Segal-Bronstein:
CHILDREN'S CHAMPION

Profile by Sheldon Gordon

Naomi Segal-Bronstein likes to keep her priorities straight. The Montreal-born activist has received numerous honours, including membership in the Order of Canada, for her work with children in developing countries, but she has never allowed the recognition to distract her from her cause.

When she received the $250,000 Royal Bank Award for Canadian Achievement (presented to a Canadian who has made "a significant contribution to human welfare and the common good") in 1997 and bank officials asked what she would like served at the dinner being given in her honour, she immediately suggested a simple meal of rice, a poignant reminder of the diet of most of the world's poorest children.

Although Segal-Bronstein eventually agreed to a less spartan menu, the incident typifies the single-mindedness she has applied to her cause—providing food, medical treatment and adoptive families for needy children in Asia and Central America—over three decades. "We estimate she has saved the lives of up to 30,000 children," says Bryan Davies, a senior vice-president at the Royal Bank.

For Segal-Bronstein, working with children has been a long vocation. As a teenager, she ran an impromptu kids' camp at her parents' home in Val Morin, Quebec, and later served as a paediatric volunteer at two Montreal hospitals. At the age of 18, she married her high school sweetheart, Herb Bronstein, and within four years gave birth to three children.

In the late 1960s, as the Vietnam War escalated, Segal-Bronstein began to read about South Vietnam's young outcasts, Amerasian children fathered by U.S. soldiers. The more she learned of them, the more she felt compelled to do something to help them. And so, in 1969, she and two other Montreal women, Sandra Simpson and Bonnie Cappuccino, formed Families for Children, a charitable organization with a dual purpose: to find families in North America to adopt abandoned Vietnamese children and to raise money and collect used equipment for orphanages in South Vietnam. Says Segal-Bronstein: "It was a lot easier in those days to raise not only money and supplies but also awareness and interest."

Naomi Segal-Bronstein. Photo by Spyros Bourboulis.

Segal-Bronstein made a series of trips to Saigon during the 1970s. Staying for three to four weeks at a time, she worked at an orphanage and did paperwork for children being adopted. Soon, she applied to adopt children herself, and after 18 months of red tape, she was able to adopt two Vietnamese orphans, Tam-Lien and Tran, who were both two.

In 1972, Segal-Bronstein visited Cambodia and discovered that the "secret war" there had created the need for a similar project. Each day she was there, she and a colleague roamed Phnom Penh, rescuing orphans from the streets.

On one occasion, a bomb exploded less than three metres from the car Segal-Bronstein was driving, leaving a crater in the road. "I'd had the silly notion that if you were there to do something good, then people would know you weren't involved in the politics and no one would bother you," she recalls.

Segal-Bronstein managed to escape to Vietnam with the orphans before Pol Pot and the Khmer Rouge seized power in 1975. Within two weeks of her escape, she had helped arrange for orphaned Vietnamese children to be airlifted from Saigon to the United States. Originally scheduled to fly out with them, she opted to go on a flight a Canadian government official had arranged for her and the Cambodian children—it meant there'd be more room for Vietnamese orphans on the evacuation flight. Sadly, the plane carrying these orphans crashed, and many of the children and their adult escorts were killed.

In 1976, Segal-Bronstein moved, with her husband and 12 children (seven of whom are adopted from countries around the world), to Guatemala, where that year she established Casa Canada, a medical clinic and orphanage, and, in 1979, Healing the Children, a program created to bring seriously ill children from Guatemala to hospitals in North America for medical treatment.

The family returned to Canada in 1981; Healing the Children not only continued in Guatemala but expanded to other countries around the world.

The peripatetic Canadian returned to Cambodia in 1989, re-establishing an orphanage called Canada House, which had closed when the Khmer

Rouge had taken over Phnom Penh 14 years before. In 1992, Segal-Bronstein was mugged on the streets of Phnom Penh and sustained severe injuries. She returned to this country to recuperate, but Canada House continued to function until 1997, by which time all of its children had been placed with families in Cambodia and abroad.

That year, Segal-Bronstein launched the charity Canadacares Children's International Foundation, whose purpose is to help children in need, such as victims of land mines or hurricanes.

In October 2000, she worked with public schools near her home in Val Morin to provide cloth bags filled with school supplies to children in a Guatemalan settlement for people who had been displaced by Hurricane Mitch two years before. The children who received the kits were fascinated by the accompanying letters and pictures from the Canadian children. This sparked the idea of Around the World Kid 2 Kid, a project that would see young people from both developed and developing countries writing to children who are living through natural disasters and wars. And in November of the same year, a small paediatric hospital Segal-Bronstein helped establish opened in a former rooming house in Guatemala City.

Currently, she is working on a project to acquire old North American school buses and convert them into mobile medical clinics that would provide immunization and other basic health-care services in rural Guatemala.

For Naomi Segal-Bronstein, children in need are the cause of a lifetime.

1. Exploring Meaning

a. Who is Naomi Segal-Bronstein? Outline some of her accomplishments.

b. To which prestigious Canadian institution does Segal-Bronstein belong? What other awards has she received?

c. With a partner, discuss your answer to the introductory question you answered before reading the profile. What qualities do people who spend their lives helping others have in common?

2. Writing   *Formal Letter*   Write a letter to the federal government proposing someone you know, or someone you've read about, as a candidate for the Order of Canada. Justify your proposal with anecdotes, facts, or information from articles you've read about the individual. Set up your letter using the formal-letter style.

As you revise your draft, examine your letter for clarity and the strength of your argument. Have you painted a clear picture of the individual and his or her accomplishments? Have you included supporting facts and details? Ask a classmate to check your use of language conventions.

Roll Me Up;
Roll Me Down/
Mobile-Mobility

Poem by Maxine Tynes

When I envy your wheels
When I'm stuck on hold
When streets are slick and frozen solid
When my path from here to there is an Olympic ice-sheet
When these post-polio feet and legs
cry out in protest of another step
  another step
When I need/don't want to plead my case for accessibility
in able-bodied heads.
For one crazy moment
that plays and plays back
like an endless tape-loop
I envy your chair
that speaks those sharp and mute and rolling volumes.

1. Exploring Meaning
a. What is the subject of Maxine Tynes's poem?
b. Explain the last line of the poem, "I envy your chair/that speaks those sharp and mute and rolling volumes."
c. Write a brief phrase that sums up the emotion or state of mind the poet is expressing.
d. Choose one effective image in the poem and explain its meaning and appeal to the reader.

2. Technique and Style *Metaphor* Identify the metaphors used in the poem. In what ways are the metaphors appropriate to the message of the poem? Develop two metaphors of your own that express the same idea.

3. Making Connections Using Internet or library resources, find other examples of Maxine Tynes's poetry. Choose one poem and write a brief review of it. Include a critical assessment of the work, as well as your personal response to it.

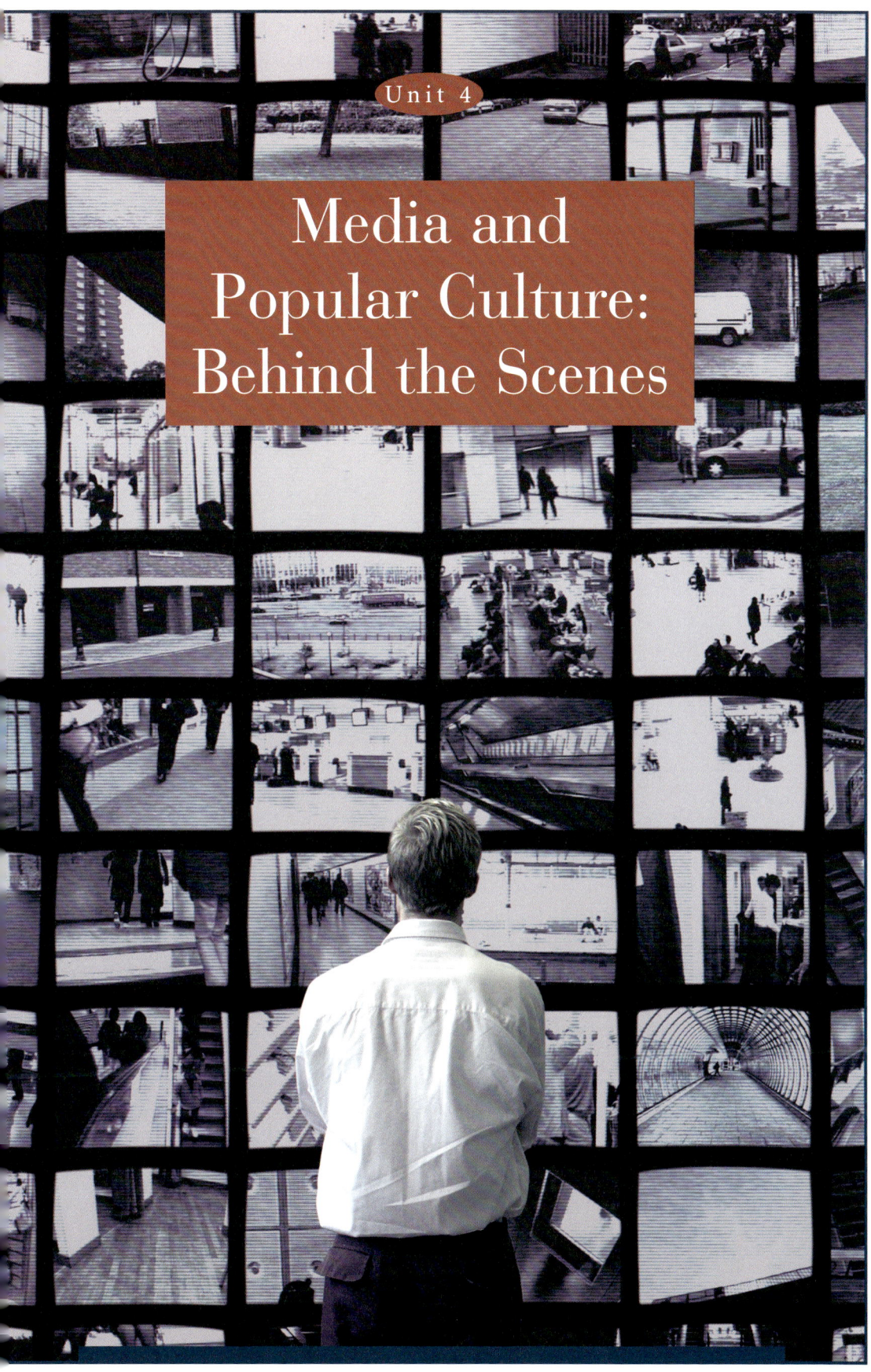

Unit 4

Media and Popular Culture: Behind the Scenes

With a partner, discuss any radio dramas you've listened to or read. What are some of the features of a radio drama?

Twenty
Thousand Ears

How-to Article by Rachel Wyatt

"Get your muddy boots off my clean floor." On stage the words would be superfluous, as he, crouching there beside his bucket, glares up at her marching across the kitchen in her boots. But on radio that line gives the listener a ton of information. It posits a floor, therefore a dwelling. It tells the sex of one of the characters, what he is doing and his mood and age. It tells something about the weather and that one person at least has just come in from outside. And when she responds, "What am I supposed to do, fly?" we have a hint of the way that relationship is going. And the beginning perhaps, of a domestic drama.

Radio writers are those people you see standing in corners at parties. Their ears are longer than other people's and they are waiting to hear that fine phrase, that remark which will set going a whole spoken drama in their minds. They appear to be modest but if they smile secretly it is because they know that they are part of a select group which includes names like Stoppard and Pinter and Eliot and Thomas and Bolt and MacLeod and Wyatt.

Beginning a radio drama is a gamble. It's part of what makes radio writing an exciting game. The writer has to catch the ear of the listener in the first moments or else all is lost and the listener has moved on or tuned out.

Take one scream. Add the sound of blood dripping onto a wooden floor, a door slamming, menacing footsteps, and a voice that says gently, "Is that you dear?" and you are into a mystery. Electronic sounds and robot voices build a distant galaxy. After some heavy breathing a voice murmurs, "He's got to come back this way." In the silence a large dog barks. Any of these things might take a listener by the throat and drag him or her into your story.

It's easy on radio to startle and amaze and frighten. But we all like to snoop, and eavesdropping on people works wonderfully on radio. Imagine a hidden microphone in the house, in every room in the house, and the listener becomes a spy watching somebody else's life. Better still, and here radio truly comes into its own, move that microphone into the mind of a character, read his thoughts and his dreams, and therein often lies the best drama of all.

So having grabbed our listeners, how to keep them? One way is to move in and out of scenes and sounds and keep the listeners on their toes (but never to the point of bewilderment). A radio script can have as many scenes as a film script, and the scenes can be as short as a couple of lines. Maria looks out of the window and sees him coming up the path and cries out "Oh no!" In the next scene, he is at the door or in the house.

And there is a little problem to solve. How do we know Maria is looking out of the window without having her say, "I'm standing here at the window of my kitchen in Leaside, wearing a sweater because it's a cold day in fall, looking out at the path and there is a man . . ."

Photo by Craig Van der Lende.

The easiest way out of that would be to have someone else in the house tell her to close the window. But since she is alone, what is Maria to do? She can talk to herself and say, "I didn't know this window was open," and close it. And then say "Oh no!" in such a way that the listener knows she has been surprised. Or she can be set up as a house-proud person with a time-consuming job and Saturday is her cleaning day—she's doing the windows . . . The ways are endless.

And then the ending? Easy to say that the ending will arise out of everything that has already happened! At the end of the stage play, the characters may not say very much but they appear to be either dead or ecstatic and the audience, able to tell which, leaves the theatre satisfied.

We don't want, at the end of our radio drama, to have Maria say, "Now I'm going into this nice orange sunset with Igor, who is wearing his black suit and . . ." or, "I have killed him. He can do no further harm and here lies his body, seeping blood onto my nice clean tiles." (It's still Saturday.)

Maria and Igor walking into the sunset can be expressed simply by such clichés as "I love you" and a swell of romantic music. And the death of Igor by a shot and a strident chord and Maria saying, "You can come out now, Brad."

It's a magic place, radio. For the price of a sound effect, a little music, and a few words, the flying carpet can take the listener to remote jungles, the top of a mountain, the dangerous backstreets of a big city, inside the palace and the hovel, into the murderer's head. And that is just Act One.

Martin Esslin has said that the listener's mind is our stage. So let's take those words, that music, a few sounds and build the scenery, create our drama, and catch the ears of ten thousand listeners at one go.

1. Exploring Meaning

a. Using information from the article and your own ideas, write a short definition of the term *radio drama*.

b. How does Rachel Wyatt grab the listener's attention at the beginning of the article?

c. Wyatt uses sarcasm when the character asks, "What am I supposed to do, fly?" Rewrite the passage without using this device. Is it as effective? Explain.

d. List the specific techniques Wyatt suggests to grab and keep the listeners' attention and help them to understand what is happening.

2. Media *Radio Scene*

Create a script for a scene in a radio play. Choose a simple event from a book you've read or from a movie you've seen recently. Jot down a list of sound effects and ideas for revealing dialogue that might help a radio listener understand what is happening. Write your scene. Review your script to ensure that the sound effects and dialogue catch the listener's ear and create a meaningful context for the action.

Record a presentation of your scene, including the sound effects. Play it to a small group and ask for feedback. Do your classmates understand what is happening? What other sound effects or dialogue do they suggest to improve the scene?

Self-Assessment: Assess the process you used to develop the scene. What advice would you give a classmate developing his or her own scene?

3. Literature Studies *Comparison*

Reread the selection, noting what a radio drama is compared to. How accurate is this comparison? Why do you think the author chose the comparison? What effect does the comparison have on the reader?

Find examples of allusions and clichés in the title, introduction, and first few lines of the script. Based on these findings, do you expect this to be a serious radio play? Explain.

NANCY CHEW
Enters the Dragon

Radio Play Excerpt by Betty Quan

Nancy Chew, famous teen detective, has the tables turned on her when she is suspected of being behind the theft of a glitzy jewel, the Last Emperor's Tear. Here she is interrogated by arch-nemesis, Bruce Lee, a good cop with a bad name.

Excerpt from Scene III
NANCY's living room.

NANCY: All right detective. Cut to the chase.

Sound of a shuffling notepad.

BRUCE: Could you go over the details of last evening, when you reported your car stolen?

NANCY: I've already given my report.

BRUCE: The details of yesterday evening, Nancy. The more you co-operate, the faster this'll take.

NANCY: I returned to my premises at about nineteen hundred hours.

BRUCE: Where had you been?

NANCY: Simon Fraser.

BRUCE: The university?

NANCY: The criminology department was having an open house. I was checking into it.

BRUCE: "Checking into it?"

NANCY: (*nonchalant*) I've been thinking about going back to school.

BRUCE: Your father'll be pleased to hear that.

NANCY: Right. Sure he will. I just have to find a way of explaining criminology to him. I'll tell him it's a new form of ESL or something like that.

BRUCE: Right. So you got home at seven. What then?

NANCY: The usual routine: parked the car in the garage, stored the Blauplunkt in the trunk. (*beat*) You know, for security I've got a portable car stereo. If you haven't noticed, Little Mountain's getting pretty dangerous. Or are you only concerned with Chinatown nowadays?

BRUCE: Then what?

NANCY: Well, the house was empty. Dad was off at one of his benevolence meetings or something like that. Georgie . . .

BRUCE: How's your cousin settling in?

NANCY: Fine I guess.

BRUCE: He's pretty young to be on his own. Kind of a shock, I'm sure, starting all over again in a new country.

NANCY: Yeah, well. God knows where he was last night.

BRUCE: So when did you discover your car was missing?

NANCY: Not until later . . . Ned, you know my friend Ned Knickers? Well he's in exams right now. So at around 8:30—I mean 20:30 hours—I thought I'd go to the 7-11, pick up some Big Gulps and some chips and drop on by.

BRUCE: He's at UBC?

NANCY: Yeah. He lives in residence. He's a gear.

BRUCE: A what?

NANCY: A gear; he's studying engineering.

BRUCE: You mean those guys who orchestrate Lady Godiva rides and hang Volkswagens off bridges?

NANCY: Affirmative. He's a really smart guy.

BRUCE: So when did you discover the car was missing?

NANCY: About midnight. Ned escorted me to the parking lot, and my car was gone.

BRUCE: So between around nine p.m. and midnight you were at this Ned Knickers'? What were you doing there for three hours?

NANCY: Hanging around.

BRUCE: Nancy. Last night at about 11 p.m., the alarms at the Sun Yat-Sen museum went off.

NANCY: You're talking about the Last Emperor's Tear.

BRUCE: The security guard there took down a plate and description. (*reading*) Dark blue hatchback, possibly a convertible, license plate N-A-N-C-Y.

NANCY: (*gasping*) That's my car!

BRUCE: Affirmative. So why don't *you* cut to the chase, Nancy?

NANCY: Evidently the thief used my wheels as the getaway car.

BRUCE: Perhaps.

NANCY: Say, Bruce, stop crowding me! I don't like where this so-called questioning is leading.

BRUCE: I'm not here to make nice with you, Nancy. Answer the question. What were you doing with this Ned Knickers between nine and midnight?

NANCY: You mean do I have an alibi? Or does this really have anything to do with the robbery? Maybe you're spying for my dad.

BRUCE: Nancy, give me a break.

NANCY: Why should I? You've never given me one. You took my dad's side when I wanted to join the police academy. You told him how it would be too dangerous for "a girl" like me. Well, I'm tough and I'm smart. And I could out-think your outdated presumptions any day.

BRUCE: It's a jungle out there, Nancy, and the only view you've ever had of it is through a silly magnifying glass and a subscription to *Ellery Queen*. You're a big girl. If you want to be a cop—

NANCY: (*correcting*) Detective . . .

BRUCE: A detective so bad you could've done it *without* my help.

NANCY: Easy for you to say. Disobey my father's express wishes? Especially when your opinion holds so much water with him?

BRUCE: You've been doing it for years. Running around the city, sticking your nose into other people's business.

NANCY: You know, I am a detective. But I don't need a badge to prove it.

I've assisted your department and the Chief of Police on numerous occasions and not once have I done them wrong. Don't you remember: *The Mysterious Disappearance of the Stanley Park Mermaid, Hidden Treasure on Wreck Beach, Secret of Fantasy Gardens . . .*

NANCY & BRUCE: (*together*) *Case of the Hitchhiking Ghost . . .*

BRUCE: (*continues impatiently*) Get off it, Nancy. The department files you in the same category as those loony psychics who insist they can find missing bicycles and dogs. They tolerate you Nancy Chew like the good Canadians they are.

NANCY: That's not true.

BRUCE: I didn't mean for it to come out that way.

NANCY: What about my Good Samaritan awards? My citations? You're just jealous because I'm good, because I got where I am today out of ability, not because of some *departmental quota*.

BRUCE: Oh, is that how you see it? I'm just a pawn for those affirmative action types? Look here, I've worked hard to get my badge. My degree in social work, first at the police academy . . .

NANCY: I wouldn't know.

BRUCE: For once, just once, Nancy, try looking at it from a perspective other than your own. You might just learn something.

NANCY: Ask me your questions, Bruce, then get the hell outa here.

Music begins under.

BRUCE: Between nine and midnight you were at your boyfriend's. What were you doing there? Helping him study?

NANCY: No.

BRUCE: Watching TV?

NANCY: No.

BRUCE: Listening to music?

NANCY: Look, Bruce, do I have to draw you a picture? Ned and I've been seeing each other a year now. (*sweetly*) If you whisper one word of this to Dad I'll kill you.

BRUCE: You're being pretty jumpy, especially when nobody's accusing you of anything. But if I've come down hard on you, I'm sorry. This piece that was stolen, the Last Emperor's Tear, well it's worth a cool million. And because Chinatown's my beat . . .

NANCY: You don't have to shout, Bruce . . .

BRUCE: I'm under the gun to produce results. So when this detective gets an eyewitness account nailing your car at the scene of the crime, well, I've got to check it out. And what's more, you've got a reputation for butting your nose into police business! Either way, you're involved in some way in this robbery, whether you like it or not! And I've got a right to ask . . . (*exasperated*) Nancy, whatya doing?

> *Sound effect of NANCY getting up and lighting incense. Rustle of paper wrappers being torn. Sound of a match not successfully igniting.*

NANCY: Could you help me with this, Bruce, please? I have to re-light the incense—see, it's gone out. It was ten years ago yesterday. So kind and giving she was. Gentle too. And very traditional. I remember every Sunday we'd *yum chah*[1] and she'd always order my favourite for dessert: *daan taat.*[2] I remember her hands. They'd be rough and calloused because she worked hard, cooking, cleaning, sewing, scrubbing.

BRUCE: I'm sorry, Nancy. I forgot. I shoulda realized . . .

NANCY: There are so many things I could have learned from my mother. She hated confrontations you know. She was just too gentle for that.

BRUCE: Really, I'm sorry.

NANCY: Yeah. So am I. (*recovering*) So when can I get my car back from the police lab?

BRUCE: Tomorrow. Maybe.

---

[1] *yum chah:* drink tea.
[2] *daan taat:* egg custard in a flaky pastry.

NANCY: Well I'm obviously not a suspect.

BRUCE: Depends on how you define obvious.

NANCY: How'd they break in?

BRUCE: The lab's not sure yet. No evidence of forced entry.

NANCY: Anything stolen? I have to let ICBC know.

BRUCE: Nothing we noticed.

NANCY: Not even my Blauplunkt? That's odd. It's probably worth an easy grand on the black market.

BRUCE: No. It was still there. Right where it should be.

NANCY: So the lab guys put it back?

BRUCE: Put what back?

NANCY: (*fast recovery*) Nothing. I was just off on a tangent.

BRUCE: What are you on about? (*beat*) You're staying out of this investigation.

NANCY: Is that a question, or a command?

Music fades.

1. Exploring Meaning

a. What is the nature of the conflict between Nancy and Bruce?

b. Nancy suggests that Bruce obtained his position because of a departmental quota. What does she mean by this?

c. Betty Quan uses several clichéd metaphors. Find two examples and discuss how the metaphors contribute to the play's tone.

d. What is a Blauplunkt? What is ICBC? Who is Ellery Queen? What is the allusion in the title "Nancy Chew"? How necessary is it to know what these references are in order to understand or appreciate the play? Reread the play and list other references that you had difficulty with. Discuss them in a small group.

2. Literature Studies *Character Sketch* What can you tell about Nancy's character from reading this scene? Make a list of her character traits and find evidence from the play to support each observation. Develop a character sketch for Nancy Chew.

Based on your understanding of Nancy, script the conversation between Nancy and her father about her plans to join the police academy. Work with a partner to present the scene to your classmates.

Self-Assessment: Assess the usefulness of a character sketch when creating a scene. How can an understanding of a character help you to plan the action and dialogue?

The following interview and editorial provide opposing points of view on how the Internet will affect newspapers and books. Read both selections and determine which one you find most convincing.

The Role of Words in the Digital Era

Interview with Peter Desbarats by Kathe Lieber

Peter Desbarats is one of the rare people who believes that the Internet will sound the death knell of the printed word. The first victim, he says, will be the daily newspapers. Journalistic practices will evolve with technology, and copyright will be at the heart of the debates, reckons the professor of journalism.

"I've been saying for over 20 years now that daily newspapers don't have much of a future. When I was with the Kent Commission[1] in 1980–1981, it was being described as a dying industry. We've had three decades of decline in readership, circulation and advertising revenue.

"The trend is quite clear. The weaker newspapers will start to close, I think, over the next five or ten years. Many medium-sized dailies in Canada now are shadows of their former selves in terms of investigative reporting. As someone who started in newspapers in the late 1950s, I find it hard to visualize a world without local daily newspapers, but there's no reason why it won't happen. Daily newspapers have only been with us for a little over a century. They were created by technology, and they can be outmoded by technology.

---

[1] **Kent Commission:** The Royal Commission on Newspapers, which concerned itself with newspaper ownership.

"*The Globe and Mail* established itself as the first truly national daily produced in Canada, then the *National Post* came into existence. Is the [Canadian] market large and affluent enough to support two national dailies? I think there's a possibility that one or the other will not survive."

What will happen when some of these papers close?
"They'll be replaced by TV and local Internet use, and by specialized weekly publications, which many cities now have. In Toronto, you have to fight your way into the subway through give-away newspaper hawkers.

"Obviously, people are still reading books. If you look at the magazine racks, people are still reading them, too. Specialized magazines find their own niches. The distinction between the printed page and the electronic page will become less important as time goes on."

How has the "digitization" of news coverage affected journalism?
"We are seeing the emergence of a new kind of journalist working for Internet-based information services for whom that is the normal, natural world.

"I recently moderated a panel at the University of Western Ontario with graduates of the journalism program over the years. The youngest member, who is from the class of 1995, was hired right out of the classroom by *The Toronto Star*. He said that the *Star* website is almost completely independent of the daily newspaper's editorial operations. Stories are constantly updated. They make some mistakes due to time pressures, of course, since they're constantly on deadline."

Do you think the speed we seem to be moving at now due to the Internet has had an adverse effect on the quality of writing?
"Not really. We all get very attached to the mechanics of writing that we've used over the years. When I left university, I still felt that if I were writing something serious, somehow it would be better to write it by hand rather than on a 'mechanical, unnatural' typewriter. Of course, then I moved to the typewriter and then the computer. I loved the computer right from the start. I write in a much more uninhibited way, and it's much more flexible and much quieter. I don't think writing in general has deteriorated with technology. The problem is that [journalism students] don't learn much about grammar."

How will books fare, compared to newspapers and magazines?
"Books will become something that people collect. They won't disappear entirely. I have a small collection of books I like because they have beautiful bindings and attractive type. People will still buy books for those reasons. But why buy a novel in book form once you have better legibility and portability in disk form?

"The same for newspapers. If someone can offer me a page that feels like a newsprint page but is lightweight and easier to read, with instant download, I'd take that instead of the newsprint page."

Gutenberg Can Rest in Peace

Editorial by Pierre Renaud

When television was introduced over fifty years ago, everyone feared the worst for the other media, from radio and the movies to theatre and novels. But the disaster never struck. Instead, television opened a new window on the world, and also created some healthy competition. Now, the Internet is stirring up the competition. There is no doubt that the web is reconnecting us with a civilization based on the written word.

The Net is not a threat. On the contrary. Users must know how to read and write in order to browse, write and send e-mail, or chat online. What a formidable learning tool this is! Perhaps we will finally be able to do something about the sad statistics on literacy in Canada: currently, one in every four children is likely to be illiterate by adulthood.

Never has so much been written since the introduction of the Internet. People "chat" online, but aren't they really doing something more akin to letter-writing? Those who communicate by e-mail have to at least take the time to proof read their messages for clarity and basic grammar.

And if you want to write well and acquire a functional vocabulary, you have to read. A lot. In other words, the Internet is not killing book culture, it is restoring its value. We were too quick to label it as a technological tool. In fact, it is a means of communication that requires literate users.

So much for content. And now for form.
Some people are very excited about the idea of the e-book, but I can't for the life of me see why. What could possibly be exciting about looking at a little laptop screen? The emotional connection we have with books is not generated by the words alone. The book itself—the physical object—also has a great deal to do with it. We feel pride in a library. Is it possible to feel such pride in a shelf of e-novels lined up in their little plastic cases? Books come in all shapes and sizes, with attractive, colourful covers that elicit an emotional response. We give books as gifts, lend them out, share them with friends.

E-books remind me of Campbell's soup tins—they all look alike. Would you be tempted to buy someone the file of Margaret Atwood's latest novel, or introduce a child to *Alice in Wonderland* online?

None other than Stephen King recently put an end to his adventure with online books, which was a resounding failure. If someone as famous and popular as King couldn't make it, what can unknown authors possibly expect?

Gutenburg can rest in peace. There's a lot of life left yet in the printed book.

---

1. Exploring Meaning

a. What is Peter Desbarats's prediction about daily newspapers? Do you agree or disagree with his prediction? Explain.

b. What does Desbarats predict about the future of books? Do you agree or disagree? Explain.

c. Who was Johannes Gutenberg? What do you think is meant by the title, "Gutenberg Can Rest in Peace"?

d. What is the thesis of "Gutenberg Can Rest in Peace"?

e. Pierre Renaud uses a number of rhetorical questions in his editorial. What do you believe is the purpose of this technique? What is the effect?

f. What is the difference between reading traditional books, newspapers, or magazines and reading on the Internet? What can you gain from each? Do you believe that one type of communication is better than the others? Explain.

2. Critical Thinking Work in a small group to critically examine each selection's point of view. Make a list of the arguments that Desbarats and Renaud make to support their viewpoints, then determine whether or not each person has adequately supported his argument. Discuss with your classmates which selection you feel is more convincing and why.

3. Technique and Style *Organization* "The Role of Words in the Digital Era" is an interview that uses questions to organize the article, while "Gutenberg Can Rest in Peace" is an editorial that uses comparison and contrast to organize the arguments. Which type of organization did you find easier to follow? In your notebook, jot down the advantages and disadvantages to each type of organization.

Marketing departments are always on the hunt to find that perfect marketing idea that will change a customer's purchasing behaviour. The following article is a practical guide to using premiums to accomplish this goal.

PREMIUMS:
The Most Abused and Misused Medium of All!

How-to Article by Alexander Hiam from *Marketing For Dummies*®

A *premium* is any product with a marketing message on it that you give away. (Okay, maybe you don't *always* give them away, but the idea is that you make getting them easy so as to spread your message as widely as possible.) Classic premiums include T-shirts with your company name or logo on them, coffee mugs with the same, pens, wall calendars, and baseball caps. But you don't have to confine yourself to these choices—nor should you, because they are often the *wrong* choices.

The problem is, *you've seen it all before.* How many pens with some company's name on them have made their way into your possession over the last five years? If the answer is too many to count, then one more won't create the slightest change in your consumption behavior.

Designing the Premium Using an "Impact Scenario"

As in any marketing initiative, the object of a premium is to *change someone's behavior.* And that's a hard thing to do with a cheap pen or mug. What you have to do in order to make a premium work is build an *impact scenario.* An impact scenario is a realistic story about the premium and its user in which the premium somehow affects that user's purchase behavior.

For example, say that you are marketing a new set of banking services for small businesses, and you want to spread the word about these services to business owners who currently have checking accounts with your bank. Specifically, you want to let them know that a variety of new services is available that they might find helpful, and you want the business owners to call or visit their branch office to learn more about these services.

This wish list of what the target customer should learn and do is the start of an impact scenario. You finish the scenario by thinking of ways that premium items might accomplish your wish list goals.

What if you have the bank's name and the slogan *servicing small businesses better* printed on pens, which you then distribute in the next mailing of checking account statements? This marketing tactic is easy and cheap. But try to imagine the scenario. Small business owner opens bank statement. Pen falls out. He grabs the pen and eagerly reads the slogan. Then, curious about what the slogan means, he immediately dials his local branch and waits patiently on hold for a couple of minutes. When he finally gets someone on the phone, he says, "Hey, I got your pen! Please tell me all about your services for small businesses!"

I dunno. What do you think? Somehow this scenario doesn't seem plausible. In fact, I think that most people would just toss the pen into a drawer or even into the trash can without reading the message or thinking about what the slogan means. Yet if you really look at most premiums, they are a part of equally unlikely scenarios. Sure, they often cost little, and so marketers often fall for them. But they usually work poorly, too.

But don't give up hope. You must be able to find some impact scenario that works—some way to use a premium so that people will actually get the message about those new small-business banking services and, as a result, take some action.

Perhaps a coffee mug would work better, because it has enough room on it to print more information about the services. The mug could be printed with a "DID YOU KNOW?" headline, followed by short, bulleted facts about the problems the bank can solve for a small business owner: "Miser National Bank offers automatic bill paying," and so forth. A customer, drinking coffee from that mug at the office, is a little more likely to be curious enough about one of the services listed to ask for details next time he goes to the bank.

Or how about this for an out-of-the-box idea? Call up American Slide Chart Corp. (in Wheaton, Illinois) to obtain a slide-chart, wheel-chart, or pop-up (it unfolds when opened to a three-dimensional object) to include in that next mailing of checking account statements. I like the idea of a slide or wheel chart because the chart is novel and interactive. The chart can easily be designed to solve a problem or give access to selected information for the user. For example, the chart may say "HOW TO SOLVE THE FIVE MOST COMMON FINANCIAL PROBLEMS OF SMALL BUSINESS" on the outside, along with a listing of those five problems. An inner sheet is then printed with black dots next to those handy solutions (each solution, of course, involving the use of one of your bank's new services).

To use the chart, the customer selects one of those five options by sliding the inner sheet until a black dot appears in a hole through the outer sheet next to a selected problem. Doing so aligns the appropriate solution in a window on the bottom of the outer sheet. If you like, you can add other pages to the charts, such as a tear-off mailer to sign up for service or request information.

Here's the impact scenario for this slide chart: The customer pulls an odd object out of the envelope, glances at it (unfamiliarity generates curiosity), sees that the object claims to solve financial problems for small businesses, and—at least sometimes—starts fooling around with the chart. Soon the customer has selected one of those five financial problems—presumably the most relevant one—and is now reading in the display window about how one of your new services will solve the problem in a jiffy. Perhaps the customer even picks up a pen (not noticing that it is imprinted with the name of a competing bank), fills in the tear-off postcard, and tosses it in the out box for mailing.

Will this premium work? Maybe—at least the scenario is reasonably plausible. You would have to run the numbers to be sure, of course. For example, if you estimate that one in twenty customers receiving the slide chart will end up trying one of your new services, will this number give you a big enough return to justify the cost of producing and mailing those slide charts?

At least you are barking up the right tree because you have a scenario that appeals to common sense. Unlike most marketers, your premium is not just wasted marketing money. Your premium at least has a chance of affecting consumer behavior according to a predesigned plan.

Considering the Premium Options
As you think about ways of using premiums, you should consider a wide range of choices. If I hadn't run across a clever slide chart recently, I would not have known about the American Slide Chart Corp. and what it can do for marketers.

Finding the Premium Options	
Old Classics	**New Classics**
Pens, pencils	Clocks, watches
Calendars	Mouse pads
Key chains	Imprinted computer disks
Note pads	Pocket knives
Rulers	Flashlights
Mugs	Calculators
Caps	Stress-ease balls
T-shirts	Frisbees
Thermometers	Leather pad holders and portfolios
Coasters	Children's toys
Balloons	Canvas or nylon tote bags
Umbrellas	Magnetic calendars
Golf balls	Packaged snacks (popcorn, candy)
Lapel pins	Sports/water bottles
	Books with customized covers
	Globe paperweights
	Kaleidoscopes

1. Exploring Meaning

a. What is a premium? What is its purpose?

b. What does Alexander Hiam believe is the problem with premiums?

c. Explain, in your own words, the term *impact scenario.*

d. Who is the intended audience for this article? How do you know?

e. Is the writing style of the article formal or informal? Find examples from the article to support your opinion. Is the style appropriate for the intended audience?

2. Technique and Style *Graphic Elements* Scan the article and note the words that your eyes are drawn to. List the graphic techniques that the writer has used to focus your attention on different parts of the text. Why do you think these words were chosen for emphasis? Next time you write an article, consider how you can best use a variety of graphic elements.

A **rhetorical question** is one that is asked for effect, and that does not invite a reply. Its purpose is to introduce a topic or to focus the reader on a concern.

3. Literature Studies *Rhetorical Questions* A writer will often use **rhetorical questions** to create an informal tone and to mentally engage the reader. Reread the article to see how Alexander Hiam has used rhetorical questions. How effective is this technique? How do rhetorical questions contribute to the tone and style of the article?

4. Media *Impact Scenario* Choose a company, a product, and a target customer, then create an impact scenario that you think would best change the customer's behaviour. To begin, brainstorm ideas with a partner, then choose the idea that has the most potential. Write a proposal describing the company, product, target customer, and the scenario.

5. Language Conventions *Sentence Fragments* Find examples of sentence fragments in the impact scenarios presented in the article. Are the sentence fragments effective in this context? When are they not appropriate? Why?

Using the impact scenario you developed in Activity 4, create a slogan to include on the premium. Experiment with sentence fragments as you create a message that is both short and effective.

With a partner, discuss Public Service Announcements [PSAs]. What are they? What are their purposes? Develop a list of PSAs you've seen on TV, on billboards, or on posters.

Bus Shelter

Public Service Announcement by Donna McCarthy
Produced for Covenant House

VIDEO: *Open up on a teenager sitting in a bus shelter. It's cold outside. People keep walking past the shelter, oblivious to him as he reaches out his hand asking for spare change.*

AUDIO: *Music throughout—"Amazing Grace."*

VIDEO: *Cut to a one-year-old baby sitting in the shelter crying. A woman walks by. She does a double take at the baby. She goes in to the shelter and bends down to soothe the crying baby.*

SUPER: How young . . . do they have to be . . .

VIDEO: *The woman picks up the crying baby and hugs him.*

SUPER: . . . before we give a damn?

SUPER: Covenant House.

1. Exploring Meaning

a. Public Service Announcements are used to raise awareness of issues of public concern. What issue is raised in "Bus Shelter"? Is it a concern in your area?

b. What advertising strategies are used in the PSA?

c. What emotional appeals are used? How did you respond to them?

d. Who is the target audience? How effectively do you think that audience is reached?

e. Examine the images that accompany the PSA. Do you find these images effective? Explain.

2. Researching Research Covenant House. Visit the organization's Web site or use other resources. What is the purpose of this organization? What other organizations help with the issue raised in the PSA? Think about other Covenant House ads you've seen. Consider whether this PSA is a typical example of ads produced by or for Covenant House.

3. Media *Design a PSA* Brainstorm a list of issues of concern in your area. Select the one that you feel is the most important. Address this issue by designing a PSA suitable for displaying in train stations or hospitals or in a doctor's, dentist's, or guidance counsellor's office. Remember to establish your target audience, use advertising strategies suitable for your issue of concern, and use emotional appeals.

Ask a classmate for feedback on your PSA. Is the issue effectively presented? Do your emotional appeals or other advertising strategies suit the message you are conveying? Revise your PSA and then publish it in a suitable format (poster, print ad, or TV commercial).

Self-Assessment: Examine the process you used to develop the PSA. What techniques worked? What did not work? How would you approach this process another time?

Examine the photos and brainstorm any questions you have about the images. Make sure to include "why" and "how" questions.

An Artist
at Work

Photos by Annie Griffiths Belt
Tinting by Jill Enfield

Under the watchful eye of her faithful companion, artist Jill Enfield hand-colors a black-and-white infrared photograph to help create evocative images like the one on pages 168–169, photographed by Annie Griffiths Belt. "Using infrared film and a dark red filter," says Belt, "breaks all the rules of standard photography. You need intense, bright light; you work with very slow film; and what you see is not what you get, because the film is sensitive to light that the eye can't see." Enfield colors the images with oil paint, pastel chalk, and colored pencil.

1. Exploring Meaning

a. How does the nature photo differ from a regular colour photo?

b. What do you think is meant by Annie Griffiths Belt's statement, "What you see is not what you get"?

c. Explain in your own words how the photo was created.

2. Visual Communication *Analyse Photo* Choose one photo from this selection and list everything that you see in it. Now view each part of the image separately. Examine the photo as a whole, and list words that describe its mood. Write one or two sentences describing what the photo communicates to you.

The Wizard of Id

Cartoon by Brant Parker and Johnny Hart

By permission of Johnny Hart and Creators Syndicate, Inc.

Visual Communication *Explore Meaning* Examine the cartoon and write a summary about what is happening. What media concepts are highlighted? What is the cartoonist's message?

Preview the title and photo in the article and make a prediction about the selection's topic.

Citytv: Now Available in Assorted Cultures

Newspaper Article by Kim Honey and Timothy Pratt

When executives from Casa Editorial El Tiempo, which owns and operates Citytv Bogota, first came to Toronto to check out the Citytv concept, they fell in love with the station's upbeat tempo and interactive, studioless format.

But company president Luis Fernando Santos, whose empire also includes the popular daily newspaper *El Tiempo*, wasn't convinced the Citytv concept would transplant into the culture of Latin America. In Toronto, Santos recalled in an interview, "80 per cent of households were wired, everyone has cable, and the income per capita was very high—it's a very, very sophisticated city, very different from a city like Bogota."

But the more he thought about the idea, the more he decided that it might just work. Now, Santos even points out how the El Tiempo building in downtown Bogota bears an uncanny resemblance to City's headquarters in Toronto's Chum building, home to *Electric Circus*, MuchMusic, *Speakers Corner*, Citytv and Bravo!—Spanish versions of which are being produced in Bogota. Located in the city's historic heart, La Candelaria, Citytv Bogota is surrounded by impressive colonial-style buildings with tiled roofs and ornate, wrought-iron balconies. And in consultation with Citytv Toronto, the El Tiempo building has been renovated to create street-front studios behind floor-to-ceiling windows, allowing passersby to watch what goes on inside, much like they do at Citytv in Toronto. Indeed, Moses Znaimer, the co-founder and president of Citytv, even helped choose the location.

Casa Editorial first decided to get into the TV business in 1993, when constitutional amendments allowed

Bogota videographer Olga Morales occasionally seeks police protection before heading out to cover a story. Photo by Eliana Aponte.

private companies to bid on new broadcasting licences. That same year, Chum Ltd., Citytv's parent company, had begun to sell its TV concept and programs to foreign markets. As a ChumCity International brochure puts it: "Now available in assorted cultures. Formats or franchises. Tailored to meet your needs. In your local language. Covering your local scene."

Through the auspices of ChumCity International, there is now Mucha-Musica in Buenos Aires, MuchUSA, Jyrki in Finland, and in Barcelona there is a Citytv-inspired and -licensed station. Franchisees usually pay royalty fees for using City trademarks, research, training techniques, and business plans; an additional annual fee can be stepped up to a percentage of the station's income. "It depends on how much of our programming they take," said Kevin Byles, head of ChumCity International. That's all in addition to Citytv's sale of individual shows, which are seen in more than 130 countries.

In 1997, Casa Editorial paid the equivalent of $15 million (U.S.) for its broadcast licence, and hammered out a deal with Citytv that requires it to pay 3 per cent of future profits in exchange for using the Toronto station's concept, training, and trademarks.

Znaimer posits that Citytv is able to make the leap from one culture to another because people are living in two places at the same time: the global marketplace and their community. "It's precisely because you have global economics that people feel a very passionate need for local culture—something that distinguishes, something that makes them special," he says. "It's a new way of organizing the television factory, and it has various aspects, some of which are aesthetic, but some of them economic. We are demonstrating that you can support the economy of a TV channel on the basis of a single city."

And Bogota is unquestionably a singular city. It's where national hang-gliding champion Jorge Abad was murdered when he accidentally landed in a bad neighbourhood. And it exists in a country that in 2000 averaged 71 violent deaths and four terrorist attacks a day. The conflict between and among leftist guerrillas, far-right paramilitary death squads, and the army has meant a steady diet of bloodshed and kidnappings on most TV news programs.

In that context, Citytv is trying something decidedly different. During a visit to the station, young journalists in jeans and sweaters, some wearing ball caps sporting the Citytv logo, ran back and forth, searching for cameras that hadn't already hit the streets. The day's editorial meeting had just ended, and assignment editor Ernesto Cortes was looking at some of the stories marked up on a storyboard grid: nine local college students killed, perhaps by guerrillas; a baby withheld by a hospital after the mother couldn't pay her bill; a march to protest against the assassination of a human-rights worker.

Asked how his reporters would cover these stories differently from other TV stations, Cortes said it would be more a matter of what City's reporters *won't* do that will make the difference.

"First of all, we're not going to show the dead bodies of the [college] kids—and we're not going to show the mothers bawling, either. And the same goes with the story about the baby: We'll interview the mother, but we're not going to show her crying or show the baby in the hospital."

Along with airing less violence, Cortes said that Citytv Bogota's goals are to listen to the viewers, and, on a broader level, to make the city a better place to live. The station strives to end its segments on a positive note, emphasizing, for example, what action is being taken to right a wrong.

It's an approach to the news that has been well-received by Bogotanos.

"They are so fed up. The country's situation is so bad, you don't have to be reminded of it every day through every broadcast," insists Cortes. "What you see elsewhere is blood from the beginning to the end . . . it's very negative news."

This day, for instance, 29-year-old Olga Luca Morales is the videographer assigned to cover the protest march listed on the storyboard. While there, she interviewed friends, family, and associates of the slain human-rights worker. Then, back in the studio, she edited out heated accusations against the 8,000-strong paramilitary army that roams the country. "In a conflict like ours, it doesn't help to broadcast these kinds of claims," she said. "We leave that up to the authorities."

Morales herself occasionally seeks police protection before heading out to cover a story. She's already had two cameras stolen at gunpoint, and in the past two years, the station has lost six cameras valued in total at $150,000 (U.S.), according to director Juan Lozano. "Right now we have only nine cameras," Cortes notes, "and often have to leave stories uncovered."

Operating under such circumstances, it's not surprising that Citytv Bogota still hasn't made a profit. But president Santos says he is right where he wants to be in terms of audience share—9 per cent of viewers in a seven-station market—and is "very happy the formula did work," claiming that revenue is now growing "faster than the other channels."

One of Citytv Bogota's most popular programs is *Arriba Bogota*, which Lozano hosts every morning between 6 and 10 o'clock, and in which public officials field questions and complaints from viewers. The day Lozano had the city's police chiefs and 17 captains on, the station was flooded with 5,000 calls. "When we had people from public works," he noted, "7,000 called."

Another popular feature is the portable video booth called—yes— *Speakers Corner*, where anyone can come in off the street and say their piece, many of which are then broadcast on television. Thanks to such features, and the station's broader approach to news gathering, says Casa Editorial's president, Bogota's residents are starting to think of Citytv as being interested in their welfare and truly dedicated to reporting local concerns.

Videographer Morales agrees. When she recently went to cover a story in a neighbourhood where the roots of eucalyptus trees were threatening to topple buildings, a community leader told her that people had been complaining to city officials, and sending press releases to local newspapers and TV stations, but that nothing had been reported because the buildings hadn't yet collapsed. After the story aired on Citytv, Bogota officials agreed to cut down dozens of trees—a controversial decision that raised the ire of environmental groups, whose anger, in turn, was duly reported on Citytv. "Local still works," boasts Byles, of ChumCity International, "and Citytv does it best."

Now Casa Editorial executives say they are looking into expanding the Citytv concept, both within Colombia and elsewhere in South America. And Znaimer, for one, seems amenable to that idea, although details have yet to be worked out: Such expansion could take the form of a joint venture, or Chum might consider licensing Casa Editorial to do it directly.

In the meantime, and in a country vexed by immense political, economic, and military problems, Citytv Bogota intends to forge ahead, inspired and informed, it would seem, by the sentiments of Znaimer emblazoned on the lobby walls of the Chum Building on Toronto's Queen Street West: "We want to create TV that is informal, urban, and positive. In doing so, we distinguish ourselves from the formality and pessimism of the mass broadcasters, who tend, especially in news shows, to view the world with alarm."

High-minded sentiments, perhaps. But in one of the world's most dangerous countries, those are brave—and potentially profitable—words to live by.

1. Exploring Meaning

a. According to the article, how does Citytv Bogota cover stories differently from other Bogota TV stations? Why does it cover the stories in these ways? Do you think this type of coverage would be appropriate in Canada? Why or why not?

b. Media have sometimes been accused of creating controversy in order to report on it. Do you think this charge is justified in the way that Citytv Bogota handled the story about cutting down the eucalyptus trees?

c. Do you think the article's title is effective? Why or why not? What alternate title would you suggest?

2. Focus on Context
List the differences between Toronto and Bogota described in the article. Why has the Citytv format worked in two very different contexts? Why do you suppose the Citytv concept works so well in Colombia and other countries without imposing Canadian culture?

3. Oral Communication
Debate View one or two TV news programs over several days, making note of the types of stories that are covered and how they are reported. Prepare an argument to support or refute the assertion that mass broadcasters are "pessimistic" and "tend, especially in news shows, to view the world with alarm." Organize a debate with classmates who have taken the opposite stance.

Self-Assessment: In a discussion with your classmates, do you listen to their opinions? Do you ask questions to find out more about what they think? How do you demonstrate respect for their ideas? How do you support your own opinions?

4. Media
TV News Story Record two TV news items that present different treatments of the same story—one that focusses on sensationalism and controversy and one that takes a more positive view and focusses on what is being done to right a wrong. Discuss with your classmates the purposes of each treatment and possible audiences that each might appeal to.

Identity Crisis

Poem by Monica Holliday

You said to be beautiful,
I had to be thin.
You said to wear that dress,
I needed perfect curves
(Whatever that meant).
You said to drive that car,
I had to have gorgeous eyes.
You said to wear that scent,
I needed flawless skin.
You said in order to get that man,
I had to have long, luscious lashes.
You said to get that job,
I needed big, pouting lips.
You said to succeed in life,
I had to be perfect.
You said to be happy,
I had to conform to all your obsessions.
And now as I lay here,
With my living breath departed,
Looking beautiful against
The creaseless silk of
My eternal bed,
I ask you why you do this,
Why I died this way,
Trying to exemplify
Perfect.

Photo by D. Bonesey.

1. Exploring Meaning

a. What do you think has caused the death of the speaker in "Identity Crisis"? What evidence can you find in the poem to support this view?

b. Identify the purpose, probable audience, and form of the poem. Use evidence from the poem to support your opinion. How would the content change if the purpose, audience, and form were different?

c. What strategies did you use to help you understand the poem? Discuss these strategies with your classmates.

2. Media *Media Images* In a small group, discuss what the poem says about the issue of conforming to media images. Jot down the poem's message, then write a statement about your view of the issue. Choose a form, such as a video, poem, collage, or personal essay that will allow you to effectively communicate your point of view. Share your final product with your classmates. **Self-Assessment:** Consider how the features of the format you chose affected your message. What are the advantages and disadvantages of the format you chose? What other format could you have chosen to communicate your message effectively?

3. Critical Thinking Discuss with a partner whether or not the media present a perfect body image for men. Consider what types of health issues affect men who try to confirm to these body images. Use "Identity Crisis" as a model to write a poem about body image from a male perspective.

Preview the selection, noting the article's organization. After reading "Video Ga Ga," comment on the effectiveness of this type of organization.

Video Ga Ga

Newspaper Article by Vinay Menon

00:01—Intro

Is this the real life? Is this just fantasy?

It's 1975, and with those words, Queen's "Bohemian Rhapsody" enters popular consciousness in London. But the pop-meets-opera tune stagnates on the charts until film director Bruce Gowers gets an unexpected call.

There's a problem: The song, with its harmonized layers, is too complicated to perform live. And the relatively unknown band needs something visual for *Top of the Pops,* a music television show.

So Gowers proposes a simple concept: He'll film the band with a prism-like lens. He'll give both the song and the band "a look."

They have no idea this visual experiment—which takes about five hours to shoot for about £3,500—is about to trigger a cultural tsunami.

00:02—The Day the Music (Died/Revived)

"Bohemian Rhapsody" might have faded into obscurity had something strange not happened.

The video propelled the song up the charts. It hit No. 1, where it lasted for 11 consecutive weeks.

And eyebrows started to raise throughout the industry.

Over the next two decades, the music video would impact every aspect of popular culture, influencing advertising, fashion, publishing, film and television.

It would be blamed for everything from shortening attention spans to poisoning youthful minds with depraved images. It would be praised for its power to exact social change, lauded as a moral compass capable of navigating gaps between gender, sex and race.

But, more than anything, the music video would change music.

00:03—The Historical Prelude

The relationship between sight and sound doesn't start with "Bohemian Rhapsody."

Not long after *The Jazz Singer* (1927), the first feature film with sound, Hollywood studios like MGM

A Eurythmics video shoot for the song "Missionary Man," 1986. Photo by Henry Diltz.

and Paramount produced "short films," featuring singing artists like Judy Garland and Cab Calloway.

In the 1950s, as detailed in the book *Thirty Frames Per Second: The Visionary Art Of The Music Video,* feature films were capitalizing on rock 'n' roll's embryonic surge. (Films like *Blackboard Jungle, The Girl Can't Help It* and *Jailhouse Rock* can be seen as precursors to the modern music video.) Britain, meanwhile, demonstrated prescience toward a new visual aesthetic with shows like *Top of the Pops* and *Ready, Steady, Go.* (In the '60s, The Beatles had already paved the way for visual literacy in music with films and short video clips.)

00:04—Hey, Hey, I'm Not a Monkee
In 1977, Michael Nesmith, a former Monkee and pioneer in the video movement, had an idea: Why not create a television channel devoted entirely to music?

He produced a video for his song "Rio," which he showed to skittish television execs. The suits found the idea of a 24-hour music network patently ridiculous.

But Nesmith was undaunted.

"I knew we had stumbled on to something," he says now. "It was more than just a discovery of one little rock, it was a discovery of a whole new land."

Nesmith produced a show called *Popclips* for U.S. cable station Nickelodeon. The new program detonated with atomic intensity; every teen now wanted a piece of the new land.

00:05—I Want My MTV
Fast forward to August 1981.

A number of factors have aligned. Shows like *Popclips* demonstrated the music video's popularity and, by extension, its commercial viability.

And cost-conscious record labels make a key observation: Making a video is a lot cheaper than touring. And with the growth of cable, a video has the potential to reach a much larger audience. Instantly and anywhere.

"When you think about it, the effect of MTV was quick. I mean it really changed the total media landscape throughout the world," says Les Garland, one of the network's co-founders, and now president of AfterPlay Entertainment.

"And in many ways, it had a 'Beatlesque' impact on youth culture."

When MTV started, it had about 200 videos in its rotation. No matter. A year after its famous 1982 "I Want My MTV" ad campaign, artists like Madonna, Mick Jagger, Stevie Nicks, Billy Idol and the Police were helping with the sell.

The feisty upstart would grow. And artists would gravitate toward the medium, seeing the music video as another arrow in their marketing quiver.

As Tonya Pendleton, music editor of Black Entertainment Television's Internet site, explains: "Those early music videos now look very primitive. There was absolutely no production value. So videos have gone from being afterthoughts to a key part of the artists' promotional package."

00:06—Rise of the Visual Image
How appropriate that the first video ever played on MTV was The Buggles' "Video Killed the Radio Star."

Director Russell Mulcahy understood that if this brave new world was to develop around a brave, new sensibility, the visual image had to be consciously separated from the music.

People already created mental sightscapes for their music. Any literal interference with the process would only detract. And unlike the past, where videos were generally relegated to performances, artists like David Bowie were now experimenting with filming techniques.

Robert Holmes, whose band Rubber Rodeo received a 1984 Grammy nomination for Best Video, remembers those epochal changes.

"In 1979, when I started making videos, most people thought of them as short-story films with music as a backdrop," he says. "Everybody was trying to be a mini-Hitchcock."

Along came Adam Ant, who spent money on costumes and make-up, attempting to create campy epics. Then came Devo, and all bets were off.

"To me, Devo was stranger and weirder than the Sex Pistols," says Holmes. "I mean, at least the Pistols you could understand—it was like rock done raw . . . But Devo seemed like a cult. They seemed dangerous they were so strange."

According to the VH1 documentary, *Video Killed the Radio Star: The History of the Music Video,* Devo was conceived as a group of "performance artists," not pop stars.

It's an important distinction because, for the first time, music suddenly became secondary to the visual image.

A few years later, when a bubble-gum pop singer named Toni Basil became the first act to sign an exclusive contract to make videos (and her song "Mickey" powered up the charts) MTV's clout was cemented.

"The network does not get the credit it deserves for making cable explode," says Robert Thompson, a television professor at Syracuse University.

"Suddenly you had all these kids who could not live without their daily dose of Duran Duran and Culture Club."

00:07—Tapping Into the Culture

Michael Nesmith explains the music video this way:

"The best way to understand what music videos were doing is to think about them as turning around the picture-sound relationship. Filmmakers have known for a long time that when you put sound under an image, the image is enhanced. But what we didn't know was that if you put a picture under sound, the sound is enhanced."

And channels like MTV and Canada's MuchMusic (started in 1984) were growing along with the videos they showed.

"In the early days, the music channels had to create a market because nobody knew if anybody would actually sit down to watch these 3-minute videos," explains George Stroumboulopoulos, a host with *The New Music*.

"So the channels had to create a market and, over the past 20 years, keep up with this market. What we've done is given the young audience a place to go. If you want to see a song, see fashion, see ideas, you come here.

"We're not creating culture, we are tapping into an existing culture and, at some level, adding to it."

00:08—This Video Is Brought To You By…

As video budgets started to rise, directors continued to experiment and push the form to the interpretive edge.

There were hyper-kinetic edits. Flash pans. Experimental camera tricks. Full-screen saturations. Seamless switching between colour and black-and-white, between animation and live action. Morphing. Different costumes in different frames.

And non-linear storytelling.

One might argue that many of the filming techniques attributed to early music videos can actually be seen in features like *Easy Rider, The Graduate, Bonnie and Clyde* and *A Clockwork Orange*.

"At first, there was this free-wheeling period, this anything goes stage," says Christopher Ward, a songwriter living in Los Angeles and a former MuchMusic personality.

"When the form was new there were no rules. People always talked about it being like a 3-minute movie. But to me, instead of being like a compressed 90-minute movie, it seemed more like an expanded 60-second commercial."

This synergy between advertising and the music video transcended mere style.

Pepsi, for instance, deftly perfected the pop sponsorship, attaching its brand to A-list stars like Michael Jackson and Madonna. (It continues to do so with Ricky Martin and the Spice Girls.)

And music video directors suddenly became the creative darlings of the ad world.

John Martin, the original force behind MuchMusic, says, "In the advertising world, these hot-shot young kids suddenly became celebrities, mainly because they were all trying to reach the same demographic."

The over-the-top links between advertising and video drew much scorn, even from within the music industry. It's not surprising then that Neil Young's "This Note's For You," a satirical montage of popular ad clips and raspy indictment of the ad-music connection, was banned from MTV in 1988 (but was played elsewhere, including Canada). But not every video endeavour was shallow or commercial.

Band-Aid's "Do They Know It's Christmas?" kickstarted a trend of "videos as popular instruments of social change." The Bob Geldof project spawned several imitators and compelled artists to actively explore themes of famine relief, racism and anti-violence.

00:09—The Point of Crossover

By the mid-'80s, music video was revolutionizing both television and film. NBC's popular *Miami Vice* actually went into production with the working title "MTV Cops."

The show's sets were wildly colourful. The opening theme became a radio hit. The leads released music videos of their own. And the cast was always on the cutting edge of fashion.

Even newspapers like *USA Today* got swept up by this cultural convergence, publishing a weekly synopsis of what "Top Songs" would appear in each weekly episode.

"*Miami Vice* was only the most obvious example of MTV's impact," says Thompson. "But in most of the dramas during the '80s and '90s, you could see at least one musical montage at some point in the program."

You could see it on shows like *Baywatch* or films like *Top Gun*.

By the mid-'80s, the music video also served a new function: It was selling tickets to movies.

Videos like "Against All Odds" were built around this concept. But the genre hit a new level when *Flashdance* was released.

"We basically got credit for making that movie," recalls Garland. "After that, the effects started multiplying through the entertainment world. MTV started affecting everything in the youth culture, from the way television commercials looked to the way films were being made and everything in between."

Popstars like Madonna and Sting made feature films. And movie stars wanted to sell CDs. Today's crossover artists include superstars like Jennifer Lopez and Will Smith.

Video directors continued to make the move to feature films. Spike Jonze, who won the MTV award for best director in 2000, made his feature debut with *Being John Malkovich.*

And highly respected directors, like John Landis and Martin Scorsese, have, at some point, moonlighted with the form.

00:10—The Beautiful Shall Inherit the Earth

Through the '80s, as bands became "better looking," they also became younger. It's important to remember that before Britney and Christina there was Tiffany and Debbie.

This "cult of youth" happened because listeners themselves were getting younger. And because of something called the "Repeated Viewing Factor." (A highly-attractive act would hold retinas longer than a less attractive one.)

From the outset, the great directors understood music videos had to be densely layered to hold up to multiple viewings from a demographic already famously short on attention.

To survive, images had to be elastic, fresh for a 15th viewing. Around this time, fashion—an interwoven part of pop—started to play a more integral role in music videos.

Models were used in videos: Christie Brinkley in Billy Joel's "Uptown Girl," Paulina Porizkova in The Cars' "You Might Think," and later, Stephanie Seymour in Guns 'N' Roses' "November Rain."

It was a logical continuation of what directors like Tim Pope already knew: A great video didn't need to revolve around the act. And sometimes scenes with nobody from the band were more compelling. George Michael's "Freedom" combines both principles, with models doing most of the lipsynching.

Accepting the "beautiful is better" principle, Robert Palmer's "Addicted to Love" featured models not really doing anything. And obeying the pop-will-eat-itself truism, the video has been successfully parodied by everybody from Tone Loc to Shania Twain.

But an emphasis on beauty didn't just affect female acts and models.

Bands like Foreigner, Styx, Chicago, Boston—none of them particularly telegenic—had railed against the video revolution.

They were ultimately replaced by video-friendly groups like Duran Duran and a-ha. (Duran Duran was so much about the visual that some of its songs, such as "Wild Boys," were actually conceived as videos before they were written.)

But by the late '80s, as the strength of the New Romantics started to wane, the big-hair, glam-rock acts of the period, such as Bon Jovi and Poison, were regaining a video foothold. Due to the strength of, ironically, concert clips on performance videos.

00:11—Morphs and Incarnations

The key to longevity in video was reinvention.

Which explains why a singer like Cyndi Lauper vanished from the cultural radar while Madonna triumphed.

Over the years, Madonna has exploited the power of the music video to transform herself through many incarnations: From non-virginal virgin, to gloved ingénue, to street urchin, to material seductress, to buxom iconoclast, to delirious nympho.

She was the first person to spend $1 million (all figures U.S.) on a music video ("Express Yourself"). And unlike many of her contemporaries, who came and went with the styles, she never looked the same.

Her videos always caused a buzz— even when nobody saw them. In this sense, Madonna realized what Frankie Goes to Hollywood already knew: *Sometimes a banned video helps sales more than one that airs.*

Michael Jackson, meanwhile, also spent money and changed his look (both in real life and on video). Despite the "Wacko Jacko" taunts from the tabloid press, Jackson's influence on the music video cannot be diminished.

The basic structure of "Beat It," for instance, serves as the genesis for most of the highly choreographed videos that exist today from boy bands like 'N Sync and the Backstreet Boys.

And though "Thriller" is often cited as the greatest video ever made, it's a popular misnomer to think of it as seminal. "Thriller" is actually the culmination of 10 preceding years of video.

(In fact, the John Landis short film was more about traditional narrative than many of the videos from that same period.)

But future attempts at grandiose production and linear storytelling would ultimately lead to video's deterioration and collapse into commercialism.

00:12—Guns, Grunge, and Hip-Hop

By the early '90s, when Guns 'N' Roses ruled the earth, the music video was already heading into serious decline. Budgets had become bloated, and there was a paucity of fresh creative talent.

But in 1991, when Nirvana's "Smells Like Teen Spirit" erupted on national airwaves, the music video (and music) was granted a temporary reprieve.

Seattle's grunge movement obliterated the previous decade's plastic images and put a dirty bullet in the glossy hubris.

The '90s would then be dominated by hip-hop acts. And though much of the music would be critically praised (says Kid Rock: "Hip Hop saved rock"), the videos themselves would collapse under the weight of clichés and unintentional self-parody.

Budgets would also reach the absurd, with Will Smith videos routinely costing more than $2 million and Michael and Janet Jackson's "Scream" eclipsing $7 million—more than some indie features.

"In the early '90s, we had a series of new directors, there was a new wave of talent that came up," says Steve Reiss, author of *Thirty Frames*

Per Second. "But by the late '90s, everything started to go south."

The end of grunge led to a resurgence of boy-girl bands. And lots of glamour, with bands such as Sugar Ray, Offspring, Ricky Martin and even the reinvented-for-America Barenaked Ladies emphasizing glam over grunge.

Videos were about shiny outfits, flattering angles and gorgeous extras. About pace and bounce. And sell. As Nesmith is fond of saying, "There are no real music videos on television anymore, just commercials."

Which is why artists like Moby and Beck—who both consider video a silly medium—spend little time or money on their projects. Their "anti-videos" are a return to a late '70s style of stock footage and/or amateur performances. (Beck's "Loser" was made for less than $5,000.)

So has video damaged music?

Observes John Martin: "There were an awful lot of bands that were bloody ugly, but which made great videos. And there were a lot of bands that had no business making music at all. But all these things settle down and there's a place on the planet for all of them."

So what is to be made of MTV's 20th birthday on August 1, 2001?

"Somebody asked me, 'Garland, if you were running MTV today, what would you do for the 20th anniversary?'" says Les Garland.

"That's quite a question, because when you are targeting the youth audience (MTV's core audience is 15–24) they don't really give a damn that it's 20 years old.

"In fact, I'm not sure they should toot that horn."

---

1. Exploring Meaning

a. What are some of your all-time favourite music videos? What is it that makes them good? Are there any common features? Explain.

b. According to the article, what different types of videos have evolved over the years?

c. What are three ways that music videos have affected TV?

d. Do you think that MTV was justified in not showing Neil Young's video "This Note's For You"? What is the responsibility of TV stations to the artists? to viewers? to sponsors?

e. Do you agree or disagree with Michael Nesmith's statement that "there are no real music videos on television anymore, just commercials"? Explain your answer.

2. Vocabulary Work with a partner to scan the article for four or five words that you would have trouble defining if someone asked you their meanings. Look up each word to find the meaning that makes sense in the context of the article. Find a synonym that would also make sense in this context and rewrite the sentence using the synonym. Does the substitution work as well as the original word?

3. Language Conventions *Co-ordinating Conjunctions* Co-ordinating conjunctions (*and, but, so, yet*) are normally used to join clauses within a sentence, but it is becoming increasingly acceptable for co-ordinating conjunctions to begin sentences. Find a few examples in the article of where this is done and discuss possible reasons the author used conjunctions in this way. Does it affect your understanding of what is being communicated? Is this usage appropriate to the tone and style of the article?

4. Media *Music Video* Working in a small group, choose a song or poem and develop a music video for it. Create a storyboard to help you develop a plan for the video. Determine your purpose and audience in creating the video. Do you want to tell a story, make the selection popular, or provide your own visual interpretation of the selection? You could use a video camera or computer software, such as PowerPoint, to create your video. **Self-Assessment:** Assess the effectiveness of your storyboard. Did it help you to plan the video effectively? How would you approach this process another time? What advice would you give to a classmate about creating a useful and effective storyboard?

Disaster as Popular Culture

Persuasive Essay by Derek Boles

The 20th century is over and, like most centuries, it was filled with catastrophe and disaster. Two World Wars and several lesser conflicts have killed over a hundred million people and have wrought incalculable economic damage. Only recently have we begun to crawl out from under the threat of thermonuclear holocaust and, in the 1980s, industrial accidents like Bhopal and Chernobyl have added to the litany of horrors. Not all of these catastrophes are human-made; nature does its part with a catalogue of hurricanes, floods, tornadoes, earthquakes and other natural disasters. Nightly, on television news, we are exposed to car crashes, train wrecks, airplane disasters and even the occasional shipwreck. In 1990 a Philippine boat disaster involving the ferry *Dōna Paz* killed almost 5,000 people but it has almost been forgotten by those who weren't directly affected by it.

Yet, one disaster of the 20th century remains etched in people's awareness and imagination. The continuing public fascination with the events surrounding the sinking of RMS *Titanic* in 1912 is testimony to the enduring hold that this disaster has on our collective cultural consciousness. Some claim that the three most written-about subjects of all time are Jesus, the American Civil War and the *Titanic* disaster. It has also been said that *Titanic* is the third most widely recognized proper noun in the English language, after *God* and *Coca-Cola*.

As a high school teacher, I'm amazed at the universal recognition whenever *Titanic* is brought up in class. The more motivated students are almost all aware of the rudiments of the event that occurred in the North Atlantic on April 14 & 15, 1912. Other students, who may be oblivious of many of the most important historical events of the last century, are at least aware of *Titanic*. What is it about *Titanic* that continues to capture people's imagination?

The Titanic Sinking on 15th April 1912 by Harley Crossley. Oil on canvas.

What really happened and why does it continue to fascinate us? The disaster was so incredible, so horrific, that it still staggers the imagination.

Trained historians sometimes condescendingly refer to *Titanic* as "popular history" in which complex processes are ignored in favour of collecting facts and emotional vignettes. Academic historians generally believe the *Titanic* disaster was relatively insignificant in the historical scheme of things. They decry the attempts of amateur historians to invest social and political significance in the disaster. School history textbooks covering the era frequently don't even mention the event.

Interestingly, *Titanic's* pop culture history began 14 years before the disaster itself. Morgan Robertson published a short novel, *Futility*, which centred on a fictional ship called the *Titan*. Robertson's ship was remarkably similar in dimensions to the real White Star liner. The fictional liner sailed in April, struck an iceberg and sank with great loss of life. Despite the remarkable coincidences, Robertson's story was widely ignored at the time and it wasn't until after the real disaster that the book attracted any attention.

The *Titanic* disaster was the biggest media event of the 20th century up until that time. *Titanic* was front-page news for months after the disaster. The event precipitated a series of responses from many of the literary luminaries of the Edwardian era including Joseph Conrad, Arthur Conan Doyle, George Bernard Shaw and Thomas Hardy. Except for anniversaries honouring the occasion and the deaths of various survivors, things were relatively quiet for the next four decades. The publication of Walter Lord's seminal *Titanic* book *A Night to Remember* in 1955 and its subsequent television and movie adaptations encouraged another round of media attention. The third time *Titanic* captured world notice was Dr. Robert Ballard's discovery of the wreck in 1985. Then we had the worldwide media frenzy generated by James

Cameron's movie, the traveling exhibition of *Titanic* artifacts and the award-winning Broadway musical. There was an unusual purity about the hype surrounding the Cameron movie. Unlike many films, the initial excitement immediately after the film's release was generated by the people themselves, rather than by an opportunistic studio publicity machine.

Undoubtedly much of this continuing interest has to do with the pervasiveness of the *Titanic* legend in our popular culture. Thousands of ditties, poems, cautionary tales, campfire songs, religious tracts, prayers, jokes, editorial cartoons, riddles and other cultural ephemera have been written about *Titanic*. Each time we are exposed to these, awareness of *Titanic* is imbedded further in our subconscious even if our interest in the historical event is marginal at best.

For example, a best-selling chronicle of the spread and politics of the AIDS disease was called *And the Band Played On*. Many who read the book and saw the subsequent TV movie were unaware that the title was a *Titanic*-inspired metaphor for institutional indifference in the face of serious adversity.

Without question, the most pervasive of these cultural manifestations are the audio-visual media of movies and television, particularly among children, teenagers and young adults. The inclusion of the *Titanic* tragedy in a movie like *Ghostbusters II* might seem gratuitous and in bad taste to serious students of *Titanic* lore, but if it serves to interest impressionable minds in learning more about the actual event, then it serves a useful purpose.

From a filmmaker's point of view, the *Titanic* tragedy is an awesome visual event. The actual sinking was not photographed by either still or motion picture cameras so Hollywood needs to recreate the event with special effects. The more successful of these recreations are among the most powerful moments on film.

No writer of fiction, no matter how talented, could spin a tale similar to *Titanic* without it being dismissed as utterly fantastic and improbable. Rarely does a story so completely combine the elements of tragedy, drama, mythology, morality play and social statement. No other historical event has been subjected to so many revisionist interpretations in the quest to find some individual or institution to shoulder the blame for the tragedy.

Several factors contribute to the allure of the event. Among them:
- The supreme confidence in a faulty technology.
- Big business' criminal priority of profit over safety.
- The arrogant disregard of every possible warning of catastrophe.
- The celebrity of *Titanic*'s 1st class passengers.
- The mathematical improbability of the *Titanic*'s collision with the iceberg.
- The breakdown of a rigidly stratified Edwardian society in which the fabulously wealthy find themselves in exactly the same predicament as the poor and destitute.

These are difficult concepts to portray in films. Movies and television are visual, not intellectual media. Ultimately, successful productions must be about people, not technology. This is why a movie such as *A Night to Remember* is celebrated over thirty-five years after it was made and the more recent *Raise the Titanic* is almost forgotten a little more than a decade later. The older movie was a testimony to the human condition; the newer one ignored it.

The *Titanic* disaster provided a cinematic prototype for numerous films which relied on a similar formula: take a group of disparate people representing a variety of ages, cultures, attitudes and socio-economic backgrounds, thrust them all together into a strange and unfamiliar environment and then test them in their ability to survive and adapt to calamity. The audience already knows that something terrible is going to happen. That's why they're there: to savor the vicarious thrills of being a part of something they hope that they will never have to experience in real life. The suspense comes in guessing who will live and who will die.

The formula enjoyed its greatest commercial success in the 1970s when it culminated in its own genre, the disaster movie. Some of the decade's most profitable films, including the *Poseidon Adventure, Earthquake* and *Towering Inferno* inspired over a dozen less successful exploitations of the formula. The best of these films managed to combine the vagaries of technology or nature gone wrong with interesting and believable characters that the audience cared about. Other genre entries such as *Deep Impact, Independence Day* and *Dante's Peak* have further mined the formula.

The disaster movie formula ran out of steam at the end of the 1970s and ultimately mutated into the drivel of television's *Love Boat,* a show that was ironically responsible for the virtual rebirth of the cruise ship industry which is now stronger and more profitable than ever.

With the public furor over the Cameron film, the *Titanic* disaster is as deeply rooted in our consciousness as ever. This seems an appropriate time to review and take stock of *Titanic* and its various representations in media and popular culture.

The disaster was directly responsible for several seminal events in the development of the mass media. It was the first time that a major news event was reported to the public primarily through electronic means. From the initial reports of the disaster on April 15 until the rescue ship's docking in New York on April 18, all of the information about *Titanic* was relayed through wireless telegraph.

The New York Times coverage of the *Titanic* disaster helped transform a local newspaper into a global voice. In 1912, there were almost two dozen daily newspapers in the New York area. In that climate of fierce competition, there was much inaccurate and misleading information in the days immediately following the disaster. *The Times* stood clear above the rest of the dailies in terms of the integrity and accuracy of its coverage. Eventually, the paper would become, in effect, the U.S. national newspaper and the paper still acknowledges that its coverage of the *Titanic* disaster was responsible for this.

The *Titanic* disaster also had a profound influence on the rise to prominence of the medium of radio. It was the first occasion that news of catastrophe reached the public over airwaves. Guglielmo Marconi, the Italian inventor who had developed wireless and who had bought a ticket for the *Titanic's* April 20th return voyage to England, was able to dramatically exploit the usefulness of the medium. Within a few years, radio would become the most powerful mass medium in the world, eventually supplanting film as the most pervasive of all media, a position usurped by television some 25 years later.

One of Marconi's employees, a Russian immigrant living in New York, was able to relay the wireless messages being sent from the *Carpathia*. David Sarnoff would greatly exaggerate the role that he had played in the rescue efforts but later, after he became the president of NBC, and one of the pioneers of television, he would claim that the *Titanic* disaster had made his reputation.

Canadian connections with the *Titanic* disaster abound. About fifty of the liner's passengers were Canadian residents or were immigrating to Canada. A member of the Molson brewing family was a victim, as was the president of a railway company that later became Canadian National. The initial wireless messages from the sinking liner were picked up in Montreal and then relayed to the rest of the world. Immediately following the disaster, the White Star Line commissioned two ships to search for the bodies of victims. Several hundred were returned to Halifax, Nova Scotia and buried in local cemeteries which can be still be visited.

Canadian poet E. J. Pratt published an epic poem about the disaster in 1935. Pratt (whose initials are hauntingly similar to *Titanic's* Captain E. J. Smith) was born and raised in a Newfoundland and Labrador fishing village and was steeped in Maritime lore. Pratt's "Titanic" chronicles the ship from its launching on May 31, 1911 to its destruction on April 15, 1912.

Ironically, the *Titanic* disaster would overshadow the greatest Maritime disaster in Canadian history. In 1914, two years after *Titanic*, the Canadian Pacific liner *Empress of Ireland* sank in the Gulf of St. Lawrence near Rimouski, Quebec and over a thousand people perished. Most of the victims were Canadian; many were from Toronto. Yet, few Canadians today are even aware of the disaster or the name of the ship.

Within a few years of 1912, the *Titanic* loss of life was overshadowed by the far more cataclysmic events of World War I. The *Titanic* disaster was all but forgotten except during the April anniversaries or whenever a local survivor passed on or was featured in a newspaper article. *Titanic* had become a minor but interesting footnote of history.

In 1938, German author Robert Pretchl published *Titanic*. The novel was the first attempt at a sustained fictional narrative of the disaster where fictional and real characters are interweaved in a generally accurate account of the disaster.

By far the most important of pop culture events was the publication in 1955 of Walter Lord's *A Night to Remember*. Lord's writing adapted a then fresh approach, which has since become a formula. The book has a "you are there" quality and a breezy writing style compared to other historical tomes. Short paragraphs, reconstructed conversations and personalized anecdotes give the book a cinematic feel. Lord's book is still considered the best among the several hundred books written about the *Titanic* disaster.

In the 1950s the new medium of television proved equally adept at exploiting the *Titanic* and the event stayed alive in the public conscience. *Kraft Television Theatre, You Are There, Telephone Time, Rheingold Theatre, The Time Tunnel, Night Gallery, Upstairs, Downstairs, The Captains and the Kings, Voyagers,* a half dozen made for TV movies and most recently, *News Radio* were among television's efforts to keep the *Titanic* legend in front of the public.

There were many *Titanic* legends that developed over the years and they were often confused with fact. Among the myths were: the *Titanic* was trying to break a speed record; there was an Egyptian mummy on board the ship; there were millions of dollars in gold in the ship's hold; several men got into lifeboats because they were dressed in women's clothing. None of these were true, except for the cross-dressing, but they continue to be reported as fact in contemporary news accounts of the disaster.

1962 saw the formation of the Titanic Enthusiasts of America. The organization struggled for a few years, was later judiciously retitled the Titanic Historical Society and received a major boost in interest with the discovery of the wreck in 1985. The Cameron movie created another membership boost and the THS remains the pre-eminent *Titanic* organization in the world, despite the formation of a rival splinter group in the 1980s. The organization sponsors yearly conferences and publishes an impressive and glossy newsletter, the *Commutator,* devoted to the *Titanic* and its two sister ships. In the 1990s they began sponsoring "heritage tours" to *Titanic* related sights in England, Ireland, the United States and Canada.

On a lighter note, the tabloid press is particularly obsessed with the *Titanic*. The *Weekly World News* reported in 1991 that Captain Smith was found in a lifeboat, "He thinks it's . . . 1912—and his pipe is still lit!" Smith would have been 133 years old. The same tabloid reported another survivor a year earlier, "She thinks it's . . . 1912—and her dress is still wet!"

In 1976, the novel *Raise the Titanic* appeared in print and in 1980 was made into an expensive Hollywood movie. The science fiction scenario has the U.S. Navy raising the liner in order to obtain a rare mineral stowed in its hold. The substance is deemed to be necessary for a new nuclear defense system. The film was a colossal flop that, in filmmaking annals, was considered a disaster in itself, though without loss of life. The film cost $40 million and its special effects budget alone was more than it cost to build the original *Titanic* in 1911.

Various preposterous schemes to refloat the *Titanic* were earnestly reported by the news media though no one was exactly sure where the wreck lay. One theory held that an earthquake in 1929 had completely buried the wreck. A Texas millionaire, Jack Grimm, financed three expeditions to locate it in the early 1980s but he was unsuccessful.

Finally, in 1985, a combined American-French expedition under the leadership of oceanographer Robert D. Ballard located the *Titanic* and photographed it using deep sea technology being developed for the U.S. Navy. Ballard returned in 1986 to take better pictures but vowed to leave the wreck undisturbed out of respect for those who had perished.

In January 1986, the space shuttle *Challenger* exploded shortly after liftoff. Several parallels with the *Titanic* disaster were striking: a fatally optimistic faith in a new technology; the deaths of an identifiable cross-section of humanity; a plunge into the North Atlantic; the possibility that ice was a factor in the failure of the *Challenger*'s O rings and the list of "what ifs" surrounding each tragedy. The *Argo*, an underwater search vehicle, was used to locate both wrecks.

In 1987, a French expedition brought hundreds of *Titanic* items to the surface. On October 28 of that year, a live TV broadcast from Paris hosted by actor Telly Savalas displayed a safe claiming that it would be opened live on television and valuable artifacts would be recovered from the interior. There's evidence that the safe was empty and stuffed with items prior to the dramatic opening. The retrieval and display of personal artifacts belonging to *Titanic* victims ignited a storm of controversy that continues to this day. The artifacts were publicly displayed in the United States for the first time in Memphis, Tennessee in 1997.

The fascination with *Titanic* also cuts across all literary genres. Arthur C. Clarke, the author of *2001: A Space Odyssey*, published a major science fiction novel, *The Ghost From the Grand Banks*, another futuristic tale about an attempt to raise the doomed liner. Romance novelist Danielle Steel set the beginning of her novel *No Greater Love* on the decks of the *Titanic*.

In the summer of 1991, a fourth *Titanic* expedition photographed the wreck in the Canadian IMAX film process for showing in the Cinesphere at Ontario Place and other IMAX theaters around the world. Dr. Joe MacInnis, a Canadian underwater specialist, who was also on the 1987 expedition, claimed that the IMAX film would give viewers the sense of diving down to the shipwreck themselves. While the underwater footage was spectacular, an interesting 45-minute documentary was bloated into a 90-minute feature and much of the padding consisted of interviews with various members of the *Titanic* lunatic fringe.

In late 1996, CBS Television, eager to cash in on the anticipation over the Cameron film, released the tawdry four-hour miniseries *Titanic*, filmed in Vancouver. The movie was mostly ignored in its first broadcast but received much higher ratings in its post-Cameron rerun in May of 1998.

In Halifax, one *Titanic* victim's gravesite, a member of the crew named J. Dawson, has become a local shrine for young fans of Leonardo DiCaprio, whose character in the Cameron movie has the same name. The modern shipboard sequences of the Cameron movie were photographed near Halifax harbour. A large piece of the *Titanic*'s internal wood panelling, retrieved from the Atlantic following the disaster, was used as a mold for a similar piece used in the film. This piece is on display at the Maritime Museum of the Atlantic. In fact, the last three *Titanic* movies have been filmed partly or wholly in Canada. I visited Halifax in 1983 looking for evidence of that city's *Titanic* connection and could find no one who was aware of it.

The Cameron film has been compared to great romantic epics of the past like *Gone With the Wind* and *Dr. Zhivago*. The movie has certainly reignited Hollywood's interest in the romance genre. Despite the monumental hype generated by and for the movie, the official license holders refrained from the more excessive attempts to cash in on a successful film. There were no *Titanic* action figures, lunch pails or plastic icebergs. Official merchandising was generally tasteful and limited to books about the real ship, the movie's special effects and poster. Others have not been so scrupulous and prices for even marginally interesting artifacts connected with the disaster have gone through the roof.

As usual, conspiracy theories about the *Titanic* abound. As with JFK's assassination and Elvis's death, people refuse to accept simple explanations for the disaster. These theories include the use of defective steel to construct the ship. One of the most fanciful conspiracies, promoted by the 1995 book *Riddle of the Titanic*, suggested that the *Titanic* did not sink at all. Instead, the authors claim, it was really *Titanic*'s sister ship that was substituted at the last minute in an insurance scheme gone awry.

Anyone interested in *Titanic*, whether seeing the movies or reading a book about the disaster, is faced with the same question. How would one have reacted under a similar set of circumstances? The sinking of the *Titanic* took 2 hours and 40 minutes and people had to make moral choices. It's the ability to relate to that situation and those choices that makes the *Titanic* story so compelling.

1. Exploring Meaning

a. Drawing on your own knowledge, generate a list of people, events, and things that are part of popular culture. Discuss your list with other students.

b. What is Derek Boles's thesis in this essay? Where does the thesis first appear?

2. Literature Studies *Essay Structure* In a persuasive essay, the writer wants the reader to accept a particular point of view. The writer does this by presenting supporting details (facts, statistics, examples, reasons, and so on) that help to prove the thesis. List the supporting details Boles uses. Do you think he proved his thesis? Explain.

3. Technique and Style *Organizational Patterns* There are several ways of organizing an essay. These organizational patterns help a writer construct a powerful argument. Here are some of the most commonly used patterns:

- *Comparison and contrast*: investigation of the similarities and differences between two or more things
- *Classification*: division of a complex topic into smaller categories
- *Cause and effect*: exploration of why something happens and the results
- *Definition*: explanation of a series of key terms or concepts
- *Chronological order*: examination of a situation or event in the order in which it occurred

Choose the pattern that you think best describes the organization of "Disaster as Popular Culture." Explain your choice.

4. Writing *Essay* Choose a person, event, or thing that is part of popular culture. Write an essay outlining the reasons the event, person, or thing has become part of popular culture. As you develop your essay, use the following process:

- Write a brief outline stating your position on the topic. Jot down notes for three or four arguments that support your thesis.
- For each point on your outline, write one or two paragraphs providing supporting details and examples.
- End your essay with a concluding statement that reflects your opening paragraph.
- Assess your essay. Did you clearly state the thesis in the introductory paragraph? Do the supporting paragraphs contain evidence (facts and statistics) proving the thesis? Is your argument reasonable and persuasive? Is your conclusion clear? Revise your essay.

Unit 5

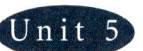

Technology and Science: On the Cutting Edge

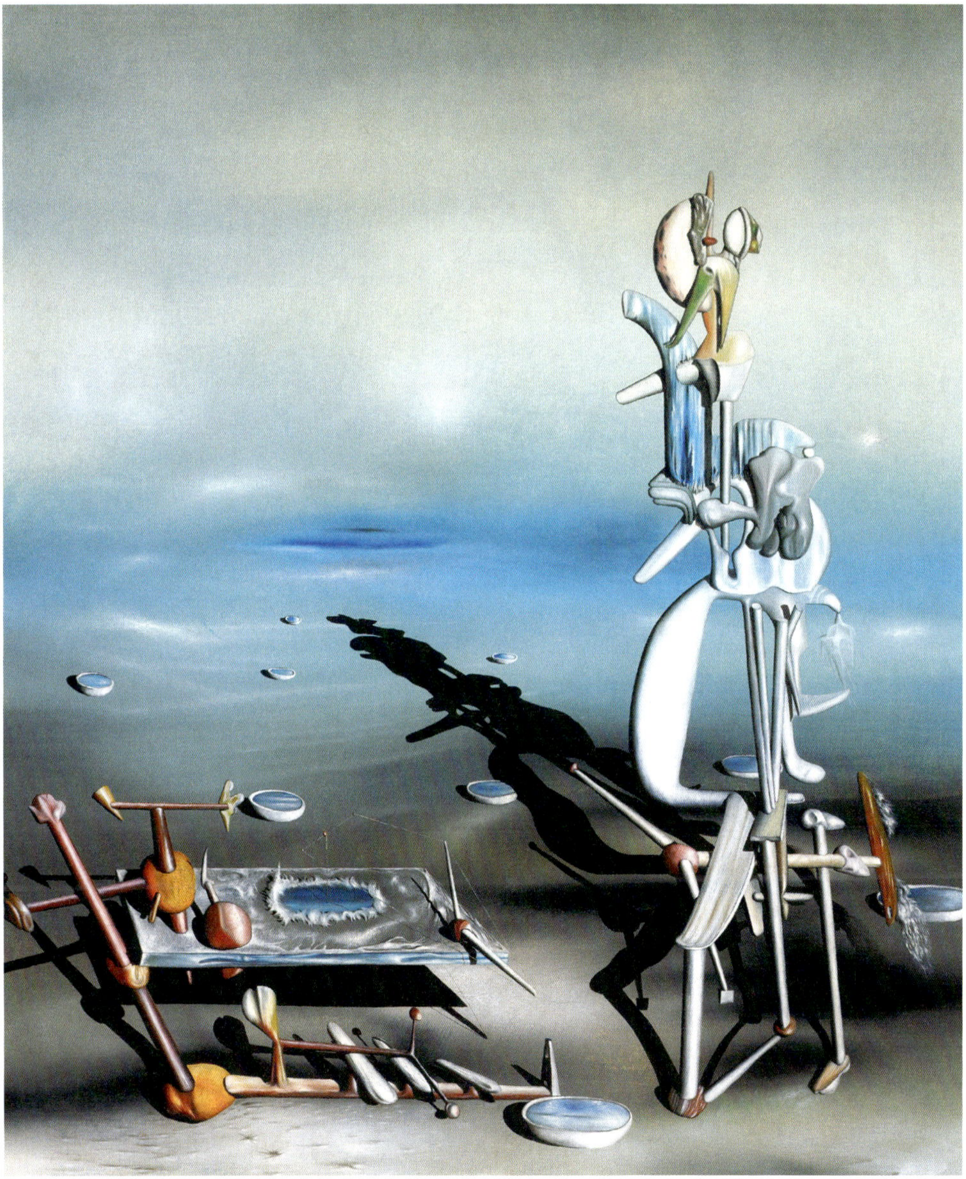

In small groups, discuss the following questions: In your opinion, have humans reached the end of their ingenuity and innovation? What is left for inventors to create? Read the following essay to find out how people might have responded to this question one thousand years ago.

It's All History Now

Essay by Bill Husted

In the year 999, the world waited for the New Millennium with excitement and fear. Scientists of the day—astrologers, monks and prophets—watched the skies for portents of disaster. The most jaded of them wondered whether all the great discoveries were in the past.

If it could be done, they reasoned, it had already been done.

After all, it was easy enough to tick off the truly important technological discoveries—and all were far in the past.

The Phoenicians had made communications easier, developing a 22-letter alphabet so many years before that the exact date was already blurred with time; wheeled vehicles for transport were in use even before that; the idea of the number "0" had come out of India in 876 B.C., making true mathematics possible; and the Chinese were using a new way to communicate and store data: writing paper.

Life was already technologically sophisticated.

The first portable digital computer had been invented and in use for centuries by 999. It was the abacus, a remarkable calculating device, easy to carry and with no battery-life problems. The abacus represented such a sturdy and useful technology that it was still being used in parts of China in 1982 to take the census.

Along with such wonders of technology, there were dangers, too.

The fearful of 999 worried that human beings were tampering with the forces of nature, imposing their egos on powers too complex to be understood, too dangerous to be harnessed.

Nor were those fears without justification. After all, the Chinese—somewhere around 868 A.D.—invented gunpowder, opening the door to a technology that took an ordinary substance and seemed to give it magical powers for destruction.

Take a bit of sulfur, some charcoal and potassium nitrate, mix well, and you have a grayish black powder that looks as harmless as a handful of dirt but holds within it the power to move mountains.

The thinkers and philosophers of the day wondered and fidgeted and questioned whether humans were smart enough to be trusted with such substances.

There was much to fear in 999 and seemingly little left to invent. Today, not much has changed.

The miracle technologies of space travel, computers, atomic energy, the telephone system and the Internet are firmly in the past. Looking ahead, it seems that all that remains for technologists is the mundane task of perfecting what already exists. Some wonder—with credibility—that human beings, in the name of science and technology, have bred the seeds of their own destruction.

Pick your poison, the fearful say.

Will it be atomic energy and one grand blast that closes the door on civilization?

Or will we all go with a sneeze and a feverish quiver because of human tampering with viruses and genes?

Those watching the skies for signs in the year 999 would have understood those fears.

At least part of the reason for our Mr. Magoo vision of technology—foggy and shortsighted—is frailty and ego. Each person's life span is short, yet history is long. We view the world as a moon that orbits around our own lives. The things that fall within our orbit become bright and important, and those outside the orbit are as dim as distant stars.

That's why, if you ask someone today about the great technological innovations of history, you'll likely hear about computers, or the Internet or even something as historically mundane as computer graphics.

The discoveries of the Pythagorean theorem and multiplication tables are quite literally ancient history, while the 600-megahertz microprocessor is a modern miracle.

Perhaps, when you think beyond a single lifetime and consider technology, it helps to find some common ground, to define and agree on some boundaries.

Little or nothing is "invented" . . . instead it is discovered.

Almost without exception, technology comes from the world and nature.

Electricity was scorching through the skies in the days when a burning torch was the latest in innovation. Atomic energy was hard at work before humans had the ability to utter their first words.

It was all there. It was just a matter of finding it.

Even the physical structure of a microprocessor—the chip that provides the real calculating engine for the computer—is no more than silicon (melt down some sand that has existed since the dawn of time and there you have it) that has been treated with some elements (boron, phosphorus or arsenic) that are bountiful in nature. Adding these elements to the silicon—called "doping" the chip—alters its electrical properties in a useful way. But the properties were not created by humans. Instead, we learned that they exist.

It has all been there—the laws of physics, the rules that govern how electricity flows, the raw materials—waiting for human beings to get smart enough to find them.

No matter what technology you name—from atomic power to the seeming miracle of a light that shines based on an invisible force traveling miles through copper wire—it's simply humans using a force that was already there.

The inventor is nature. Humans are the discoverers.

But if humans are little more than scavengers, searching the world for bits and pieces that we can use, we have been resourceful and ingenious ones.

Each new-found technological discovery leads to the next, like the pieces of a giant jigsaw puzzle that slowly form a beautiful picture as they are put together. Signal flags and smoke signals created the working knowledge of communicating in code, which opened the door for the telegraph, which taught the lessons of communicating over a network, which made it possible to build the Internet.

The most frightening part of technology may not be its potential for destruction, but its potential for change.

Just as we get used to the idea of horse-drawn carriages, the automobile comes along—and everything you once knew is suddenly wrong. Once humans grasped the idea of sailing ships, the steam engine made them too slow for useful work.

There's a practical loss—skills and careers built on one technology become useless almost overnight.

Each new technology seems to kill off an old one, even technologies that appeared too powerful and important to die.

Take, for instance, the first truly digital method of communicating . . . the telegraph and Morse code.

It was a network that erased time and distance. Messages that took days and even weeks or months to deliver by messenger, train and boat moved almost at the speed of light over the telegraph lines. One of the marvels of technology was the laying of great undersea cables that let messages move by telegraph from Europe to America. Surely it would last forever.

Or so people thought.

But wireless communications and the wired telephone turned the telegram into a relic, an antique that now seems quaint and cumbersome.

Petroglyphs at Canyonlands National Park, Utah. Photo by Harvey Lloyd.

New technologies force out the old.

And not all the losses are practical. Some of the losses—perhaps the most important losses—are deeper and more fundamental.

One of the most enduring of all human traits has been storytelling. In the earliest days, stories, poems and songs were passed down orally from generation to generation. But as the printed word became more important, people's memories faded. Few people memorize stories anymore; family histories are passed down on videotape and computer disk, not in stories by the fire.

At one time, music stores sold sheet music and many families spent the evening gathered around the piano, singing together. While singing and storytelling haven't died, they've more and more become the work of professionals and less a part of ordinary life.

Instead, there are books, movies, CDs and television. It would be difficult to argue that the new technologies are bad. It would be equally impossible to say that what we lost had no value. We don't sing as a family as much anymore.

Before you judge all this and decide whether you think it's good or bad, keep in mind that technology doesn't care what you think.

Since technology has such power over our lives, our jobs and even over the future of the human race, it is tempting to give it a human face—to label some technologies as evil, others as good.

No matter which technology you discuss—the Internet, atomic energy, missiles and satellites, commercial television or cellular phones—you'll have no trouble finding opposing opinions.

Technology doesn't have a soul. Your television set is no more good or evil than atomic energy. Each technology has the potential to be anything humans assign to it because technology is no more or less than a tool.

And anyone who has used a hammer can tell you that a tool can be used to do good or to bring pain and destruction.

The only firm rule—when it comes to predicting the future of technology—is that the experts are usually wrong. Just a few decades ago, there were predictions that you'd commute to work in a car with fold-down wings, that there would be a colony on the moon, that almost all electricity would come from atomic and wind power.

All these things are technologically possible, but proved impractical, socially unacceptable or just plain not wanted by the consumer.

Perhaps the best way to look at the future of technology is to study the past.

1. Exploring Meaning

a. What does Bill Husted suggest might be the most frightening thing about technology? Support your answer with quotations from the text. Discuss his ideas, offering your own opinion.

b. Develop a T-chart listing the major technological advances humans made in the first and second millenniums. Use your chart to compare and contrast the way people lived before 1000 C.E. and before 2000 C.E.

c. Husted frequently uses the second-person point of view ("Before you judge all this and decide . . ."). Suggest some reasons for using this point of view.

d. What main point does Husted make about the future of technology? Do you think he proves his point? Why or why not?

2. Oral Communication *Speech* Prepare a five-minute speech in which you explain what you believe was the single most important technological advance made in the last two thousand years. Include the reasons for your choice. Present your speech to a small group and ask for feedback about its clarity, delivery, and effectiveness. Revise and rehearse your speech, then present it to the class. You may wish to include props, images, diagrams, or other presentation aids.

3. Visual Communication *Technology Images* Examine the cave painting on page 201, and the surrealist painting by Yves Tanguy on page 197. How has each artist represented technology and human innovation? Which do you think best reflects humans' relationship with technology? Explain.

4. Focus on Context From the perspective of a student in a Canadian school at the beginning of the twenty-first century, record your personal response to the cave painting. Now, imagine you are a friend of the original artist, and he or she has just unveiled this work. How do you respond to the cave painting?
Self-Assessment: What did you find most difficult about this task? Which strategies did you find most effective in helping you complete this task?

5. Language Conventions *Double Negatives* Examine the following statement and explain what it really means:

> Nor were those fears without justification.

Identify the two negatives in the statement and discuss why the author has phrased the sentence in this way. Would you change the sentence? If so, how? With a partner, brainstorm six sentences that use double negatives. Discuss their effect or effectiveness.

Prometheus Carrying Fire

Painting by Jan Cossiers

1. Visual Communication *Story Through Image* In a small group, discuss what you already know about the myth of Prometheus. Why is it appropriate for a Technology unit? What does this painting reveal about the myth? Using the Internet or library resources, research the myth of Prometheus. How effectively does the painting tell the story of Prometheus? What part of the myth would you have chosen to illustrate? Explain.

2. Making Connections Use Internet or library resources to find other images that represent the myth of Prometheus. Create a display of these images with text to incorporate highlights from the myth.

Alternatively, find other myths or folktales related to fire and its discovery and discuss any similarities.

3. Writing *Perspectives* Imagine you are Prometheus as portrayed in the painting on page 204. Write a short piece in a format of your choice exploring your experiences, thoughts, feelings, dreams, and desires.
Self-Assessment: Assess your writing and consider how effectively you have captured the experiences and probable thoughts and feelings of Prometheus. Is your chosen format an appropriate vehicle for your content?

4. Film Study Assume that you work for a company developing a movie from the Prometheus myth. Choose one aspect of movie development— costumes, set design, storyboard, script, promotional materials, or advertising —and develop an appropriate presentation to highlight your work on the Prometheus movie.

The Flying Machine

Short Story by Ray Bradbury

In the year A.D. 400, the Emperor Yuan held his throne by the Great Wall of China, and the land was green with rain, readying itself toward the harvest, at peace, the people in his dominion neither too happy nor too sad.

Early on the morning of the first day of the first week of the second month of the new year, the Emperor Yuan was sipping tea and fanning himself against a warm breeze when a servant ran across the scarlet and blue garden tiles, calling, "Oh, Emperor, Emperor, a miracle!"

"Yes," said the Emperor, "the air is sweet this morning."

"No, no, a miracle!" said the servant, bowing quickly.

"And this tea is good in my mouth, surely that is a miracle."

"No, no, Your Excellency."

"Let me guess then—the sun has risen and a new day is upon us. Or the sea is blue. That now is the finest of all miracles."

"Excellency, a man is flying!"

"What?" The Emperor stopped his fan.

"I saw him in the air, a man flying with wings. I heard a voice call out of the sky, and when I looked up, there he was, a dragon in the heavens with a man in its mouth, a dragon of paper and bamboo, coloured like the sun and the grass."

"It is early," said the Emperor, "and you have just wakened from a dream."

"It is early, but I have seen what I have seen! Come, and you will see it too."

"Sit down with me here," said the Emperor. "Drink some tea. It must be a strange thing, if it is true, to see a man fly. You must have time to think of it, even as I must have time to prepare myself for the sight."

They drank tea.

"Please," said the servant at last, "or he will be gone."

The Emperor rose thoughtfully. "Now you may show me what you have seen."

Aeronautical engineer Otto Lilienthal in a glider, around 1896. Photographer unknown.

They walked into a garden, across a meadow of grass, over a small bridge, through a grove of trees, and up a tiny hill.

"There!" said the servant.

The Emperor looked into the sky.

And in the sky, laughing so high that he could hardly hear him laugh, was a man; and the man was clothed in bright papers and reeds to make wings and a beautiful yellow tail, and he was soaring all about like the largest bird in a universe of birds, like a new dragon in a land of ancient dragons.

The man called down to them from high in the cool winds of morning. "I fly, I fly!"

The servant waved to him. "Yes, yes!"

The Emperor Yuan did not move. Instead he looked at the Great Wall of China now taking shape out of the farthest mist in the green hills, that splendid snake of stones which writhed with majesty across the entire land. That wonderful wall which had protected them for a timeless time from enemy hordes and preserved peace for years without number. He saw the town, nestled to itself by a river and a road and a hill, beginning to waken.

"Tell me," he said to his servant, "has anyone else seen this flying man?"

"I am the only one, Excellency," said the servant, smiling at the sky, waving.

The Emperor watched the heavens another minute and then said, "Call him down to me."

"Ho, come down, come down! The Emperor wishes to see you!" called the servant, hands cupped to his shouting mouth.

The Emperor glanced in all directions while the flying man soared down the morning wind. He saw a farmer, early in his fields, watching the sky, and he noted where the farmer stood.

The flying man alit with a rustle of paper and a creak of bamboo reeds. He came proudly to the Emperor, clumsy in his rig, at last bowing before the old man.

"What have you done?" demanded the Emperor.

"I have flown in the sky, Your Excellency," replied the man.

"What have you done?" said the Emperor again.

"I have just told you!" cried the flier.

"You have told me nothing at all." The Emperor reached out a thin hand to touch the pretty paper and the birdlike keel of the apparatus. It smelled cool, of the wind.

"Is it not beautiful, Excellency?"

"Yes, too beautiful."

"It is the only one in the world!" smiled the man. "And I am the inventor."

"The only one in the world?"

"I swear it!"

"Who else knows of this?"

"No one. Not even my wife, who would think me mad with the sun. She thought I was making a kite. I rose in the night and walked to the cliffs far away. And when the morning breezes blew and the sun rose, I gathered my courage, Excellency, and leaped from the cliff. I flew! But my wife does not know of it."

"Well for her, then," said the Emperor. "Come along."

They walked back to the great house. The sun was full in the sky now, and the smell of the grass was refreshing. The Emperor, the servant, and the flier paused within the huge garden.

The Emperor clapped his hands. "Ho, guards!"

The guards came running.

"Hold this man."

The guards seized the flier.

"Call the executioner," said the Emperor.

"What's this!" cried the flier, bewildered. "What have I done?" He began to weep, so that the beautiful paper apparatus rustled.

"Here is the man who has made a certain machine," said the Emperor, "and yet asks us what he has created. He does not know himself. It is only necessary that he create, without knowing why he has done so, or what this thing will do."

The executioner came running with a sharp silver ax. He stood with his naked, large-muscled arms ready, his face covered with a serene white mask.

"One moment," said the Emperor. He turned to a nearby table upon which sat a machine that he himself had created. The Emperor took a tiny golden key from his own neck. He fitted this key to the tiny, delicate machine and wound it up. Then he set the machine going.

The machine was a garden of metal and jewels. Set in motion, birds sang in tiny metal trees, wolves walked through miniature forests, and tiny people ran in and out of sun and shadow, fanning themselves with miniature fans, listening to the tiny emerald birds, and standing by impossibly small but tinkling fountains.

"Is it not beautiful?" said the Emperor. "If you asked me what I have done here, I could answer you well. I have made birds sing, I have made forests murmur, I have set people to walking in this woodland, enjoying the leaves and shadows and songs. That is what I have done."

"But, oh, Emperor!" pleaded the flier, on his knees, the tears pouring down his face. "I have done a similar thing! I have found beauty. I have flown on the morning wind. I have looked down on all the sleeping houses and gardens. I have smelled the sea and even seen it, beyond the hills, from my high place. And I have soared like a bird; oh, I cannot say how beautiful it is up there, in the sky, with the wind about me, the wind blowing me here like a feather, there like a fan, the way the sky smells in the morning! And how free one feels! *That* is beautiful, Emperor, that is beautiful, too!"

"Yes," said the Emperor sadly. "I know it must be true. For I felt my heart move with you in the air and I wondered: What is it like? How does it feel?

How do the distant pools look from so high? And how my houses and servants? Like ants? And how the distant towns not yet awake?"

"Then spare me!"

"But there are times," said the Emperor, more sadly still, "when one must lose a little beauty if one is to keep what little beauty one already has. I do not fear you, yourself, but I fear another man."

"What man?"

"Some other man who, seeing you, will build a thing of bright papers and bamboo like this. But the other man will have an evil face and an evil heart, and the beauty will be gone. It is this man I fear."

"Why? Why?"

"Who is to say that someday just such a man, in just such an apparatus of paper and reed, might not fly in the sky and drop huge stones upon the Great Wall of China?" said the Emperor.

No one moved or said a word.

"Off with his head," said the Emperor.

The executioner whirled his silver ax.

"Burn the kite and the inventor's body and bury their ashes together," said the Emperor.

The servants retreated to obey.

The Emperor turned to his hand-servant, who had seen the man flying. "Hold your tongue. It was all a dream, a most sorrowful and beautiful dream. And that farmer in the distant field who saw, tell him it would pay him to consider it only a vision. If ever the word passes around, you and the farmer die within the hour."

"You are merciful, Emperor."

"No, not merciful," said the old man. Beyond the garden wall he saw the guards burning the beautiful machine of paper and reeds that smelled of the morning wind. He saw the dark smoke climb into the sky. "No, only very much bewildered and afraid." He saw the guards digging a tiny pit wherein to bury the ashes. "What is the life of one man against those of a million others? I must take solace from that thought."

He took the key from its chain about his neck and once more wound up the beautiful miniature garden. He stood looking out across the land at the Great Wall, the peaceful town, the green fields, the rivers and streams. He sighed. The tiny garden whirred its hidden and delicate machinery and set itself in motion; tiny people walked in forests, tiny foxes loped through sun-speckled glades in beautiful shining pelts, and among the tiny trees flew little bits of high song and bright blue and yellow colour flying, flying, flying in that small sky.

"Oh," said the Emperor, closing his eyes, "look at the birds, look at the birds!"

1. Exploring Meaning

a. What does the emperor's machine (the garden of metal and jewels) represent to him? Quote the line(s) that support your answer.

b. In the emperor's mind, what danger does the flyer's invention pose? Explain why the emperor feels this way.

c. In your own words, explain what the following quotation means:

> But there are times . . . when one must lose a little beauty if one is to keep what little beauty one already has.

d. Give an example of **foreshadowing** from the story.

e. In your opinion, does the photo on page 207 adequately or effectively represent the story? What other image would you suggest to illustrate this selection? Explain.

> **Foreshadowing** is a plot technique in which a writer plants clues about events that will happen later in the narrative.

2. Focus on Context

The overt theme of this story is that certain knowledge should be suppressed for the good of the majority. Given that the author, Ray Bradbury, lives in the twenty-first century, what is the underlying message or theme of "The Flying Machine"? Discuss the story and its message in small groups.

3. Critical Thinking

As a class, discuss the following questions: Do you believe the emperor is justified in executing the flyer? Why or why not? What would you have done in his position? How do you think Bradbury feels about the emperor's actions? Explain your answer.

4. Researching

Research the Great Wall of China. Remember to look at the 5W's (*who, what, when, where, why*, and *how*). Present your findings to the class.

Alternatively, work in a small group to list examples of inventions that, while revolutionary and exciting, also contain an element of danger if inappropriately used. Consult outside resources if necessary. Discuss whether or not it is ever possible or advantageous to suppress knowledge.

5. Drama

Present a Scene With a partner, prepare and present the dialogue between the flyer and the emperor. Try to make the dialogue as realistic as possible by using appropriate tones, voices, gestures, and expressions.

As It Is

Poem by Dorianne Laux

The man I love hates technology, hates
that he's forced to use it: telephones
and microfilm, air conditioning,
car radios and the occasional fax.
He wishes he lived in the old world,
sitting on a stump carving a clothespin
or a spoon. He wants to go back, slip
like lint into his great-great grandfather's
pocket, reborn as a pilgrim, a peasant,
a dirt farmer hoeing his uneven rows.
He walks when he can, through the hills
behind his house, his dogs panting beside him
like small steam engines. He's delighted
by the sun's slow and simple
descent, the complicated machinery
of his own body. I would have loved him
in any era, in any dark age; I would take him
into the twilight and unwind him, slide
my fingers through his hair and pull him
to his knees. As it is, this afternoon, late
in the twentieth century, I sit on a chair
in the kitchen with my keys in my lap, pressing
the black button on the answering machine
over and over, listening to his message,
his voice strung along the wires outside my window
where the birds balance themselves
and stare off into the trees, thinking
even in the farthest future, in the most
distant universe, I would have recognized
this voice, refracted, as it would be, like light
from some small, uncharted star.

1. Exploring Meaning

a. What is the attitude of the speaker to the man she is talking about in the poem? Quote words or phrases to support your opinion.

b. Explain what you think the title "As It Is" means.

c. Discuss the meaning and effectiveness of each of the following examples of figurative language:

> . . . slip/like lint into his great-great grandfather's/pocket . . .
>
> . . . his dogs panting beside him/like small steam engines.
>
> . . . sun's slow and simple/descent . . .
>
> . . . the complicated machinery/of his own body.
>
> . . . this voice, refracted . . . like light/from some small, uncharted star.

d. What is the theme of this poem?

e. If you had a choice about what time period you could live in, would it be the past, present, or future? Explain why you feel this way. Poll the class for their opinion.

2. Visual Communication *Collage* Create a collage that evokes the past in conflict with, or in juxtaposition with, the present or future. Your collage can be any combination of visuals, lines from this poem or other poems you know, and your own words.

3. Language Conventions *Relative Pronouns* Reread the first line of the poem and consider the effectiveness of the words, "The man I love hates technology . . ." Note how the poet has used unconventional grammatical structure by using an *adjective clause* (a dependent clause that modifies a noun or pronoun in the main clause) without a *relative pronoun* (a pronoun that shows relationship, such as *that, who, whose, whom, which*). Why would she not have started the poem: "The man *whom* I love hates technology . . ."? Examine the poem for other clever uses of language, and for other instances of unconventional grammatical structures. Discuss any of these with a partner.

Clocks, Computers and Why We Play God

Editorial by Jay Bookman

Barely 50 years after its invention, the computer is already listed with the wheel, the printing press and the steam engine as a technology that has changed the world.

Like the printing press, the computer has greatly accelerated the flow of information.

Like the steam engine, the computer can be applied to a variety of industrial uses, making the entire economy more efficient.

But in its impact on how human beings live, the computer is best compared to a humble technology called the clock.

Like the computer, the clock simply generates information—in its case, the time of day—and shares that information with a large number of people. Yet historians credit the clock as one of the most influential inventions of all time, because it changed the human mind-set.

Its unique power lay in its ability to synchronize millions of human beings, to create out of many independent individuals one smoothly functioning organism.

Without the clock, it would be impossible to agree to meet a client at 3:30 p.m., get to work by 9 a.m. or turn on the TV for *Friends* at 8 p.m.

The clock has given us all a common framework and, in the process, has become our conductor. We humans are mere members of its orchestra, playing to its beat.

That's what the computer is doing, too. In the next few years, as it transforms from a large, stationary object to something that many of us carry around throughout the day, the computer will make us more accountable to each other, more connected.

Through its various and intertwined communications media—e-mail, the Internet, cell phones, etc.—it will synchronize human activities far more closely, in many more ways than the clock ever has.

We will each become a node in a wireless, highly synchronized network, sending and receiving electronic information almost constantly.

Just what you needed, right?

But that's only the beginning. As a catalyst for change, the computer's potential is almost limitless. And the transformations it has caused to date are relatively minor compared with what the future holds.

After all, the computer was designed to mimic, extend and eventually challenge the most potent force for change on the planet: human intelligence.

Most scientists seeking to create some form of artificial intelligence explain their goals in relatively practical, non-threatening terms.

They want to make computers smarter and thus more useful.

They want to use computers to help human beings who have been paralyzed by disease or accidents. They want to build computers that feel less mechanical and more friendly to their human users.

Each of those goals is feasible and each offers practical benefits for human beings. But there's also something deeper going on.

Author John Horgan, in his 1996 book, *The End Of Science*, argued that the days of discovery are largely over. Scientists have pretty much explained the secrets of the world around us, he wrote, leaving little to be explored or explained.

And while he has a point, the two largest questions—puzzles that have dogged human beings for aeons—remain unanswered in scientific terms.

Big questions typically come in stark little packages. In this case, the two biggies can each be expressed in three words:

Who are we?

What is "life"?

When you talk to scientists in their laboratories and read their journals, it gradually becomes clear that at some level, perhaps even an unconscious one, this is what they're really after.

They're trying to understand life and consciousness and, in science, that is done most convincingly by creating life and consciousness artificially.

There is nothing new about this impulse. Humankind has always had the drive to create, to try to mimic if not duplicate the godlike power to give life.

Cro-Magnon humans drew lifelike images of their prey on cave walls. Medieval Jewish mystics told the story of the Golem, a creature molded out of clay by a powerful rabbi and then given the breath of life.

In the 18th century, inventors used the new art of mechanics to build life-like animals that moved and behaved like their real-life counterparts, even to the extent of eating food and excreting waste.

The pioneering work in robotics, artificial intelligence and other computer-related fields is a modern expression of that ancient drive. So are the Human Genome Project and ever more sophisticated cloning experiments.

Such research sends a chill down the spines of many people, which is not surprising. We may be compelled to recreate life, but we're terrified at the thought of succeeding.

That fear takes several forms. Mary Shelley, in her classic novel *Frankenstein*, captured the fear that technology will somehow slip our control and turn against us. That story, published in 1818, expresses a fear that has never gone away. In fact, it has grown more real over time.

Bill Joy, chief scientist at Sun Microsystems and one of the most respected figures in Silicon Valley, echoed Shelley in the cover piece of the April 2000 issue of *Wired* magazine.

Noting that fully intelligent computers are likely to arrive by 2030 and that biotechnology, genetics, cloning and robotics are coming into full flower, Joy wrote: "We are on the cusp of the further perfection of extreme evil."

Joy is afraid that his work, together with that of other scientists, eventually could enable "the construction of the technology that may replace our species."

But he offers no concrete means of avoiding that fate.

The *Wired* article kicked off considerable controversy among those who follow technology, with some of the most spirited debate taking place in Internet chat rooms.

While some participants reacted with horror to the future Joy depicted, others greeted it with surprising enthusiasm.

"Humanity, as we know it, SHOULD become extinct," one person wrote.

"We have spent the past 10,000 years adapting our environment to suit our needs—now it is time to take the final step and make our minds and bodies as subject to our whims as our outer world is . . ."

But while technology may give human beings godlike powers, it cannot give us the godlike wisdom and restraint we need to use that power well.

A scene from *2001: A Space Odyssey.*

The problem was best expressed by social critic Lewis Mumford.

"One does not make a child powerful by placing a stick of dynamite in his hands," Mumford wrote in 1934. "One only adds to the danger of his irresponsibility."

A little more than a decade later, humans had invented and used the atomic bomb.

There's also the fear that in making machines more lifelike, we threaten to dilute those traits that make our species special.

At the Massachusetts Institute of Technology, theologian Anne Foerst professes a certain puzzlement at that concern.

"It's curious how people insist on defining themselves as unique, because that's apparently important to us," says Foerst, who serves as a sort of spiritual adviser to MIT's Artificial Intelligence Laboratory.

"First, we said it was language that made us special. Then, it turned out that some of the higher forms of life, like the chimps, could also communicate through language.

"So, we turned to genes. But it turns out that we share 99 per cent of our genes with the chimps, and even 50 per cent with yeast. I love that fact."

With language and genes no longer defining us as special, Foerst says, intelligence has become the last human bulwark. And that might help explain why people get so queasy at the idea of biocomputing, the fusing of living brain cells with silicon to create a hybrid computer.

Scientists in that field are doing what human beings have always done—taking what we find in nature and turning it to our own purposes.

From that perspective, using rat neurons to make a computer should be no different than using cow leather to make shoes.

Yet for most people, there's something instinctively unnatural about linking life and silicon so intimately: It blurs the clear demarcation between us and them, or more accurately, us and it.

Foerst argues that the idea of human singularity will have to be abandoned in the face of what's coming. Even the soul, she says, is not inherent to us as human beings but rather something that develops "an interactive quality between God and his people."

Even machines might somehow acquire a soul, she speculates.

While that seems extremely unlikely, Foerst's assertion does illustrate the gravity of the questions now being raised.

In debating the impact of technology, historians often cite something called the "technological imperative": that if something can be done, it will be done—that human beings lack the discipline needed to turn our backs on a tempting but dangerous new technology.

We are always eager to reap the rewards of progress, always eager to dismiss any danger as the price of doing business.

Champions of progress point out that every generation since the late 1700s has had its prophets of technological doom.

For example, doctors in the early 1800s warned that travelling faster than 25 m.p.h. on steam-powered trains would endanger the human heart.

With the nagging exception of atomic weapons, every forecast of technological doom since then has proved equally groundless.

The same might be true—probably *is* true—about the dire fears raised about the computer.

Our great-grandchildren likely will look back at us and get a good chuckle out of our silly little worries, just as we snicker at the good doctors' warning about rail travel.

It does seem reasonable to wonder, however.

In our apparent compulsion to exercise godlike powers over life—in our insistence that we, too, can endow our creations with intelligence—we're playing with things we cannot fully comprehend.

It all smacks of arrogance, and arrogance can reap a bitter harvest.

1. Exploring Meaning

a. In this article, Jay Bookman draws an analogy between clocks and computers. How does he see these two inventions as similar? Do you agree? Why or why not?

b. Bookman states that humankind has always tried to mimic God's power to give life. What examples of this does he mention?

c. For what audience is this article intended? Support your answer.

d. Scan the selection to find examples of parallelism and rhetorical questions. Discuss the effectiveness of these devices. Now list examples of gender-neutral or gender-inclusive language.

2. Film Study Choose and view one of the films mentioned in the Introductory Activity on page 214. Discuss how this film deals with similar themes to those in the editorial.

3. Visual Communication *Analyse Image* Develop a short essay to explain how the photo on page 217 reflects the theme and message of the editorial. Consider colour, composition, content, and mood.

4. Making Connections Jay Bookman states, ". . . historians often cite something called the 'technological imperative': that if something can be done, it will be done—that human beings lack the discipline needed to turn our backs on a tempting but dangerous new technology." How do you think the emperor, in Ray Bradbury's story "The Flying Machine," would respond to this statement? How do you think the inventor of the flying machine would have responded?

5. Language Conventions *Pronoun Use* Note the pronoun used in the above quotation in the phrase ". . . human beings lack the discipline needed to turn our backs . . ." How would you correct the pronoun or phrase?

What is the difference between *phobia* and *fear*? Consult a dictionary for clear definitions.

Virtual Therapy, Real Results

Newspaper Article by Clive Thompson

Linda Manassee Buell's panic disorder was getting out of control—and nothing, it seemed, could help her.

Whenever she tried to leave her neighbourhood in San Diego, she'd be overcome by agoraphobia, with a racing heartbeat and cold sweats. "I would just be overwhelmed with a need to go back home, to get into a safe zone," says the 46-year-old. Even though she had risen to be a division director of a Fortune 500 company, her inability to travel had caused friction with management.

She'd even been too afraid to attend family functions out of town. "I'd missed a stepson's graduation, I missed another's wedding," says Buell. "I didn't go on vacations because I couldn't handle the travel."

Despite years of therapy, her phobia wasn't getting better. Then she met therapist Brenda Wiederhold, who suggested a radical new form of therapy: virtual reality.

To get Buell to face her fears, Wiederhold put her in a virtual-reality headset, the same type you'd find in a high-end video arcade. Goggles would project a 3D scene directly into Buell's eyes, and a computer program would place her in a virtual car, driving around simulated cities like Chicago.

She could head out into strange new areas, wrestle with virtual traffic and even get stuck in a virtual tunnel. A different program let her roam around a virtual mall.

"The first time I tried it, I was just blown away. It felt very real," she marvels. "You could look up, down, around—it was just like being there." She laughs, and adds, "which is to say, terrifying!"

After a few months of treatment, Buell noticed an improvement, and is

Illustration by Brian Hughes.

now able to drive anywhere across town. "I learned to watch my symptoms, to see how my body would start panicking, to control it," she says. "You learn that in the simulator and it transfers out into the real world."

The technique of desensitizing people to situations that scare them is a traditional and often successful way to treat panic disorders. But now virtual-reality systems are offering therapists a unique new tool to achieve this goal.

Wiederhold was at the cutting edge, beginning to experiment with virtual reality two years ago. Now, a handful of companies worldwide are manufacturing the systems for therapeutic use and a dozen or more clinics use them across North America, including one that opened in Kitchener.

"We're always looking for ways to use new technologies to help treat people,"

Wiederhold says. "And we're already seeing that virtual reality works."

Indeed, after using the technique on 120 patients, Wiederhold's success rate is an impressive 90.6 per cent. It also works more quickly than traditional phobia therapy. Her virtual-reality patients have needed an average of only six sessions to gain control of their fears, as opposed to 14 sessions with traditional styles.

In addition to treating agoraphobia, she uses simulations to treat everything from fear of flying to fear of heights and fear of public speaking.

Panic disorders are a crippling and often undiagnosed problem. While psychologists estimate that one in 10 Canadians suffers from one, only 15 per cent of those ever seek treatment.

Part of what makes virtual reality successful, Wiederhold says, is the increased realism. With traditional phobia therapy, patients are encouraged to imagine the situation that they fear and then practise relaxing.

The problem is many people's imaginations aren't strong enough to truly conjure the situation. It certainly didn't work for Buell, who had tried for years. "I'd try imagining it but real life was always so much more overpowering," she recalls.

Virtual reality, in contrast, gives patients a much more intense stimulus. Wiederhold monitors her patients' vital symptoms and can see the effect: "When we switch on the simulation, you can see their heart rate spike immediately and their sweat glands start to kick in," she notes.

Virtual reality also lets the therapist have much more control over the experience. When treating fear of flying, the therapist can use the simulator to ease someone into the experience—having the plane taxi for a long time and take off only when the patient feels ready.

That's impossible to do in real life, "unless you rent a 747 for the afternoon so you can practise flying—which is a little expensive for the average patient," jokes Charles Pierce, a Kitchener psychologist who recently bought a virtual-reality system.

Pierce's simulator costs $150 an hour and patients can take off and land as many times as they want. As well, Pierce remains alongside the patient, another thing that's impossible in real life, unless he or she can afford to pay for a therapist to accompany him or her on a flight.

"This puts all sorts of new possibilities in people's hands," says Pierce. "I'm extremely excited by it."

Advances in technology are likely to make virtual-reality systems even cheaper and more ubiquitous, says Ken Graap, CEO of Georgia-based Virtually Better, which makes the systems that Wiederhold and Pierce use. "It's all because of video games. They've driven incredible advances in 3D graphics," he says. His systems, which went on the market in 2000, cost about $5,000 U.S. and $400 U.S. to lease the software per module—the fear-of-flying software is one module, the driving simulator is another.

Graap has also created a "Virtual Vietnam" simulator for a local hospital, to help treat victims of post-traumatic stress syndrome, including Gulf War Syndrome. "We put a bass shaker in a platform beneath the chair, so when a gun goes off, you feel it in your whole body," he notes.

You don't need high-end virtual reality to do treatment, either. Wiederhold has even used off-the-shelf, $40 video games to help treat disorders. She used Microsoft's Midtown Madness to help get agoraphobics used to driving, and The Sims—a game in which players create and control families of virtual people—to help treat children with social disorders. "Your average everyday computer is more powerful now than the stuff NASA used to send people to the moon, so it's just getting cheaper to offer this stuff to everyone," she adds.

And there are other treatments on the horizon. Later this year, Wiederhold will begin treating eating disorders with software that scans patients' bodies so that they can view them objectively. "People with eating disorders are always saying, 'I look fat,' and even when you get them in front of a mirror they still see it that way. With this software, it helps them step outside their bodies and see them as they really are," she says.

Granted, virtual-reality treatment is still rare. "Most psychologists are unaware of it," Pierce adds. "It's very, very new and they're pretty cautious. They like to check things out before they use them." He heard about the technique by accident— when he was shaving in the morning and heard Graap being interviewed on the radio.

For her part, Buell now swears by the therapy.

"I got my life back and I want to help others get theirs, too," she says.

---

1. Exploring Meaning

a. According to Clive Thompson, what makes virtual-reality therapy successful in the treatment of phobias? Why is it more successful than traditional therapy? Support your answer with details from the article.

b. Describe in your own words how virtual-reality therapy can be used to treat other psychological disorders. How else do you think virtual reality could be used to help people? Discuss any ideas with a small group.

c. This article can be divided into two sections. Where would you put the dividing line? Why?

2. Researching With a partner, use the Internet or other resource material to research a common fear/phobia, such as claustrophobia or agoraphobia. What does conventional medicine or psychology say about the fear's origins, treatments, and so on? Present your findings to the class.

3. Film Study Alfred Hitchcock's thriller *Vertigo* is a movie that explores the fear of heights. View the movie and critique how effectively the director portrayed the main character's phobia. Compare the movie's treatment of the symptoms of this phobia with what the class researched in Activity 2.

4. Visual Communication *Newspaper Illustration* The editor of the newspaper in which this article first appeared commissioned Brian Hughes to illustrate the article. With a partner, discuss the illustration and what it adds to the article. What fear do you think it represents? Imagine that you are the illustrator who has been asked to illustrate an article about virtual-reality technology being used to treat phobias. Find or create a suitable illustration.

Assessment: Share what you have done with a small group. Explain what you hoped to achieve, and together assess how successfully you think you have represented the article.

What meaning and connotations does the word *scanner* have? What do you think an article about "body scanners" will focus on? Record your thoughts.

Body Scanners

Magazine Article by Kimberley Noble

For Alex Briglio, the routine is familiar. Returning from a ski and snowboard show in Las Vegas, the vice-president of ROI (Recreation Outfitters Inc.) of Burnaby, B.C., entered the high-ceilinged immigration hall at Vancouver International Airport and turned away from the lines forming at a dozen booths. Stepping to a kiosk similar to a bank machine, Briglio inserted a card. Following prompts on a screen, he placed his right hand in a recess and aligned his fingers against five small pegs. Touching the screen to indicate he had nothing to declare, he received a paper slip confirming his entry into Canada. In less than a minute, he was on his way. It was the kind of experience that has made Briglio a big fan of the Canada Customs and Revenue Agency's pilot Canpass automated-entry program for low-risk air travellers: "The biggest attraction is being able to get off the plane, put your card in and just go. It's great."

Canada Customs hopes to introduce a service similar to the Vancouver pilot project by year-end at seven more airports, including Toronto's Pearson and Montreal's Dorval. The expanded service may scan travellers' eyes, instead of their hands, to confirm their identity. But whatever body part it traces, the technology is only the forerunner of a wave of new biometric devices designed to identify people by lines in their skin, the tone of their voice, the shape of their face—even the tempo of their typing. All use unique individual variations in physical features, or such recognizable behaviours as walking, talking and signing a name, to authenticate identity. Uses range from the humble—doing away with the inconvenience of remembering multiple online passwords—to the controversial—such as facial scans of the Super Bowl crowd by police. Other applications may soon provide some Canadians with the ultimate personal ID for dealing with everything from government to vending machines.

Plummeting computing costs and an explosive growth in digital transactions have fuelled the new push to bring biometrics to market. With as many as 100 companies pursuing various methods, a race is on among the leaders to win acceptance as de facto standards in the most valuable market niches. Any technology tapped by the airlines to identify travellers, for instance, stands to earn a share of global biometrics revenues that some analysts put at $4 billion within five years. And several Canadian companies are among the front-runners.

At the head of the pack is a small Vancouver firm with some big names in surveillance behind it. Former RCMP commissioner Norman Inkster and Reid Morden, an ex-director of the Canadian Security Intelligence Service, are advisers to Imagis Technologies Inc. in its development of face-recognition software. To experience it at work, you could drop in to any of Gateway Casinos' three B.C. locations and try to cheat at one of its slots, roulette wheels or game tables. If you display the obvious signs of a cheater that security staff look for, operators in a darkened room off the casino floor will train a discreetly placed video camera on your face. Using complex calculations based on the relationship of features around the nose and eyes, Imagis's software will compare your face to those of more than 2,000 known or suspected cheats already on file, and report any match in under a second. "If you are going to compromise the integrity of the game," says general manager Monique Wilberg, "we're going to catch you."

The software guarding the one-armed bandits is actually a spin-off from Imagis's primary market: law enforcement. RCMP detachments in North Vancouver and Surrey, B.C. were proving grounds for a computerized arrest and booking system that replaces binders of mug shots with a database of digital images. Given a new face, Imagis's software can find any matches in seconds. In North Vancouver, it exposed one man who had previously been arrested three times under three different names. "It's pretty amazing," says detachment identification officer Sandy Ferris. "We have put in composite drawings and come up with a list of suspects." The company has since sold the system to police forces in Ontario, Alberta, California and Mexico's Chihuahua state.

Another Canadian company is betting on the biometrics of typing. Yukon-registered Net Nanny Software International Inc., which markets out of Bellevue, Wash., and does its R and D in Vancouver, recently released BioPassword, a program that works on office systems to provide security based on what the company says are unique "keystroke dynamics" of people's typing. By analyzing the time between each keystroke and how long fingers dwell on each key, the software claims to be able to distinguish an imposter typing your name and password.

Toronto's Mytec Technologies Inc. is in a crowded field of companies promoting fingerprint sensors as the basis for security devices for everything from cellphones to handguns, including a prototype Smith and Wesson electronic "smart gun" that has gained wide attention. But president Pierre Donaldson sees an even bigger market among computer, cellphone and luxury-car owners. "We're in the business of replacing passwords and any type of key," he says.

Basing identity on distinguishing physical features, of course, is as old as humankind. But computer power, and the ability to record minute physical details using non-invasive probes of laser light, have vastly increased the number of features to measure. Technologies based on physical patterns in the eye, face, finger and hand are well proven. New approaches go beyond biology to measure unique patterns in how people move, especially in repetitive tasks. Holland's LCI Technology Group NV claims to identify unique finger movements through a sensor-equipped ballpoint pen. A University of Maryland study predicts police will soon be able to pick any individual out of a crowd by his or her stride. British researchers claim to have detected personal calling patterns distinctive enough to know when a thief is using your phone instead of you.

And air travel is set to get easier. Computing giant Unisys and Air Canada are among players in talks with Canada Customs to expand the Canpass airport service as it moves east (the technology is also offered by U.S. immigration to pre-clear low-risk travellers at Canadian airports). In the grand vision, a single biometric-backed smart card (dubbed the ConciergeCard by Unisys) would be used for automated seat and baggage check-in on airlines and tasks like booking car rentals and hotels, as well as for clearing Canadian customs.

But the expanding reach and improving precision of biometrics leave some people queasy. Ontario Provincial Police and the province's casinos roused controversy when they used face-recognition software to run pictures of casino patrons through police mug files (B.C.'s Gateway searches only its own database). Critics also blasted Tampa police for using similar software to scan the faces of fans at the Super Bowl game in 2001.

To get his Canpass, Briglio willingly parted with his physical information. "I have no problem when the government runs it," he says. But, the businessman admits, "I have a real problem when private industry would have your fingerprints. For banks to have them? I wouldn't give it to them." In fact, Dutch-owned ING Bank of Canada in 2000 gave out more than 300 thumbprint-reading biometric computer mouses to its customers as a test-cum-promotion. But officials say most are no longer in use—abandoned in favour of conventional passwords. Biometrics may be fast establishing itself as a safe bet for cops and casinos. Whether it will find ready acceptance among consumers is more of a wild card.

1. Exploring Meaning

a. What kinds of advantages and drawbacks to biometric technology are mentioned in the article? How do you feel about this technology?

b. List all of the uses for biometrics mentioned in the article. How else do you think biometric technology could be used? Discuss your ideas and the possible outcomes of such uses.

c. When you are introduced to a person for the first time, what is usually the first thing you notice about him or her? Poll the class for their answers. Do you think that biometrics will significantly change how people identify each other?

2. Focus on Context
This article was published in March 2001, before the attacks on the World Trade Center in New York City. Do you think people's views of biometric technology have changed since this event? Do you think people still have the same objections to the uses of such technology? Explain. What new uses do you think biometric technology may have?

3. Making Connections
Skim "Body Scanners" and "Clocks, Computers and Why We Play God." Consider what each article has to say about identity. In a small group, discuss the ideas from each selection, as well as your own thoughts.

4. Vocabulary
Use the word's origin or structure and the context in which it appears in the article to define five of the following: *biometric, scanners, tempo, ID, de facto, face recognition, proving grounds, R and D, keystroke dynamics, smart gun,* and *wild card.* Discuss the strategies you used to work out the meaning of these and other unfamiliar words.

Paper cell phones, self-focussing glasses, "smart" shoes with tiny motors, cars that repair themselves . . . they're closer than ever.

ZAP!

IT'S THE FUTURE

Magazine Article by Chris Wood

Dana opened her clothes closet. It was a double-wide, since these new self-cleaning fabrics had allowed her to do away with laundry. Reaching in, she selected a business suit in her favourite shade of midnight blue with a hint of purple. A moment later, she slipped into a pair of low heels and watched as they changed from stone grey (yesterday's outfit) to midnight blue . . . with a touch of purple. That still blew her away.

In the kitchen, she tore a packet open and poured the contents into a bowl. She crushed the empty paper into a ball quickly, before it could launch into its audio instruction on how to pour boiling water over cereal. This talking packaging thing was getting out of hand, with "talkie" strips even appearing in magazines. On the way out the door, she paused to rip a fresh cellphone from the roll by the fridge.

In the elevator, Dana frowned as she remembered the jerk who yesterday left a deep gouge in her new car. But the plastic body panel had done what its maker promised. Overnight, it had regained its original shape; the deep scratch had healed over. She felt a touch on her left arm and raised it to see who was calling. It was only an e-mail. "Have a surprising day! XO, Ben," scrolled across the midnight-blue silk before twinkling out. Dana smiled.

Dana's day is still in our future, but not as far off as you might think. The technologies depicted exist, though some are in their infancy. Among scientists, engineers and designers in every industrial country, it's now mostly a matter of putting the pieces together—and making parts small and cheap enough to appear in everyday items.

How about starting the day putting on a jogging suit that hasn't budged from where you threw it, damp and smelly, last night? Only now it's fresh and clean. State university biotechnologists in Dartmouth, Mass., have raised the possibility with fibres that contain living bacteria. Their idea: textiles impregnated with micro-organisms that eat dirt, perspiration and body oils. "You could end up having to feed your shirt instead of wash it," jokes researcher Alex Fowler. After leaving the bugs to chow down on your sweats, maybe you'll pull on a T-shirt made from fabric that Japan's Fuji Spinning hopes to be selling soon. It exudes your daily dose of vitamin C, to be absorbed through the skin, through more than 30 washings. Other vitamins and medicines are promised.

And the layer next to your skin may do more than merely dispense vitamins. Researchers in Ventura, Calif., have shown a prototype of a vest that measures the wearer's blood pressure, heart rate and other vital signs—and can transmit that information to a doctor or nurse. Sensor threads will report the location and extent of any new wound. Also in the works for military or police use: memory chips that hold the wearer's medical history.

Then there's the technology that could be folded into fictional Dana's messaging jacket. Jeans maker Levi-Strauss & Co. collaborated with Royal Philips Electronics last year to demonstrate one vision of "electronic" fashion: rather crude couture that inserted cellphones and personal electronic notebooks into special pockets. Companies in Canada and Israel may have the components of a more elegant solution. Israeli Visson Enterprises Ltd. puts video on textiles by weaving them with fibre-optic threads that glow where they crisscross. Tactex Controls Inc. of Victoria makes a thin rubber film, likewise embedded with optics, that can be placed beneath fabric to make it responsive to touch. Tactex president Rob Inkster imagines his technology married to a fabric display like Visson's: "There's a patch on your T-shirt or sleeve. It looks like a cellphone and you can use it like a cellphone. A moment later, it looks like a video game and you can play it." Or maybe it just goes back to looking like a T-shirt.

Australian researchers are working on a "smart" bra that will sense the movement of its wearer's body. The material will stiffen to provide the kind of extra support during activity that a sports bra offers, then relax for greater comfort at rest.

Personal accessories have been another target for innovation since long before Buck Rogers's secret decoder ring. Recently, IBM researchers have built voice recorders into necklace pendants. They also envisage brooch cellphones not far removed from the communicators worn by later-generation crew members of television's *Star Trek* programs.

Researchers have made giant strides in identifying, purifying and, in a growing number of cases, manufacturing complex materials that can sense, adapt

Illustration by Leif Peng.

to—or even act upon—their environment. Some new creations detect radio waves, sound or air pressure, and respond with bursts of light, electrons or magnetic energy. Others glow, change their shape or initiate specific chemical reactions on command. Many new materials make use of earlier discoveries in optics and ways of assembling molecules one atom at a time. Other advances, in microcircuitry and manufacturing, are making it possible to combine new materials with computer processors in places never before imagined, for example, in colour-changing clothing, self-adjusting spectacles or a motorized suitcase that follows its owner.

"There are no smart materials," insists David Zimcik, a National Research Council expert who uses ceramic like that in barbecue lighters to reduce vibration in helicopters. "There are," he says, "smart systems." Those have four critical components: sensors, some kind of processor, a program to guide it, and what Zimcik calls "actuators," parts that act on their surroundings. In his helicopter system, one lot of ceramics detects vibration in the chopper blade; instructed by a computer chip, another set expands or contracts to stiffen or relax the blade to reduce vibration.

Much of what makes this new stuff so smart happens at the level of molecules—even atoms. Often there's little to see outside a microscope. Among the most promising new super materials are carbon nanotubes—cylinders of the common element just a few atoms across. The tubes are five times stronger than steel and 500 times as long as they are wide. But they're so small that even under a conventional microscope, they look like so much grey dust (and cost $1,000 a gram). Montreal native Pascal Hubert is among researchers at a NASA centre in Hampton, Va., trying to figure out "how to take nanotubes and twist them to make nanotube ropes," the way cotton fibres are spun into thread. By one calculation, such ropes could be strong

Smart Walls and Windows

"Thick as a plank." "Dumb as a post." When it comes to smarts, building materials don't generally get much respect. University of Manitoba engineering professor Aftab Mufti hopes to change that. With colleagues across the country, he has installed sophisticated fibre-optic sensors in two dozen structures, including the elegant arches of the 13-km Confederation Bridge between New Brunswick and Prince Edward Island as well as oil pipelines and a nuclear reactor. "We are trying to build structures that will be smart like your body," the civil engineer explains. "We're putting sensors inside that tell us what sort of loads are going over a bridge, what sort of stresses and strains are inside it."

In the Confederation Bridge's case, engineers can call up the sensors—made of glass fibre and scattered about the structure—via an integrated wireless modem, to check in on its condition. Or, says Mufti: "If there is something unusual, it will call us."

Materials for homes and offices may soon show off startling new talents as well. German scientists have demonstrated windows that darken—and clear again—at the touch of a button. A Toledo, Ohio, glassmaker has developed self-cleaning panes that break down specks of dirt, allowing the grime to rinse away in the rain. Other American designers forecast entire walls of glass coated with active film that can switch from transparency to showing floor-to-ceiling videos, and exterior bricks that change molecular structure with the weather to admit more or less heat and humidity. At Shanghai University in China, researchers have unveiled paint that changes from (heat-reflecting) blue in summer, to (heat-absorbing) red in winter. Thick as a brick? More like sharp as a tack.

enough to hoist payloads to a space station by elevator, instead of by rocket.

Making the little big is one way to go. Electrical engineer Kris Pister of the University of California at Berkeley goes another. He wants to make *dust* smart. He imagines things the size of a few grains of sand that will be able to monitor light and temperature across whole cities and report back to utilities. Pister, understand, lives in a state preoccupied with its power supply. He concedes his "smart dust"—working models are closer in size to Smarties—could also spy on other things, such as when people get up or go to bed, by sensing movement and temperature changes. "Like it or not," he shrugs, "this is the future."

A remarkable common thread to this explosion of human ingenuity is that much of its inspiration comes not from abstract human theory at all. At NASA, says Pascal Hubert, the hot new topic is "biomimetrics"—the art of copying nature. In Victoria, aeronautical composites expert Ansel Suleman dreams: "If we have wings that can change shape by twisting like a bird's wing, maybe we can emulate bird flight."

Meanwhile, technology is already turning lessons from nature into the newest, as well as smartest, stuff under the sun.

Buy Me! Bake Me!

And you thought shopping aisles were already busy enough. Imagine this: as you push your cart down the bakery aisle, boxes on either side come to life, iridescent squares on the front of each one bursting into a full-motion, full-colour, full-throated sales pitch. The aroma of fresh-baked cake wafts into the aisle. Suppose you take one of these chatty boxes home. Rip off the top and the screen launches into a different video—this one demonstrating how to turn the package's contents into a moist, frosted layer cake. Back at the store, meanwhile, the bakery shelf has noted the box's departure—and automatically reordered it.

The full-video cake-mix box may never come to the grocery aisle, but it easily could. All the ingredients, so to speak, already exist. Americans have marketed a synthetic aroma generator. A Russian has invented a vodka bottle cap that delivers toasts when it's opened. Video-on-the-box is just a matter of adding a display and more computing power. Scottish and Irish researchers have developed thin-film video displays that promise to be cheap and easy to apply to most surfaces—including packaging. An Israeli group has figured out how to print batteries in a layer no thicker than a Band-Aid. And Canadian Ross Hill, at Simon Fraser University in Burnaby, B.C., is one of several inventors with rival processes for printing cheap, powerful microcircuits on paper or plastic.

Packaging that reports when it's been sold is also today's technology, not tomorrow's. Several companies are testing implants smaller than postage stamps that can be hidden in a box to track the source, product details and shipping history of its contents. Such so-called smart tags reveal their information through hand-held radio-frequency or magnetic scanners (allowing retailers to take inventory by walking down the aisle with the scanner). Fancier tags can be updated with sales information, recording such items as special warranty terms.

So how about a box "that has the Betty Crocker commercial going on it?" wonders Hill. He answers himself: "I'm not going to say you won't walk down the aisle in five years and see that."

1. Exploring Meaning

a. The thesis of this article develops through the use of examples and illustrations. What is that thesis? List three examples that support it.

b. For what audience is this article written? Support your answer.

c. The tone of this selection is optimistic and enthusiastic about the future of technology. Does the author see any disadvantages or problems with the new products? What does this reveal about Chris Wood's objectivity?

d. What do many of the innovations listed in the article have in common? Discuss any other innovations that you can think of that might be based on similar technologies.

e. Briefly describe your response to the image on page 230. How effectively does it reflect the content of the magazine article?

2. Literature Studies *Writing Types* This selection combines narrative and expository elements. Identify and discuss an example of each type of writing. Why has the author used two types of writing? What effect does it have on the reader?

Next, discuss the article's structure, layout, and content. How is or isn't the article effective or appropriate? How is it like or unlike other magazine articles you have read?

3. Writing *Story* Write two more episodes exploring Dana's life in the future. Use information about cutting-edge innovations from this and other articles, as well as from your own imagination. You could choose to look at future inventions optimistically (often called *utopian fiction*) or pessimistically (often called *distopian fiction*). Share your writing in small groups.

4. Language Focus *Idioms* Skim the sidebar on page 231 and identify at least two **idioms** such as "thick as a plank." Discuss their use and the author's intentions. With a partner, generate similar examples of idioms that could be used in the future, for example, "smart as a shoe" or "clever as a car."

An **idiom** is a fixed expression whose meaning is different from the literal meaning of the words.

Next, search the article for other examples of effective language use or word play (such as pun), and discuss their effectiveness, and why the author has used them.

Future Tense

Interview with Faith Popcorn from *Flare* Magazine

What will the next 20 years and beyond bring? We asked Faith Popcorn. Through her New York-based company BrainReserve, Faith Popcorn gives companies and consumers the tools to help them meet and manage the future. As a trend forecaster, Popcorn "brailles the culture" to find out what's going on. Here's the futurist's report.

The Future of Shopping

Cocooning, a trend I identified in 1981, has been a dominant force in the way retail has evolved. And cocooning's influence continues to intensify: it's becoming the "Armoured Cocoon." People are hunkering down in their homes. They're shopping at home, working at home, schooling at home and socializing at home.

E-commerce (shopping on the Internet) is really the logical extension of this trend. Already, online sales are $43 billion annually. I predict that by 2010, 90 percent of all consumer products will be home-delivered. Over the next decade, e-commerce will explode. We'll order medical procedures, homes, even our spouses from the Web. There will be e-privacy devices to keep online chats top secret, e-cheques will make paper cheques obsolete, college degrees will be earned entirely online and consumers will use prewritten e-complaint letters to picket companies that have done them wrong.

Middlepeople everywhere should be watching their backs, as the Web offers consumers direct access to lots of products that were mediated in the past. Travel agents, brokers and sellers of all stripes are quickly reassessing their businesses—look at what's happened, just in the past year, to stock trading, with the movement to online trading versus traditional broker/client relationships. Even Merrill Lynch, the bastion of full-service brokers, has moved 180 degrees to embrace online trading. But I don't think middlepeople will disappear completely. The smart ones will begin selling a much deeper level of service, a long-term relationship with customers that blends quality information with personal attention. We're moving into what I call a "high-tech, high-touch" era where technology and the human-added value will develop side by side in the marketplace.

The Future of Customer Service

The basic idea here is that men and women are different and, for too long, we've been marketing to them the same way. In general, men's approach to consumption is transactional while women's is relational. Women don't just buy brands, they join them, or at least they do when the brands have done enough things right to merit their trust. And customer service has an enormous role to play here. When businesspeople wake up and realize that women control 80 percent of consumer spending in Canada, they will finally confront the challenge of how to win, and keep, the female consumer.

My answer to the age-old question, "What do women want?" is simple: relationships. And customer-service reps are the frontline response team. The way they respond to customer (and potential-customer) queries is crucial to the health of the brand and, likely, to have a far greater effect on the brand image than any advertising that a customer sees. Word-of-mouth is the best advertising. And women pass on brands in both directions—up to their parents and down to their kids.

The Future of Technology

Technology is extremely jarring to us: we love what it can do and its potential, but we're afraid, because we often don't understand how it works. It can be abstract, impersonal and out of our control. The *Frankenstein* and *2001: A Space Odyssey* myths—that our own tools will eventually turn on us—haunt us.

One way I think we're going to deal with technology in the future is by transforming high-tech into "My-Tech." Our initial fascination with technology's power will be replaced by our desire to domesticate it. We'll want to make it ours, make it serve us more closely. The move from stand-alone computers to smart appliances of all kinds reflects this. Today, we don't necessarily want an omniscient box sitting on our desks, but we do want devices better equipped to follow our very human movements and desires—and we want technology as a whole to recognize us as unique and individual.

Biometric identifiers that analyze fingerprints, hand geometry and the voice are either already in use or being tested around the world as secure identification methods. Each offers the convenience of not having to know codes or carry various cards and keys, as well as the promise of perfect ID.

With the growing fear of identity theft—where a thief steals a driver's license and credit cards and takes on the person's identity—people are increasingly eager to protect themselves in this way.

This process can get a bit surreal, though. Need guidance or wisdom from a higher authority at the office? Marketplace Ministries Inc. places beeper-equipped chaplains in corporate settings across the country to offer support and confidential discussions to employees who want them. Time will tell whether consumers enjoy interacting with such intermediaries, but the drift is clear: technology is working its way deeper into our lives every day.

"Access Anxiety" is another version of our tech fears. As access to information explodes and boundaries that were once secure are threatened, we are anxious to protect our individual rights and our privacy. Researchers at the University of California at Berkeley have cracked a widely used encryption code in cell phones—and it only took them about 10 hours of computing to do it. If criminals were to crack the method, they could "clone" phones—that is, detect confidential identification information about a cell phone and use it in another phone to bill calls fraudulently.

A new development in the privacy wars: there is a new invention that could singlehandedly reverse the tide of tabloidism. A miniature device that is worn on a cap or as jewelry can, whenever a photographer tries to take the wearer's picture, emit a picture-ruining flash. Call it the "paparazzi blocker."

Despite our fear of technology, we are increasingly dependent on its power. American neuroscientists Dr. Philip R. Kennedy and Dr. A. E. Bakay of Emory University School of Medicine in Georgia have entered the world of science fiction by implanting electrodes in the brains of people so that they can control a computer with the power of thought. The implants have enabled two people who are paralyzed to move the cursor on a computer screen simply by thinking about moving a part of their bodies. They were also able to convey messages such as "I am thirsty" and "It was nice talking to you" by pointing the cursor at different icons.

The Future of Fashion

People are craving personalization in every aspect of their lives, particularly in fashion and beauty. It's a trend I call "Egonomics." It's about the economics of marketing to one's ego. In addition, today's consumers are living 99 lives. They barely have time to take a breath between all of the items on their to-do lists.

When retailers look at these two consumer directives, they'll understand the message their customers are sending them: "I don't have time to buy mass-market clothes and to have them tailored. I need customization from the point of purchase." Retailers that can satisfy that craving for customization, but give it without the hassle, will be the companies that thrive in the future.

There will be increasing "multitasking" of health and beauty services: more and more, we'll see therapy during makeovers, financial planning at the treadmill and wardrobe consultants in the doctor's waiting room.

We'll see the independent fashion scene continue to thrive because of its ability to respond to the individual tastes of consumers. In such places as Tokyo and New York, tiny shops with their own distinctive sensibilities offer alternatives to the bland mainstream. Indie designers are offering one-of-a-kind pieces to cure boredom. They make customers part of the process, allowing them to pick styles, colours and fabrics to create their own pieces.

In the future, we'll be watching *Ally McBeal* (or another show), see an outfit we like, put our hand on the screen and tell Ally that we'd like to buy the suit she has on. She'll stop and say, "Hi, Faith. You like my suit?" and I'll say, "Yes, Ally, but I'd like to see it in other colours." So Ally will show me all the other colours it comes in. I'll tell her I want it in black and navy and Ally will say, "Faith, you are not going to order one more black or navy suit. That's all you have in your closet!"

Also in the future, we'll have doorways equipped with scanners that function like the tailor's tape. We'll walk through the door and our measurements will be stored in the scanner. When we order something off the TV, we'll simply e-mail those measurements so that our clothes fit precisely. We're already on our way to mass customization: Levi's Original Spin Program allows the customization of a five-pocket jean that is perfect for the buyer. The client chooses the style (classic, low-cut or relaxed), fly type, leg opening, colour and inseam length. In about 2–3 weeks, a customized pair of jeans is delivered to your door.

Polish Mood Shades nail polish (P.M.S. for short) changes colour depending on what your mood is. Its two-tone, temperature-sensitive polish (worn by the likes of Madonna and Naomi Campbell) will turn from a shade such as "Gotta Have Chocolate" to "Estrogen Emerald" at the first sign of a mood swing.

We already have designer estrogens and "pharmacogenetics" (the application of DNA science to prescription medicines to customize them for individual effectiveness). This will open the field of herbal supplements and beauty products to mass customization. "I'd like my lipstick with ginseng and vitamin C, my foundation with St. John's wort and collagen and my shampoo with ginkgo biloba, please."

The Future of Food

In the future, our glasses will be filled with what looks like a reassuring, familiar drink, such as milk. Except it will be "milk plus": a vaccine booster with customized doses of vitamins and supplements, depending on what our bodies need. We'll fill our glasses with beverages that come directly from our household tap—no more going to the store to buy cartons of milk or bottles of juice; instead, the distributors will bring it to us. Our milk will be branded, perhaps by Coca-Cola or McDonald's, to guarantee purity. And it will carry an "ethical ingredients" list, detailing the health and treatment of the cows from which it came, the labour policies covering everyone from the milkers to the delivery-truck drivers and the wider corporate profile behind the brand.

As for the food on our plates, it will have lots of value-adds: antibiotic spices, bioengineered vegetables with our daily dose of vitamins, themed foods (such as Biblical cuisine) that carry stories and spiritual meanings. Next to the plate will be a compact little instrument that tests for everything from E. coli to influenza. Finally, the food will be patented (potatoes and spinach by Monsanto, beef by ConAgra) and with exotic elements—for example, a fruit with its colour by Versace.

The Future of Travel

The future lies in virtual travel. We'll step into our virtual-reality rooms at the office or in our homes and "travel" to the meetings we need to attend. We'll feel like we're in a boardroom in Los Angeles but really we'll be at home in Toronto.

People will get tired of the schlepp. Airlines should factor in the ride to and from the airport as part of their total experience. Whoever owns that—and eliminates the hassle and stress of getting to an airport on a mass-market level—will be successful. People will pay for convenience. Virgin Atlantic Air already offers limousine service to and from the airport for first-class customers. In the future, airlines will shuttle VIP passengers to and from the airport via helicopter or limousine to keep their passengers for life. The successful airlines of the future will have planes that are cocoons. There will be lounges, dining areas, aromatherapy chairs, CD libraries, real libraries, massage therapists and entertainment other than movies, such as cabaret, poetry readings and lectures.

People are looking for the added value in all aspects of travel, from the financial (frequent-flyer programs) to the experiential (educational/adventure vacations). My "Clanning" trend (people seek out the comfort and familiarity of people with like interests) could be key here. Wild Women Adventures, a tour operator in California, now has 25 all-women trips per year. Also, think of "salon" cruises, sponsored by such magazines as *The Nation*. Airlines could add this sort of thing to certain flights and turn six hours of dead time into networking/spiritual/experiential gain.

Photo by Jake Rajs.

The Future of Feminism

As "EVEolution" takes root, feminism will change course. Its central focus will shift from politics to economics. The culture, overall, is headed in this direction (look at the increase in financial shows, everybody on the Web checking their stocks, businesspeople as the new celebrities). Feminism will become all about the market power of women, both as consumers and as business owners and entrepreneurs. It will no longer be looked at as an F-word or as a stigma but as a badge of making it.

Just look at what the feminists of tomorrow are doing today: women own and/or operate 30 percent of all firms in Canada and their numbers are growing at twice the rate that men's are. Women-owned and women-led businesses employ approximately 1.7 million Canadians. The growth in women-led businesses is especially fast in higher knowledge areas—those requiring higher education levels.◆

1. Exploring Meaning

a. Faith Popcorn believes that in the next ten years ninety percent of all shopping will be home delivered. Do you agree? How do you feel about this?

b. Do you agree with Popcorn when she says that women want relationships with the brands they choose? Do you consider that statement sexist or stereotypical? Explain.

c. Discuss other ideas the selection raises that you find particularly interesting.

d. The introduction to this interview indicates that Popcorn is based in New York City. List any evidence from the selection that reveals that it was written for a Canadian audience. How do you think the article would change if it were written for another audience—American, Chinese, or British for example?

e. The title of this article can have more than one meaning. Give two possible interpretations of what *future tense* means.

f. What does the image on page 239 represent? In your opinion, is it a suitable choice for inclusion with this selection? What techniques has the photographer used?

2. Vocabulary
Faith Popcorn uses a number of new business- and technology-related terms. Explain in your own words what each of the following terms means: *cocooning, e-commerce, identity theft, egonomics, clanning,* and *access anxiety*. What other words from the selection would you add to a list of business or technology terms? Choose two words and investigate their origins and how they developed.

Write a short speech that explains your opinion or forecast for one of the aspects of society mentioned in the selection—shopping, health, beauty, vacations, and so on. Use at least five business or technology terms from the selection.

3. Media
Advertising Create an ad (TV, radio, brochure, billboard, or Web site) for one of the services or products mentioned in this article, for example, the paparazzi blocker, Polish Mood Shades nail polish, or Wild Women Adventures. Consider your audience, purpose, form, and production options carefully as you develop the ad. You may want to develop a **slogan** or **logo**.

A **slogan** is a short, catchy phrase used to advertise a product or service. A **logo** is an identifying symbol or image, sometimes including a name or a word, used in advertising.

Peer Assessment: Ask two or three classmates to assess how effectively your ad persuades a consumer to purchase the product or service. In their opinion, is your target audience obvious? Have you used your chosen form skilfully? Are there media techniques which you could use more effectively?

The following two selections give the reader some insight into the amazing scientific breakthroughs that could change the way we live.

Written in the Body

Newspaper Article by Marni Jackson

If narrative is the true road to revelation, then the decoding of the human genome may turn out to be the greatest story ever written.

Last year I had a chance meeting with one of the world's greatest readers: Sydney Brenner, a molecular biologist of international distinction. He is a haunter of bookshops as well as a legendary decoder of the human genome, and it turns out that these activities are closely related.

As we learned on June 26, 2000, the genome is a linear, coded text inscribed on the molecules of our DNA, just like a book. On the page, the script of life looks like something banged out by an over-caffeinated writer on a broken typewriter: ACT ACC ACG CAG CGA, and so on, for another billion words. The genome is about the length of 800 Bibles, and so far, quite a page-turner. It uses an alphabet of only four letters—A, C, G, and T—combined into three-letter sequences known as *codons*, a term Brenner coined himself.

Together, these "words" comprise what science writer Matt Ridley has called "the autobiography of our species." Each gene in our cells contains data traces from the earliest days of life on Earth, etched in us like a psalm on a grain of rice.

It makes you think twice about that famous opening line, "In the beginning was the word."

Brenner, along with Francis Crick, was one of the earliest translators of the human and animal genome. He's famous for his work on RNA, a worm called C. elegans, and the gene sequence of the pufferfish, among other things.

I ran into this bibliophile/biologist at the Gairdner Foundation International Awards, a symposium held each year in Toronto to honour advances in medical sciences. He was easily recognizable by his eyebrows, thick little shelves of reddish-brown fur above intelligent eyes. Brenner was also wearing a ratty green T-shirt in a room full of suits. We began to chat about the genome, which in my case was an astonishingly brief conversation. In two sentences, one of which Brenner had to correct, I exhausted my knowledge of this subject.

"So the genome is really a sort of narrative," I ventured brightly.

"No," he said, "it's more of a description of nature, just as the laws of society are a kind of social DNA, which is to say, a description of how we should conduct ourselves." However, he was willing to accept my next analogy, which compared the genome to a hieroglyph—a kind of cave painting in miniature, that tells who we are and where we have travelled.

Then we talked about his other passion: reading and collecting books. He has a vast private library, and in Cambridge, England, he lives above a bookshop. He also writes a rather elegant and playful column called "Loose Ends," for the otherwise unplayful journal *Current Biology*. Light years ahead of the rest of us in genetics, when it comes to print, Brenner is crabby about e-mail and old-fashioned about the physical presence of paper.

"I tried amazon.com once," he said dolefully, "and all they ever do is ask for my credit card. But when I go into a bookstore, I always discover something I wasn't looking for." Readers, like scientists, are always hoping for a new plot twist.

Then Brenner had to race off to deliver a paper at the symposium. I followed and sat in the audience, where I listened to him compare our new grasp of the genome to the early days of astronomers, when they were learning how to read the starry heavens. He cast the same spell as an author reading from a novel.

It was not like a science paper; I felt I was listening to something very old, and very new—a modern bedtime story.

In fact, the Gairdner Awards happened to overlap with the International Festival of Authors, and as I shuttled back and forth between these two forums, I was struck by their similarity. Where science once immersed itself in isolated detail, the genome has now uncovered an underlying narrative. A molecular biologist such as Brenner is engaged in an immense plot, like a historical writer.

In his 1999 bestseller, *Genome*, Matt Ridley tracks the story of the genome through the 23 chromosomes, giving each one a character and theme. It's a simplification, thank God, and one that works well for readers who still think that DNA is a clothing label.

Photo by D. Hallinan

"Until the genetic code was cracked in the 1960s," Ridley writes, "we did not know what we now know: That all life is one; seaweed is your distant cousin and anthrax is one of your advanced relatives. The unity of life is an empirical fact. [In 1794] Erasmus Darwin was outrageously close to the mark: One and the same kind of living filaments has been the cause of all organic life."

All of which brings me to my New Year's prediction: As a result of the "publication" of the human genome, we are going to see a dramatic new convergence between science and the humanities.

Narrative is already becoming an important new tool in medical diagnosis. And at the University of California in Los Angeles, a new department that brings together scientific research with history has been created.

Writers used to be the storytellers, while scientists were more like journalists or reporters. But readers of the genome have changed that. The book of life is not just a metaphor—which puts us all on the same page.

Genome Sequence
Just the Beginning

Essay by David Suzuki

As a geneticist, I could not help but feel a sense of wonder and awe after last week's release of the completed human genome sequence. Never, during my 25 years of genetic research, had I anticipated this would occur in my lifetime.

The determination of the sequence of all three billion letters in the DNA blueprint of human cells is a stunning technical achievement. Now the really interesting and difficult work of trying to make sense of it all begins. That task will take much, much longer.

The human genome is incredibly complex, and the genome project has elucidated just 2 per cent of it (the other 98 per cent is non-coding "junk" DNA, the function of which has yet to be determined), but that didn't stop some newspapers from running misleading headlines such as, "Revealed: The secrets of who we are." Others turned this scientific advance into a triumphant business story with headlines like, "Private sector wins genetic-code race."

For the most part, however, newspapers got the story right—pointing out that the sequenced human genome has opened up more questions than it has answered.

For example, although it now appears that humans only have about 35,000 genes (the lowly fruit fly has more than 13,000), we have little idea how these relatively few genes are harnessed and orchestrated to transform a fertilized egg into an organism as complex as a human being. It suggests that the basic biological differences between fruit flies and human beings are not nearly as great as differences in mere size or appearance would suggest.

In fact, comparisons between the human genome and the sequenced genomes of other species reveal remarkable genetic similarities. For example, we share as much as 10 per cent of our genes with much simpler organisms like the fruit fly and the worm. We also share some 233 genes with bacteria that are not found in the genomes of the fruit fly, the worm or yeast. So at some point in our evolutionary history, our ancestors must have taken on bacterial genes, or vice versa.

Even more enlightening will be the comparison of our genes to other, more closely related species whose genomes have yet to be sequenced, such as mice and even chimpanzees. Determining the mouse genome (which is nearly complete) is an important step because it is expected to be similar to the human genome, so genetic experimentation with mice could yield important medical advances for humans. And since humans and chimpanzees share about 99 per cent of the same DNA, a comparison of the two genomes should inform us about what genetic factors make us human.

Still, in comparing the genomes that have been sequenced so far, it is the similarities that are most striking. Evolution has been remarkably efficient, exploiting the same genes over and over throughout life. The fact that a few genetic differences are all that separate humanity from the rest of the animal kingdom ought to give a much-needed dose of humility.

Similarly, the finding that genetic differences within racial groups are greater than those between racial groups strikes a final nail in racism's coffin. Genetically, race consists of superficial physical similarities, nothing more.

With the human genome sequenced, scientists can now turn to a vastly more complicated process, determining what the three billion bases that make up our genes do, how and when they are turned on and off, and how the proteins they design collaborate to carry out various functions. That is the real challenge, for the sequenced human genome merely represents a list of parts.

As geneticist Eric Lander has said: "We've called the human genome the blueprint, the Holy Grail, all sorts of things. It's a parts list. If I gave you the parts list for a Boeing 777, and it has 100,000 parts, I don't think you could screw it together, and you certainly wouldn't understand why it flew."

1. Exploring Meaning

"Written in the Body"

a. Who are the two people Marni Jackson quotes in her article? What do they have in common? What does the addition of these quotations add to her argument?

b. For what audience is this selection written? What is Jackson's purpose for writing this article? Explain.

c. Jackson tries to simplify the complex idea of the genome by putting it into simpler language. How does she do this? Find two examples from the article.

d. What connection does Jackson see between science and the humanities? Do you agree? Why or why not?

"Genome Sequence Just the Beginning"

e. What is David Suzuki's thesis in this essay? Where does it first become apparent?

f. What is the tone of this essay? Give an example that you believe demonstrates it clearly.

An **analogy** is the illustration of one idea or concept using a similar idea or concept.

g. Suzuki quotes another geneticist, Eric Lander, in the last paragraph. Explain the **analogy** Lander uses and how it applies to the human genome.

h. What kind of audience is this selection written for: scientists, educators, or a general audience? Explain your choice.

2. Researching Use the keyword *genome* to research this subject on the Internet. Find out who discovered the genome, when, and what it is. Make a few jot notes to summarize your findings. Develop a short written report that includes visual aids, and cite your sources.

Alternatively, research Suzuki's life and work, developing a short biography. Present your findings as an oral presentation for the class. You might include clips from his TV series *The Nature of Things* to enhance your presentation. In your presentation indicate why Suzuki would be interested in genome research.

3. Focus on Context As a class, discuss how the context of each selection affects its content. How do the selections vary? What is the purpose and audience of each? How does the author's background and interests affect his or her content? Does the identity of the author affect your response to either article?

Self-Assessment: Do you usually consider the context (author's background, purpose, and audience, for example) as you read and respond to a selection? Do you reflect on how context can affect content? When is considering the context of a selection important? Explain your response.

4. Film Study With a small group, brainstorm ideas for a science fiction or horror movie that incorporates some aspect of human genome research revealed in these selections. Choose one idea and create one of the following:

• a script for one scene
• a storyboard for one scene
• a trailer
• a movie poster
• a videotaped presentation of one scene

Unit 6

Issues: Justice

Justice

Poem by Rita Joe

Justice seems to have many faces
It does not want to play if my skin is not the right hue,
Or correct the wrong we long for,
Action hanging off-balance
Justice is like an open field
We observe, but are afraid to approach.
We have been burned before
Hence the broken stride
And the lingering doubt
We often hide

Justice may want to play
If we have an open smile
And offer the hand of communication
To make it worthwhile

Justice has to make me see
Hear, feel.
Then I will know the truth is like a toy
To be enjoyed or broken

1. Exploring Meaning

a. What metaphors does Rita Joe use in the poem? What similarities does she identify between the things she compares?

b. The word *hence* is used in the first stanza to show transition from one idea to the next. What other words in the poem connect ideas or show transition?

c. In the last stanza, the author presents the concepts of *justice* and *truth* as interconnected. Discuss the relationship between truth and justice.

d. Do the last two stanzas present a pessimistic or optimistic view of justice? Explain.

2. Writing *Memoir* Write a memoir in which you recount a time when you experienced an injustice. Explore why the injustice occurred and what impact it had on your belief in the possibility of justice for all. Do you think justice for everyone is possible?

3. Film Study Find a film that addresses the theme of injustice. In what ways are the characters' attitudes to injustice similar to, or different from, the attitudes presented in the poem? How do the characters demonstrate their attitudes?

A Matter of Balance

Short Story by W. D. Valgardson

He was sitting on a cedar log, resting, absentmindedly plucking pieces from its thick layer of moss, when he first saw them. They were standing on the narrow bridge above the waterfall. When they realized he had noticed them, they laughed, looked at each other, then turned their backs. In a moment, the short, dark-haired one turned around to stare at him again. His companion flicked a cigarette into the creek.

Bikers, he thought with a mixture of contempt and fear. He had seen others like them, often a dozen at a time, muscling their way along the road. These two had their hair chopped off just above the shoulders, and from where he sat, it looked greasy and hung in tangled strands. They both had strips of red cloth tied around their heads. The dark-haired boy, he thought, then corrected himself, man, not boy, for he had to be in his middle twenties, was so short and stocky that he might have been formed from an old-fashioned beer keg. They both wore black leather vests, jeans and heavy boots.

He was sorry that they were there, but he considered their presence only a momentary annoyance. They had probably parked their bikes at the pull-off below the waterfall, walked up for God knows what reason—he could not imagine them being interested in the scenery—and would shortly leave again. He would be happy to see them go. He was still only able to work part-time and had carefully arranged his schedule so that his Wednesdays were free. He didn't want anything to interfere with the one day he had completely to himself.

The tall blond man turned, leaned against the railing and stared up at Harold. He jabbed his companion with his elbow and laughed. Then he raised his right hand, pointed two fingers like he would a pistol and pretended to shoot.

The action, childish as it was, unsettled Harold, and he felt his stomach knot with anxiety. He wished that he were on the other side of the bridge and could simply pick up his pack and walk back to his station wagon. The only way across the river, however, was the bridge, and he had no desire to try to force his way past them. They reminded him of kids from his public school days who used to block the sidewalk, daring anyone to try to get by. He had been in grade two at the time and had not yet learned about fear. When he had attempted to ignore them and go around, they had shifted with him to the boulevard, then to the road and, finally, to the back lane. As his mother was washing off his scrapes and bruises and trying to get blood off his shirt, he had kept asking her why, why did they do it? Beyond saying that they were bad boys and that she would speak to the principal, she had had no answers. Only later, when he was much older, had he understood that their anger was not personal and so could not be reasoned with.

Every Wednesday for the last six months, he had hiked to the end of this trail and then used his rope to lower himself to the riverbank. Before the winter rains began and flooded the gorge, he wanted to do as much sniping as possible. The previous week, he had discovered a crack in the bedrock that looked promising, but before he had a chance to get out all the gravel, the day had started to fade and he had been forced to leave. The gorge was no place to spend the night. Even at noon, the light was filtered to a pale grey. He dressed warmly, wearing a cotton shirt, then a wool shirt and, finally, a wool jack-shirt; yet within a few hours, he was always shaking with cold. As strenuous as the panning was, it could not keep him warm. The air was so damp that when he took a handful of rotting cedar and squeezed it, red water ran like blood between his fingers. On the tree trunks, hundreds of mushrooms grew. At first, because of their small size and dark grey colour, he thought they were slugs, but then he pried one loose with his fingernail and discovered its bright yellow gills.

Although he had been nowhere near the bottom of the crack, he had found a few flakes of gold, which he meticulously picked out of his pan with tweezers. Panning in the provincial parks was illegal, so he always went right to the end of the path, then worked his way along the river for another hundred yards. Once, he had taken a quarter-ounce of dust and small nuggets out of the river, and he wondered if someone had found out, but he immediately dismissed the idea. Only his psychiatrist knew. When they met each Thursday, he always showed Conklin his latest find. As far as his friends and colleagues were aware, he spent his days off hiking, getting himself back into shape after having been ill for over a year.

As he studied the two men below, he told himself he was letting his imagination run away with him again and to get it under control. There was no good in borrowing trouble. He stood up, swung his pack onto his shoulders and, being careful not to look like he was running away, resumed his hike.

From this point on, the trail was a series of switchbacks. If the two on the bridge were planning on following him and stealing his equipment or wallet, they would probably give up after a short distance and wait for easier prey. Unless they were in good condition, the steep climb would leave them gasping for breath.

Large cedars pressed close to the path, blocking out the light. Old man's beard hung from the branches. The ground was a tangle of sword fern, salal and Oregon grape. In a bit of open space, an arbutus twisted towards the sun. Its bark, deep earth-red, hung in shreds. Here and there, the new pale green bark was visible. That was the way he felt, like a snake or an arbutus, shedding his old skin for a new, better one. The previous year, when nothing else had seemed to work, he had taken his pack and hiked from sunrise to sunset, exhausting himself so completely that he could not stay awake. The sniping, looking for gold in cracks, under rocks, among the roots of trees, had come when he had started to feel better.

At the next bend, he stopped and hid behind a rotting stump. In a couple of minutes his pursuers—he told himself not to be foolish, not to be paranoid—appeared. They were walking surprisingly fast. If the trail had been even slightly less steep, they would have been running.

He wished there was a cutoff that would allow him to circle back. He could, he realized, use his equipment, if necessary, to lower himself to the river, but to do so he would need to gain enough of a lead to have time to untie and uncoil the rope, to set it around a tree, to climb down and then to pull his rope down after him so that it could not be taken away or cut. He then would be faced with the problem of finding a route up. He had to be back by seven. It was the agreed-upon time. Since their mother had been killed, the children became upset if he was even a few minutes late.

He looked at his watch. It was ten o'clock. It was a two-hour hike to the end of the trail, but he could hike out in an hour and a half. That did not leave him much time. First, he wanted to clean out the crack and, if possible, begin undercutting a large rock that sat in the centre of the river. Undercutting was dangerous. It would require that he move rocks and logs to divert the shallow water to either side of where he was going to work. Then he would need more logs to prop up the rock. He didn't want to get the work partly done and have half a ton of stone roll onto him. The nuggets that might be clustered around the base were worth some risk, but there was no sense in taking more chances than necessary.

Ahead, through a gap in the trees, he saw the railway trestle. The two behind him would, he told himself, stop there. Hardly anyone went farther.

The trestle was an inexplicable focal point. Every weekend, dozens of people hiked to it, then dared each other to cross over the gorge. Many, terrified of heights, balked after the first few steps and stood, rigid, unable to force themselves to go farther.

That, he reassured himself, was what those two were coming for. They would cross the trestle and scare each other by roughhousing like a couple of adolescents.

He had hoped, unreasonably, that there would be hikers or a railway crew on the tracks. Normally, it was a relief when there was no one there. Hikers were inclined to talk about their experiences, and in the past, he had been afraid that if he was frequently seen on the same trail, his weekly visits might come to the attention of the park warden. To avoid that, he had deliberately arranged to come when the park was empty.

He did not stop but crossed over the tracks and entered the forest on the far side. The path dwindled to a narrow line of crushed ferns. The trees were shagged with windblown moss, and deadfall was everywhere. It was old forest, and in all the time he had come, he had never seen a bird or animal. As a child he had dreamed of living in the forest. In his dreams, his hunting had always been rewarded with game. The discrepancy between what he had hoped for and reality still astounded him.

While he was able to see the railway tracks, he stopped and waited. His legs had begun to tire and cramp. He stretched them, then kneaded his right calf with his thumb and forefinger. Always before, he had valued the silence and isolation. Now, however, as he watched the two bikers look up and down the roadbed, then cross the path, Harold felt the forest close around him like a trap.

He hurried away. Even as he fled, he reassured himself that they had done nothing. Anyone was free to hike wherever he wanted. If he just stopped, they would catch up and pass him by without paying any attention to him.

He kept his eyes on the path. He had no intention of tripping over a vine or slipping on a log. His fear, he chided himself, was not rational. If a Mountie suddenly appeared and asked him what was the matter, what could he say? That he didn't like the way they had looked at him earlier? That they had threatened him? And how was that, sir? He could hear the question. And the answer? The blond one pointed his finger at me. Any Mountie would think him mad.

The moss was so thick that his feet made no sound. There was only the creak of his pack, the harsh sound of his breathing. He would, he decided, abandon his plans, and when he got to the end of the granite ridge that ran along on his left, he would double back through the narrow pass on its far side. People don't assault other people without good reason, he told himself, but it did no good. His panic fluttered like dry leaves in a rising wind.

He wished that he had brought a hunting knife. It would have made him feel better to have a weapon. His mind scurried over the contents of the pack as he tried to determine what he could use in a fight. The only possibility was his rack of chock nuts. It wasn't much. A dozen aluminum wedges, even clipped together on a nylon sling, would not be very effective.

As he came to the end of the ridge, he turned abruptly to the left. The pass was nearly level and, unlike the area round it, contained only a few scattered trees. There were, he remembered, circles of stones where people had made campfires. One day he had poked about and discovered used condoms, some plastic sandwich bags and four or five beer bottles. A broken beer bottle, he thought, would serve as a weapon. He was just beginning to search for one when he saw a movement at the far end of the pass.

He became absolutely still. He felt so weak that he thought he was going to fall down. He craned his neck for a better look. If there were two of them, he could circle back the other way. In a moment, he realized that there was only one. That meant the other was on the path he had just left. He spun on his heel and ran back to the fork. No more than a quarter of a mile away the path ended. At that point, there was nothing to do but return the way he had come or descend to the river. In either case, he was trapped. His mouth, he realized, was so dry he could not spit.

Behind him, he heard someone ask a question that sounded like "Where did he go?" and a muffled reply, but he could not be sure of the words. The ground was nearly level. He was running when he burst out onto an area where the rock fell from the side of the trail like a frozen set of rapids. There were few places here for trees to root. Leaves and pine needles were swept from the pale green lichen by the winter rains. Rather than continue to what he knew was a dead end, he clambered down the slope. He had not explored this area. In the back of his mind was the hope that the rough rock continued all the way to the river. By the time they found out he was no longer on the path, he could have climbed the other cliff. All at once, he stopped. The rough black rock turned into sixty feet of smooth slab.

There was no time to go back. He glanced over his shoulder, then at the slab. It was, he realized, deceptive. It angled down toward the river, then stopped at a ragged edge. No steeper than a roof at the outset, it curved just enough that every few feet the angle increased. Patches of lichen and the smooth texture of the stone guaranteed that anyone who ventured out on it would be engaged in a test of balance.

There was a chance, because of his friction boots, that he could work his way onto the steepest part of the slope. If the two behind him were not pursuing him, they would pass by and he would never see them again. If they were, for whatever reason, meaning him some harm, they would have great difficulty reaching him.

Quickly, he unzipped the right-hand pocket of his pack and pulled out a section of three-millimetre rope. He tied a figure-eight knot in both ends, wrapped the rope around his left hand, then crept down to a small evergreen. Ten feet to the right, in a completely exposed area, there was a gnarled bush. Here and there, stunted trees, their trunks nearly as hard as the rock itself, protruded from cracks.

There was little room for error. If he began to slide, it would be difficult to stop before he went over the edge. At this part of the river, the fall would not be great, but height would not make any difference. Even a twenty-foot fall onto the scattered boulders of the riverbed would certainly be fatal. He leaned out, brushed away some dust that had collected on the rock, then took his first step.

Above him, someone whistled sharply. It startled him, but he kept his eyes fixed on the surface of the rock. He fitted the toe of his boot onto a small nubbin, then his other toe onto a seam of cracked quartz. The greatest danger was that, for even a split second, he would allow himself to be distracted. For his next move, he chose a pebbled area no bigger than a silver dollar. From there,

Photo by Bill Hatcher.

he moved to a depression that was only noticeable because of its slight shadow. He had crossed more difficult areas than this but always with the security of a harness and rope and a belayer he could trust. A fall in those circumstances meant no more than some scraped skin and injured pride.

When he was within two feet of the bush, he felt a nearly overwhelming urge to lunge forward. He forced himself to stay where he was. On the rock there could be no impetuous moves. Patience, above all else, was to be valued. There seemed to be no place for him to put his foot. He scanned the surface. Just below him there was a hairline crack. If he pressed down hard on it, it would hold him long enough for him to step to the side and up and catch hold of the bush.

Slowly, he pirouetted on his left foot, then brought his right foot behind it. He took a deep breath, forced the air out of his lungs, then in one fluid movement, stepped down, up and across. Even as his hand grasped the wooden stem, he felt his feet begin to slide.

When he unwrapped the three-millimetre rope from his arm, he sat with his legs on either side of the stem. He fitted a loop of rope around an exposed root, then slipped the second loop around his wrist. Unless the root gave way, the farthest he was going to fall was a couple of feet.

Only then did he allow himself to look back. There was still no sign of anyone. The area of tumbled rock ran on for a fair distance and, he realized, would take a while to search. He cursed himself for not taking a chance and running back the way he had come.

He hooked his pack to the bush, took out the sling with the hardware on it, then eased himself out onto the steepest section of slab he could reach. Here he crouched, with his back to the trail, his hands splayed against the rock.

There was a sharp whistle above him. It was immediately answered from some distance back toward the trestle. With that, he realized that they had split up. One had blocked the trail while the other had done the searching.

He looked back again. Thirty feet behind him was the dark-haired biker. His blond companion was swinging down from the left. Both of them, Harold could see, were tired. He had, he thought, with a distant kind of pleasure, given them a good run for their money. If they had been carrying packs, he would have outdistanced them.

They both stopped at the rough edge, some ten feet apart, looked at each other and smirked.

"Did you want something?" he asked. He had meant to make it a casual question, even offhand, as though he had no idea they had followed him, but panic sharpened his voice.

They both laughed as if at a joke.

"What do you want?" He was no longer sure that what he had planned would work.

The blond man had a small leather purse attached to his belt. He unsnapped it and took out a bone-handled clasp knife. He pried out the wide blade.

"Are you crazy?" Harold cried. "What's the matter with you? I don't even know you."

They both grinned foolishly and studied their boots. They looked, he thought wildly, like two little boys caught in the middle of a practical joke.

Panic made him feel like he was going to throw up. "Are you nuts?" he shouted. "Are you crazy or something?"

Their answer was to start down the slab, one on each side of him. Their first steps were confident, easy. The surface of the rock was granular and bare at the edge and provided plenty of friction. He could see that neither was experienced. They both came down sideways, leaning into the rock, one hand pressed to the surface. He gripped the nylon sling in his right hand and concentrated on keeping his balance.

The dark-haired one was closest. He was coming down between the tree and the shrub, taking little steps, moving his left foot down, then his right foot, then his left, dangerously pressing all his weight onto the edge of his boot and, even more dangerously, leaning backward, throwing off his centre of balance. Suddenly, a piece of lichen peeled away and his left foot slid out from under him. Instead of responding by bending out from the rock and pressing down with his toes, he panicked. He was sliding faster and faster. His body was rigid, his face contorted with fear, his eyes, instead of searching for a place he could stop his slide, were desperately fixed on the safe area he had just left behind. He made no sound. When he was finally even with Harold, he reached out his hand as though expecting it to be taken. There was, Harold saw, on the back of the hand, a tattoo of a heart pierced by a knife. A red and blue snake wound up his arm and disappeared beneath the sleeve. It was only by luck that his one foot struck a piece of root and he stopped. He was no more than a foot from the edge.

The blond man had come at an angle, picking his way along by fitting his knife blade into a crack. Just before his companion lost control, the blond man had started to work his way across an area where there were no cracks. He seemed frozen into place.

"Why?" Harold shouted at him.

The sound seemed to wake the blond man from a stupor. He turned his head slowly to look at Harold. He squinted and formed his mouth into a small circle, then drew his chin down and ran his tongue along his lower lip. For a moment, Harold thought the biker was going to turn and leave.

"Get me out of here," his companion cried. Fear made his voice seem as young as a child's.

The blond man shook his head, then half-snarled, stood up and tried to walk across the intervening space. It was as though momentum and will held him upright; then Harold swung the nylon sling over his head, lunged forward and struck his opponent on the upper arm. The blow was not powerful, and normally it would have been swept aside. But here, as they both teetered on the steep surface, it was enough to knock them both off balance.

As the blond man skidded down the rock, he jabbed at it with his knife, trying to find an opening. Six feet from the edge, he managed to drive the blade into a crack. The knife held. He jammed his fingers into the crack.

Harold had slipped, fallen, then been caught by the rope around his wrist. He pulled himself back to the shrub and knelt with his knee against the stem.

"Help us up," the dark-haired man begged. He looked like he was on the verge of weeping.

Harold loosened the rope, then untied it. Carefully, giving his entire attention to the task, he retraced his original route. Once at the evergreen, he knew he was safe. His sides were soaked with sweat and he could smell his own fear, bitter as stale tobacco. The two men never stopped watching him.

When Harold reached the top of the slab, the blond man called, in a plaintive voice, "For God's sake, don't leave us here."

Fear had softened their eyes and mouths, but he knew it was only temporary. If he drew them to safety, they would return to what they had been.

"Pull us up," the dark-haired man whined. His red headband had come off and was tangled in his hair.

Around them, the forest was silent. Not a bird called, not an animal moved. The moss that covered the rock and soil, the moss that clung thickly to the tree trunks, the moss that hung in long strands from the branches, deadened everything, muted it, until there were no sharp lines, no certainties. The silence pressed upon them. Harold had, for a moment, a mad image of all three of them staying exactly as they were, growing slowly covered in moss and small ferns until they were indistinguishable from the logs and rocks except for their glittering eyes.

"Tell somebody about us," the dark-haired man asked.

The words tugged at him like little black hooks. He looked down. Their faces were bleached white with fear. He could tell someone, a park warden, perhaps, but then what would happen? If he could be certain they would be sent to prison, he might dare tell somebody, but he knew that would not happen. If charges were laid, he would have to testify. They would discover his name and address. And from then on, he would live in fear. Afraid to leave his house. Afraid to go to sleep at night. Afraid for his children. And what if they denied everything, turned it all around? He had had the necessary equipment to rescue them and had refused. What if one of them had fallen by the time someone came? He could be charged with manslaughter, and the children would be left without mother or father. No matter how he tried to keep his psychiatrist out of it, Conklin would become involved. Harold knew how people thought. His short stay in hospital for depression, his weekly visits to a psychiatrist to siphon off pain and, automatically, he was crazy.

"You bastard," the blond man screamed. "You bastard. Get us out of here." He kept shifting his feet, trying to find a purchase where there was none. "If you don't, our friends will come. They'll get us out. Then we'll start looking for you. There's thousands of us. We'll find you."

The screaming startled him for a moment, but then he thought about how soon the little warmth from the sun would disappear, of how the fog would drift down with the darkness, of how the cold would creep into everything, of how few people came this way.

He wondered if his wife had screamed like that. Six of her fingernails had been broken. *Unto the third generation,* Conklin had said. His children, and his grandchildren should he have any, would feel the effects. Alone in a dark parking lot, desperately fighting for her life, and he had been sitting in his study, reading. "Help never comes when it's most needed."

Then, with real regret for the way things are, he hefted his pack so that it settled firmly between his shoulders and returned the way he had come.

---

1. Exploring Meaning

a. What significant events or details in the story are revealed through flashbacks?

b. What inferences can you make regarding the fate of Harold's wife? about the nature of his illness?

c. From the beginning of the story, Harold's behaviour is motivated by feelings of uneasiness. How does the author develop these feelings?

d. How does Harold rationalize his leaving the bikers in such a dangerous position? What other reasons might he have? Do you think his actions are justified? Discuss.

e. Comment on the appropriateness and effectiveness of the title.

2. Technique and Style *Point of View* This story is written from the limited omniscient point of view. It allows the author to choose what he reveals about the thoughts of the protagonist and reveals nothing about the thoughts of the antagonists—the bikers. Why is this point of view effective? Discuss your ideas with a partner.

Write a short story that tells the events of this story from the perspective of one of the bikers. Use a limited omniscient point of view in your retelling.

3. Focus on Context At what point in the story do you know that the threat is real and not a result of Harold's paranoia? Do your classmates agree? Discuss how a reader's background or personal experience might influence his or her interpretation.

4. Writing *Technical Writing* Using the information W. D. Valgardson presents in his story, write a short how-to piece about either rock climbing or sniping for gold. As you develop your instructions, use parallel structure for clarity. You could express ideas using the same grammatical form, or balance words with words or phrases with phrases. Ask a classmate for feedback. Are the instructions clear? Can a reader using these tips accomplish the task? **Self-Assessment:** Assess the importance of parallel structure when developing any type of technical writing. What purpose does parallel structure have?

5. Language Conventions *Subordinating Conjunctions* W. D. Valgardson uses various sentence types in "A Matter of Balance," including *complex sentences* (sentences that contain one main clause and one or more dependent clauses). Skim the story and jot down five examples of complex sentences. Note the subordinating conjunctions that are used to introduce the dependent clauses, and begin a list in your notebook. Develop five complex sentences of your own.

List five adjectives to describe bullies.

Calvin and Hobbes

From *Scientific Progress Goes "Boink"*
Comic Strip by Bill Watterson

1. Exploring Meaning

a. What visual or written details does Bill Watterson use to characterize Moe as the bully and Calvin as the victim?

b. Calvin is met with a dilemma: Should he steal the truck back or give up and let Moe keep it? Which alternative would you choose? Are these the only possible solutions?

c. Calvin's statement, "The forensic marvel has reduced my logic to shambles" is quite ironic. How does the meaning of the word *forensic* help create this irony?

2. Writing *Continue the Story*

The conflict between Moe and Calvin is unresolved. Continue the plot to bring the story to a resolution. How will Calvin solve his problem? How will Moe react? Use both visuals and text to conclude the story within three to six frames.

3. Drama *Script*

In a small group, discuss a situation you've seen or experienced which involved bullying or peer pressure. Develop and perform a script about the event. Present your script to the class.

Performance Tip: Prepare for your performance by considering how you will use gestures, facial expressions, and movement to portray the characters' emotions effectively. What is the purpose of these gestures or movements? Practise displaying various emotions in front of a mirror.

Self-Assessment: Identify the strengths and weaknesses of your presentation. Create an action plan to improve future oral presentations.

Have you ever been discriminated against because of your age? Have you ever discriminated against someone else because of his or her age? Is age discrimination ever justifiable? Explain.

The Truth About Sharks

Short Story by Joan Bauer

The noise seemed faraway at first, like a foghorn blaring in the distance. It was a persistent, ringing, irritating sound. I hated it. I pulled my down comforter over my head, but the noise got louder. It would continue to get louder, too, until I did something. I lifted my head from beneath the covers and saw unhappily that it was morning. I did not do morning, being a devout night person. I gripped the sides of my bed to steady my angst-ridden body and lumbered toward my closet as the noise got louder.

"I hate this!"

I threw open the closet door, lamely stretched my arms upward to find the source of the noise and turn it off, but my mother, the rat, had hidden it well this time. I searched through shoe boxes, purses, then I found it. I grabbed the alarm clock and pushed the on button to off.

Silence.

I dropped to the floor ignoring the knock on my door. All noises were unwelcome in the morning. My smiling mother opened the door and regarded me slumped on the floor.

"There you are."

I shook my head. "It's a mirage."

"Beth," said my mother, "the day has begun; I suggest you do the same. You have to go shopping, wash the dog . . ."

My mother is a morning person. I made a pitiful noise and curled into a ball.

"Don't push my buttons, Beth. The party starts at five."

I sighed deeply, indicating my level of stress. I didn't see why I had to go to Uncle Al's birthday party that would be nothing but torture because Uncle Al was, basically, subterranean.

"And," my mother ordered, "don't say anything about this party either because Al is my brother who has his faults like all of us do . . .""

I don't tell sexist jokes at the dinner table.

I don't suck food through my teeth.

"And we're going to go and honor him and make it very clear that we love him."

Nothing came from my lips.

Mother stared at my lips just to make sure nothing would. "You can have the car, Beth, from now until one, then I absolutely have to have it."

"It's ten-thirty already."

"Then you'd better get cracking."

"I hate mornings."

"What a joy you are to me," Mom said and walked off.

I pulled my best black pants from their hanger, the pants I had spent a fortune on, the black pants that now hung dull and lifeless, hopelessly stained by guacamole dip that was dumped on me and them in sheer hostility by Edgar Bromfman while he was doing his Ostrich in Search of a Mate imitation at Darla Larchmont's party. I loved those slacks. They had power.

Once.

They went with my best beaded vest that I wanted to wear to Uncle Al's party because Bianca, my hideous cousin who always dressed to kill, would be there with her latest gorgeous boyfriend to snub me and make me feel insignificant and toady. She learned this from Uncle Al, her father.

Reingold, my black toy poodle, whined torturously at the door. I let him crash in, a rollicking, teeny ball of fur. I picked him up.

"Reingold, you who see all and know all, tell me where in Fairfield County, Connecticut, I can get a vastly important pair of black power pants."

Reingold licked my neck and wiggled.

"Reingold, your wisdom exceeds even your cuteness. Of course, I will go to that new store on Route 1 in Norwalk. And there I will find them."

Reingold followed me into the bathroom. I gave him a drink of water from a little Dixie cup, washed my face fast, brushed my oily brown hair that hung exhausted on my shoulders; I threw on gray sweats. There was no doubt about it, I looked seedy.

"You're going out like that?" Mom asked, staring.

"Yes." Beauty would come later. All I had going for me now was personality.

Mom touched my bangs. "Maybe if you just—"

I put on sunglasses. "I won't see anyone we know."

Mitchell Gail's was a huge store; five stories, to be exact, with too many choices. My mother said that was the problem with the world today—too many choices. Paper or plastic? Regular, premium, or super? Small, medium, or grande?

I walked past the stocky, stern security guard who was picking her teeth, a visual reminder of Uncle Al's bash tonight. Maybe they knew each other. She glared at me through frigid, gray eyes and touched her name tag, MADGE P. GROTON, SECURITY GUARD. The woman needed a life. The sign above her read, SHOPLIFTERS WILL BE PROSECUTED TO THE FULL EXTENT OF THE LAW. I should hope so. I caught sight of myself in a full-length mirror. Who would know that beneath the greasy hair, sallow skin, and baggy sweats there lived a person of depth and significance? I groaned at my vile reflection and headed for the pants section.

I found four pairs of black slacks, size 10, and one pair, size 8. Hope springs eternal. I walked into the dressing room, past another larger, more threatening sign—SHOPLIFTERS WILL BE PROSECUTED TO THE FULL EXTENT OF THE LAW—just in case any thieves missed the first warning. A sweet, round saleswoman showed me to an empty changing room. Her name tag read HANNAH. She had sad eyes.

"If you need anything I'll help you," Hannah said.

"Thanks."

She looked down.

"Must be the pits working on Saturday," I offered.

She shook her head. "I'd rather work. It's better than sitting home. My boyfriend was cheating on me with this manicurist. I saw them kissing in his apartment."

"I'm sorry."

She laughed, not happily. "He said he never really loved me; I was too fat." She looked at her plump arms.

"He's a jerk. You're not fat."

"I'm just going to work, save my money—"

"— Hannah!" It was the store manager. Hannah shrugged stiffly, let out a long, painful breath, and left.

Males. I was between them at the moment. Probably just as well given my last boyfriend's sizzling attraction to blondes—a little problem we were never able to work out since I'm a brunette. I observed a moment of silence for Hannah's pain. Then I tried on the size 8 pants. I could zip them up exactly one-eighth of an inch.

Okay . . . size 8 is still a dream.

On went a size 10.

No.

Another . . .

Thunder-thighs.

The fourth pair hit me mid-calf.

I tried the fifth. Not bad. I turned in front of the mirror. Not perfect, but doable. And with my beaded vest these could be downright smashing. I put on my shoes, left my coat and sweatpants in the changing room with my purse underneath them. I shouldn't leave my purse there, but I was in such a hurry. I said to Hannah, "I'll take these, but I'm going to keep looking."

"They look nice on you."

They do, don't they? I smiled at the beckoning sale sign over a rack of pants right by the elevator that I'd not seen before. I walked toward the rack and was just reaching for an excellent pair of size 10 black silk pants marked 50 percent off, which would keep me within my budget, which would be a miracle, when a rough hand came down hard on my shoulder and spun me around.

"That's not the way we play the game," Madge P. Groton, Security Guard, barked.

"What?"

"That's not the way we play the game," she repeated, pulling my hands behind my back and pushing me forward.

"*What are you talking about?*"

She was strong. She pushed me past a line of staring customers, into the elevator. She squeezed my hands hard. A cold fear swept through me.

"*What,*" I shouted, "*are you doing?*"

"You were going into the elevator wearing pants you didn't pay for. We call that shoplifting around here."

"*No, I was—*"

She pressed my hands tighter.

"*You're hurting me!*"

"*Shut up!*"

Tears stung my eyes. My chest was pounding. I had seen a TV show about what to do if you're falsely arrested. You don't fight, you calmly explain your position. There was an explanation. I would give the explanation to this person at the right time and I would go home and never set foot in this store again. If I panicked now . . .

The elevator door opened and the guard shoved me forward past the jewelry counter like a mass murderer, past Mrs. Applegate, Uncle Al's nosy neighbor, who stared at me like she wasn't surprised.

"Ma'am, I'm *innocent,*" I said.

"Yeah, and I'm the Easter Bunny." She opened a door that read SECURITY, and pushed me inside to a dingy beige windowless room with the now-familiar sign: SHOPLIFTERS WILL BE PROSECUTED TO THE FULL EXTENT OF THE LAW.

"Please, Ma'am, Ms. Groton . . ."

My whole body was shaking.

"Take them off," she snarled.

"What?"

"Take the pants off. Now."

I stared at her. "You mean here?"

She put her hand on her gun. This was crazy.

"I get a phone call, right?"

"You are in possession of stolen property."

"Ma'am, I know you're trying to do your job. Just listen to me. I was going to buy these pants. I told this to the saleswoman. I left my coat and my pants and my purse in the changing room. Believe me, this is a big—"

"Take them off." She leaned back in her chair, enjoying her power.

I felt my face shaking like tears were exploding inside. I was sick and terrified. My mind reached for anything.

I remembered that article I'd read about sharks. If you're swimming in the ocean and a shark comes at you to attack, hit him in the nose, the expert said.

I looked at Madge P. Groton, Security Shark.

"No, Ma'am. Not until I get my pants back."

She leaned toward me; her face was tight and mean. "You do what I tell you."

I took a huge breath and looked at her hard.

"No, Ma'am."

Her face darkened. She punched a button on a large black phone, said into the receiver, "I've got one. Send a car."

Nausea hit. I choked down vomit. My heart was beating out of my chest. Madge P. Groton, Security Guard, took her handcuffs off her belt and clinked them on the cracked linoleum floor again and again.

"If we could just talk to that saleswoman," I tried, "I think we could clear this—"

"That's not the way we play the game."

I leaned against the wall and pushed down the screaming voice inside that shouted I was innocent because Madge P. Groton had made up her mind and the Easter Bunny himself couldn't change it. And a car was coming for me with police, probably, which meant jail, probably. I could get thrown into jail with dangerous people and no one was going to listen. I'd never get into veterinary school, never see my dreams fulfilled. My life was over at seventeen.

"I need to make a phone call, Ma'am. I need to call my mother."

"I bet you would."

"The law says I get to make a phone call."

"You can do it at the station."

"Ma'am, my purse and coat and pants are still in the changing room."

Nothing.

I checked my watch: 1:10. My mother was waiting for the car. She wouldn't be getting it soon. I lowered my head and started to cry.

"I've seen you kids," she snarled. "You think you can take anything you want, call your parents, cry some fake tears, and it's over, huh? You think wrong."

"I didn't do it."

I jumped at the harsh knock on the door. A big policeman with leathery skin entered with his hand on his gun. He listened to the security guard's story. I told him she'd made a mistake, but it didn't seem to matter. No one believes prisoners.

"Don't ever set foot in this store again," warned Madge P. Groton.

Don't worry, lady.

The policeman took my arm firmly and we walked out of the store, past Mrs. Applegate, past jewelry, and purses, and leather gloves, and scarves, past the Clinique counter with those white-jacketed technicians, to the waiting police car.

"You have the right to remain silent," he said the sickening words to me. "You have the right to an attorney. If you do not have an attorney, one will be appointed for you."

He opened the back door of the squad car, I got in crying.

The door shut like a prison gate.

"It wasn't worth it, Miss," he said, got into the front and drove off with Mrs. Applegate staring after us.

I slumped down deep in the seat and looked at my feet because I was sure everyone I'd ever met in my entire, complex life saw me in the prisoner section of the squad car.

"Officer," I whispered, "I know you're doing your job. I know that security guard was doing hers, but I've got to tell you, if we go back to that store, I've got a witness who knows that I didn't do it."

This was a definite gamble. I didn't know if that saleswoman would remember me.

"Who?" he asked.

I told him about the saleswoman. "Officer, I am really scared and I don't know what else to do. Would you let me try to prove I'm innocent?"

He stopped the car and stared at me through the grill.

"Look, sir, I know I look really weird. I had to buy some slacks for my uncle's stupid birthday party and my mother needed the car in a hurry, so I just jumped out of bed and hadn't figured on getting arrested. I mean, I normally bathe. I normally look better than this. Corpses look better than I do right now. I sound like an idiot."

The policeman searched my face. "Which salesperson?"

I put my two innocent hands on the grill. "Her name was Helen. No. Hortense. Wait—*Hannah*. Yes! She had just broken up with her boyfriend who had been cheating on her for months with this manicurist and he said he'd never really loved her because she was too fat, which she wasn't—a little plump, maybe, but definitely not fat—and she was giving up men. At least for the moment."

He stared at me.

"Not that men are bad. I mean, some are. But you know that. You arrest bad people and that's a really good thing."

I was digging my own grave. He would take me to the psychiatric hospital. I would be locked in a room with no sharp objects. I looked away.

"*Please* believe me, Officer. I'm not really this strange!"

The officer sighed deeply. "I don't have time for this." He rammed the patrol car into gear, did a perfect U-turn, and headed back toward Mitchell Gail's.

"Oh, thank you, Officer! You are a wonderful person, a—"

He held up his hand for me to stop. I bit my tongue. I didn't ask what would happen if Hannah wasn't there or didn't remember me or was Madge P. Groton's best friend.

"Don't try anything funny," said the officer as he opened the squad car prisoner door and I got out.

"I won't." This was the most humorless situation I'd ever been in.

"I do the talking."

I nodded wildly. We walked through the front door, past jewelry, purses, and Madge P. Groton, who nearly dropped her fangs when she saw us.

"Just checking something out," said the officer to her and kept on walking to the elevator.

"What floor were you on?" he asked me.

I held up four trembling fingers.

"You can talk when I talk to you."

"Right," I croaked.

The elevator came and Madge P. Groton glared at us with poison death darts as we got in. I figured an actual policeman was more powerful in the food chain than a security guard, but I decided not to ask at this moment.

The elevator stopped at every floor. A little girl got on with her mother, looked at me and said, "What's the matter with her, Mommy?"

"Polly," said the mother, "don't be rude."

The elevator opened at the fourth floor. We got out. My eyes searched for Hannah. The policeman walked up to a gray-haired saleswoman.

"We're looking for Hortense," he said.

"*Hannah!*" I shrieked.

The woman pointed to Hannah who was folding sweaters and arranging them on a shelf. We walked toward her. Remember me? I wanted to shout. I am the person who took time from my busy schedule to listen to your problems with your scuzzy boyfriend; the person who cared enough to show you the healing touch of humanity during a particularly stress-packed morning in my life.

"Do you know this young woman?" the policeman asked Hannah.

Hannah looked at me and smiled. "I waited on her this morning. She left her purse and coat and stuff in the changing room. I've got them for you."

Madge P. Groton stormed up. "What's going on?"

"Just clearing a few things up," said the officer.

Madge P. Groton dug in her spurs. "This girl is a shoplifter. I caught her trying to leave the store wearing merchandise!"

Hannah looked shocked. "Then why would she leave her purse in the changing room?"

Why indeed?

I smiled broadly at Madge P. Groton, Security Guard, whose face had turned a delightful funeral gray.

"And why would she leave her coat?" Hannah continued. "It's worth at least as much as the pants. You made a mistake, Madge."

"Can I see the purse?" asked the officer.

Hannah ran to get it. I winced as he pulled out Tums, dental floss, breath mints, two hairbrushes, my giant panda key ring, a box of Milk Duds, three packs of tissues, my sunglasses, four lipsticks.

"You got a wallet in here?"

I reached deep within and pulled it out. He checked my driver's license. He counted the money. Seventy-five dollars.

"I think," said the officer, "we've got things straightened out here, wouldn't you say so, Ms. Groton?"

Madge P. Groton sputtered first. Her wide jaw locked. Her thick neck gripped. Her nose mole twitched. She turned on her scuffed heel and stormed off. The officer gave me back my purse, coat. "You're free to go," he said. "Just give the store back the pants."

"I never want to see these pants again. Thank you for believing me, Officer . . . um . . . I don't know your name."

"Brennerman."

What a wonderful name. I thanked him again.

I thanked Hannah.

I thanked God.

I ran into the changing room, put on my dear, old gray grubbies, drew a penetrating breath of freedom, and raced toward my mother's Taurus. It was two-thirty. All I had to worry about now was the flaming war spear my mother would have singeing the lawn in honor of my late return.

I floored the Taurus, most unwise, since I'd had one brush with the law already today. I drove home, three miles under the speed limit (a first), thanking God I was a free American.

I turned left at the Dunkin' Donuts on Route 1 feeling something wasn't quite right.

I stared at the poster of the cholesterol-laden Dunkin' Munchkins nestled cozily in their box as the unrighteousness of it grew in my soul.

I'd been publicly humiliated.

Falsely accused.

I have my rights!

I rammed Mom's car around and headed back for Mitchell Gail's.

I am teenager, hear me roar.

I parked the car, stormed into the store past the SHOPLIFTERS WILL BE PROSECUTED TO THE FULL EXTENT OF THE LAW sign, right past Madge P. Groton, Security Neanderthal, to the Clinique counter.

"I need to see the store manager," I announced to a blond woman demonstrating face cream. "Immediately."

"Third floor, left by Donna Karan, left by lingerie, you're there."

Madge P. Groton was now guarding the elevator. I took the stairs two at a time, rounded left by Donna Karan, left by lingerie to the store office.

"Can I help you?" asked a tired receptionist with too red hair.

"Only if you're in charge, Ma'am. I need to see the manager."

She looked me up and down. "He's busy now." She looked toward the manager's closed office door. The sign read: THOMAS LUNDGREN, STORE MANAGER.

"It can't wait."

"I'm afraid it's going to have to, dear, you see . . ."

"No, Ma'am. You see. I was falsely arrested in this store by Madge P. Groton, Security Witch, and in exactly two seconds I'm going to call a very large lawyer."

"*Oh, Mr. Lundgren!*" the woman's bony hands fluttered in front of her face. She flew into his office. I walked in behind her. "We have a little problem."

Thomas Lundgren, Store Manager, appraised my grubby gray sweats, unimpressed. "What problem is that?" he said coarsely, not getting up.

I told him. The policeman, Hannah, Madge, the lawyer.

He got up.

"Sit down," he purred at me. "Make yourself comfortable. Would you like a soda? *Candy?*"

"I'd like an apology."

"Well, of course, we at Mitchell Gail's are appalled at anything that could be misconstrued—"

" —This wasn't misconstrued."

"We'll have to check this out, of course."

I folded my arms. "I'll wait, Mr. Lundgren."

"Call me Tom." He snapped his finger at the receptionist. "Get Madge up here."

I crossed my legs. "I'd call the police, too, Tom. Officer Brennerman. He's probably the most important one, next to the lawyer."

Tom grew pale; the receptionist twittered. "Make this happen, Celia," he barked. Then he smiled at me big and wide.

"We certainly pride ourselves on treating our customers well."

I smiled back and didn't say he had a long way to go in that department. The phone buzzed and Tom lunged for it. Maybe I'd can veterinary school and become a lawyer. Lawyers have power. No one gets worked up when you say you're going to call a veterinarian.

"I see." Tom said into the receiver. "I see . . . Yes, Officer Brennerman, it was most unfortunate . . . a vast misunderstanding . . . thank you." He pushed a stick of Wrigley's toward me and mouthed, "Gum?"

I shook my head. Madge P. Groton had seeped into the hall. I said, "By the way, Tom, in addition to false accusations and public humiliation, your security guard told me to take off my pants in her office."

"Pardon?"

"It was a low moment, Tom."

"Tell me you kept them on."

I nodded as Tom moved shakily to the hall, his arms outstretched. "Madge, what is this I'm hearing?"

He shut the office door.

There were hushed, snarling words that I couldn't make out.

I racked my brain to think if I knew any lawyers, large or otherwise. I sort of knew Mr. Heywood down the street, but he was a tax lawyer.

The door opened. Tom grinned. "Madge is truly sorry for the misunderstanding."

Madge glowered at me from the hall. She didn't look sorry.

"Mitchell Gail's is terribly sorry for the . . . inconvenience," he murmured.

"Um, it was a bit more than an inconvenience."

"We would like you to accept a $250 gift certificate from the store for your trouble."

I thought about that.

"We'd be happy to make it $500 for all your trouble," Tom added quickly.

"I'll think about it, Tom."

"We'd really like to get this worked out here and now."

"I'm sure you would, Tom, but I'm going to think about it."

I walked into the hall, past Madge P. Groton, who was so penitent she looked like she'd bitten into a rancid lemon; past Celia, who was fluttering by the receptionist desk. I walked down the stairs and out the door.

Yes!

It was three thirty-seven. All I had to fear now was my mother. I rehearsed my poignant speech all the way home. I was encouraged pulling into the driveway that there was no flaming spear on the lawn. Only a mother spitting fire.

"Mother, you're never going to believe what happened to—"

"You're dead."

I wasn't, of course. Even a profoundly angry parent cannot stay that way long when their beloved child has been falsely accused. It was all I could do to prevent Mom from driving back to the store and personally annihilating Madge P. Groton.

I was the hit of Uncle Al's party. I wore an old black dress, but there was something shining in my face that I could feel—something, Mom said, that money could not buy—empowerment. Mrs. Applegate had called my Aunt Cassie to report on my shoplifting, and even though Aunt Cassie had questioned my innocence, when I told her about Officer Brennerman, she turned pink and flustered and hurried away. I even took Uncle Al aside and told him that the joke he told before dinner offended me and all women through the ages and he *apologized*.

As for my cousin Bianca, she will probably always have a more glamorous life than me, but for a few brief moments that night it really didn't matter.

And regarding Tom and Madge, I decided to not call a lawyer. Tom upped the gift certificate to $650 and had Madge P. Groton personally apologize to me, which was like watching a vulture telling a half-eaten mouse that he didn't really mean it.

"I'm sorry for the trouble," she snarled.

Tom glared at her.

"It was wrong of me," she added flatly.

"Thank you," I said.

Madge P. Groton backed out the door fast and ran down the hall. It was a great moment. Tom said she was going to work in another store and hoped that I would come in often and bring all my friends. I hoped the store was in Antarctica.

I clutched my $650 gift certificate and embraced budget-free shopping. I found the black pants that had started all the trouble—they were marked down 40 percent now—so I got them along with a cherry-apple-red pants suit and a leather jacket and four pairs of shoes and a silk blouse for my mother, who kept saying how proud she was that I had handled this by myself.

I guess I'd learned the truth about sharks: If one comes barrelling at you, the best thing to do is hit it in the nose.

SOMETIMES I FEEL JUDGED.

1. Exploring Meaning

a. Does the beginning of this story present a realistic view of family relationships? Is the dialogue realistic? Support your answer with examples.

b. Comment on the realism of Beth's character. Do you think she is a typical young adult? Explain.

c. What contributed to Madge Groton jumping to the conclusion that Beth was shoplifting?

d. Beth sees a similarity between her predicament and being attacked by a shark. How are the two situations similar? Do you think this is a good analogy? Why or why not?

e. Do you think Beth was adequately compensated for the injustice done to her?

f. Discuss the cartoon accompanying the story. In a group, brainstorm labels that could be printed on the mallet.

2. Writing *Performance Report* In role as the store manager, write a half-page performance report to place in Madge Groton's employment file. Before developing your report, discuss as a class what categories might be included, such as job knowledge, quality of work, ability to get along with others, initiative, and so on. Develop an overall grade such as Outstanding, Meets Expectations, or Marginal.

3. Language Conventions *Non-Standard Language* Joan Bauer uses several slang or non-standard words. Find three or four of these terms and define them. How does using non-standard language enhance or detract from the effectiveness of one's writing? In which formats is non-standard language appropriate? inappropriate?

4. Researching Research the rights of young people and find information about lobby groups that protect them. Consider young people's roles in society, such as consumers, employees, students, drivers, and so on. In a small group, develop a "know-your-rights" manual for young people. Clarify what their rights are and identify and describe situations in which young adults might need to challenge authority in order to protect their rights. Give advice on how young adults should respond in such situations.

Publish your manual using appropriate computer software. Select the most effective type faces and type sizes, and experiment with borders, shading, colour, and page layout to help you organize the content and communicate ideas.

Self-Assessment: Assess your manual and consider how effectively you have used design elements to communicate your ideas. Do your design elements hinder or help the reader?

5. Film Study In small groups, consider movies you have seen that portray teen or child empowerment (for example, *Finding Forrester*). What is the appeal of these movies? What similarities do they share? Are they more or less believable than this story? Why? Write a comparison-and-contrast essay comparing one of these films to "The Truth About Sharks."

During World War II, on August 6, 1945, Allied forces dropped an atomic bomb on Hiroshima. On August 9, another bomb was dropped on Nagasaki. Over a hundred thousand Japanese people died, and by the 1950s a further two hundred thousand died from their injuries or radiation.

Floating Lanterns XII

Poem by Iri Maruki and Toshi Maruki
Translated by Nancy Hunter and Yasuo Ishikawa

On August sixth every year
   the seven rivers of Hiroshima
   are filled with lanterns
Painted with the names of
   fathers, mothers, and sisters
   they float on their way to the sea

Almost there, pushed back
   flame snuffed out
Darkly coming back in pieces
Tossed by ocean waves

That time, years past
   these same rivers were filled
With the corpses of those
   fathers, mothers, and sisters

1. Exploring Meaning

a. How does the imagery in the first and last stanzas help you to understand the enormity of the tragedy at Hiroshima? Explain.

b. How does the second stanza symbolize the events of August 6, 1945?

c. The names of fathers, mothers, and sisters appear on the lanterns. In your opinion, why would the poet not have mentioned the names of sons?

d. What purpose would a memorial such as the one described in the poem have? Are similar purposes achieved by celebrations like Remembrance Day? Explain.

2. Researching Use the Internet to research the bombings of Hiroshima and Nagasaki. Begin by answering these questions: What led to the decision to drop the atomic bombs? What was the strategic objective of these actions? What judgments have historians made about these events? What other questions do you have about Hiroshima or Nagasaki?

Find descriptions, photos, or films of the aftermath of the bombings. Using the information you have researched, write your own poem about the bombings of Nagasaki or Hiroshima. Use the images you found in your research to illustrate your poem.

3. Oral Communication *Debate* In a small group, debate whether or not the Allies were justified in bombing Nagasaki and Hiroshima. Remember to listen to the arguments of your opponents and to respond to their arguments. **Group Assessment:** As a group, assess and discuss the effectiveness of your debate. What was the overall effect of the debate? Were the arguments coherent? supported? How effectively did you work together as a debating team?

In the aftermath of the attacks on the World Trade Center and the Pentagon in the United States, some Muslim Americans and Muslim Canadians found themselves fearing for their safety and questioning their place in society.

At War With Oneself

Essay by Ali Hossaini

Can I be at war with myself? Watching the World Trade Center collapse, then living through the aftermath, begs that absurd question. I'm American, with a Muslim name but nondescript appearance. No one takes me for Middle Eastern—I was born in West Virginia, and I'm only a quarter Arab. But thanks to the peculiarities of history, and naming, I have an Arab-American identity.

The attack on the World Trade Center puts me in an awful place. On the one hand, I've been deeply fortunate. Neither my loved ones nor I were injured. Like everyone else, I am horrified. I could have been there, munching a bagel on the observation deck. I can't imagine how someone could have planned such an attack, and my shock is turning to anger and mourning. At the same time, I feel excluded from the national unity that happens after such a tragedy. Why? As an Arab-American, I'm subject to reprisals. I'm nervous, wondering if I will somehow share the blame. Slurs, threats and even violence have already been levelled against anyone associated with Islam, and I wonder what will happen to me. I'm looking for work—will I be denied a job? What if a wider war breaks out? Will I lose my liberty?

Some friends have said I should go to Egypt for safety. They meant well, but their comments betrayed a misunderstanding that verges on racism. Hard as it is for the safely white to comprehend, there is only one place for me and other hyphenated Americans: the United States. America produced me. My grandparents hail from four different countries. Where else could they have created a family? If I'm out of place here, thanks to my name, I'm certainly out of place in the Middle East, where I stick out as an American. What is left for me? Do we have to pick sides in the end? And what can I do if neither side will have me, if both treat me as the enemy?

I'm at a loss to answer these questions, at least under the current logic. Some of my fellow citizens are striking out at American Muslims. Some are even calling for a firestorm to be rained upon Islamic nations. Don't they see that the terrorists had the same inspiration? The Afghans were caught between the Soviet Union and the United States for decades. Their country has been reduced to rubble. They have no hope. Violence occurs in cycles, and if we respond senselessly, striking innocent people in our search for criminals, then we'll create more radicals, more suicide bombers who embody the despair of poverty and war. The monopoly on violence is broken, and I shudder to think what comes next.

I'm living in fear, and my identity leaves me no shield. I often fly from Newark to San Francisco. Was the attack a one-time event or the first of many? Will I step onto a doomed jet? Will our cities ever feel safe? Then, again, what will I face in my day-to-day existence? Will I get mocked and beaten up? Are my tears for the dead less potent? Will my name become a Yellow Star that excludes me from society? Will I share in the collective healing that must come?

We are asked to choose sides, but my situation brings a clarity that opposes cries for war. From my hyphenated perspective, I see the absurdity of labels, indeed, of the whole idea that race, religion or flags divide humanity. I have a Muslim name, but my grandfather was Serbian. How would that fly in the Balkans?

I've wondered if I will ever have to choose a side. If so, here is my choice: pacifism and dialogue. I choose love; I choose humanity. I may symbolize Islam to some, and America to others, but I transcend these distinctions. I am proof that love conquers hate. My grandparents conquered tradition to found my family, and I stand tall as an American born from a unique and tolerant soil. What race produced me? The human race. Let me plead for understanding and compassion. Chase the criminals if you must, but let us then begin to fight. Let us fight not for oil, money or revenge, but for a world where hatred and weapons belong to a distant, barbaric past.

Exploring Meaning

In a small group, discuss the issues raised in "At War With Oneself." What is Ali Hossaini's thesis? What is his message? Respond to his views in your journal or another format of your choice.

The Right Honourable John G. Diefenbaker (prime minister from 1957 to 1963) moved the second reading of Bill No. C-79, to provide for the recognition and protection of human rights and fundamental freedoms. The following is an excerpt from his speech to the House of Commons on July 1, 1960.

Human Rights

Speech by the Right Honourable John Diefenbaker

Mr. Speaker, on this Dominion Day once more we think of the genius of the fathers of confederation and the contribution they made in their day and generation to the setting up of a national political organization which, despite the many vicissitudes of national and international events, has proven one of the most forward-looking constitutional accomplishments among the nations of the democratic world. Today we have reason for celebration when we look back over the years and recall that the purpose of the legislation which brought about confederation, in the words of its major architect, Sir John A. Macdonald, along with Sir George-Étienne Cartier, was "to make a great people and a great nationality."

We have been able during the intervening years to add steps which more and more have expanded the democratic rights of Canadians as a whole. At the present session, we have passed legislation which provides for the first citizens of Canada, the Indians, the full right of the exercise of the franchise, thus removing any suggestion that they or any other Canadians are in the position of being second-class citizens.

It is in this context that I rise for the purpose of speaking on a subject on which I have spoken through the years, which has to do with the maintenance and preservation of freedom against governments, however powerful they may be, for in the words of an organization which was set up some years ago by our great neighbour, the United States, "freedom is everybody's job." On this day there should be a realization of the responsibilities of citizenship, with pride in the achievements of the past, and the added assurance that individuals will know that henceforth under law they will at all times have preserved to them the rights and benefits of that institution.

These ten amendments cover the fundamental freedoms of religion, speech, and security of the individual. In general, they are those which, with the necessary additions that have to be made in the light of present day conditions, are in the bill of rights which I now bring to Parliament.

The bill in question can be summed up in a few words. In clause 2, the following fundamental freedoms are provided:

a) the right of the individual to life, liberty, security of the person and enjoyment of property—and the right not to be deprived thereof except by due process of law;

b) the right of the individual to protection of the law without discrimination by reason of race, national origin, colour, religion or sex—

Pausing there, Mr. Speaker, may I say that above everything else in the world today, there is no element more dangerous to the legions of freedom everywhere and to the nations which espouse freedom, than the practice of discrimination.

Clause 2 continues:

c) freedom of religion

d) freedom of speech

e) freedom of assembly and association; and

f) freedom of the press

I am going to set out some of the abuses which have taken place. I am not going to be partisan. I am going to quote from the submission of the committee for a bill of rights.

Why, then, is it now necessary to state explicitly in the constitutional document what is already implicit? The answer is that experience has shown that what is only implicit is in fact endangered by lack of recognition and acceptance, and that an explicit statement of rights is not only advisable to create public recognition of the fundamental basis of our society but also to prevent definite infringements of those rights. The exigencies of total war and the inevitable growth in the functions of government have naturally and inevitably resulted in a tendency to the abrogation of these civil rights.

Then it goes on to point out a few examples, and I know all of us regret those examples today. It says:

Under the sweeping powers conferred by the War Measures Act, the executive (or cabinet) in December 1945, some months after the cessation of hostilities and without reference to parliament, passed three orders in council, which if they had been enforced . . . would have exiled . . . to Japan some 11,000 or more persons of Japanese origin, a large proportion of whom were Canadian born citizens.

When we talk about discrimination and its dangers we recall that the only offence committed by these people in 99 percent of the cases, as it turned out subsequently, was their colour.

I wish to say that the bill of rights, as I see it, will deny the right of any government to interfere with my right to speak within the law, my right to be free from the threats of the activities of a police state, whether consciously or unconsciously administered. It will deny anyone the right to prevent me living my own life within the limits of the law without regard to race or colour or creed. It will remove from any government the right to deny me the right to belong to an unpopular minority anywhere in the country. It will deny any government, however powerful in the future, the right to deny recourse to the courts.

Those are some of the benefits that will come from the passage of this legislation.

I hope the house will support this measure. It is introduced on Dominion Day. It is one of those steps which represent the achievement and the assurance of that degree of liberty and freedom under law that was envisaged by the fathers of confederation. I think it embodies a pledge for all Canadians, a pledge which I place before you not as something original but changed to meet the fact that I am speaking in the Canadian Parliament.

I am a Canadian, a free Canadian, free to speak without fear, free to worship God in my own way, free to stand for what I think right, free to oppose what I believe wrong, free to choose those who shall govern my country. This heritage of freedom I pledge to uphold for all mankind and myself.

---

1. Exploring Meaning

a. In this speech, *July 1* is referred to as *Dominion Day*. What do we call this day now? Why does John Diefenbaker consider this date to be significant?

b. As Canadians, we often take pride in our country's reputation in regard to human rights. What evidence is given in this speech that our human-rights record has not been perfect? Are there other examples of Canada violating human rights? Explain.

c. Discuss what is meant in the following statement: "freedom is everybody's job."

2. Technique and Style *Audience and Purpose* With a partner, discuss the audience and purpose for Diefenbaker's speech. How does Diefenbaker's language reflect the formality of the occasion? What are some other occasions that would require formal language?

3. Oral Communication *Speech* Choose one of the following roles to respond to this speech:
- the leader of the Opposition
- a First Nations Chief
- a representative of any other group with a special interest in Bill C-79

As you develop your speech, reflect on how the context will affect your content. Consider your audience and purpose and what oratory devices you might use. Consider using repetition, rhetorical questions, and anecdotes.

4. Writing *Essay* Write an essay about a current human-rights issue. It could be a Canadian concern or one with a worldwide focus. You may need to research the situation further so that you can present all sides of the issue. As you develop your essay, choose one of the following organizational patterns for your thesis and arguments: cause and effect, problem-solution, comparison and contrast, or general to specific. Revise and edit your essay, ensuring that you have used punctuation to clarify meaning.
Self-Assessment: Assess the strengths and weaknesses in your writing skills. Are you stronger in developing ideas and weaker in the mechanics, such as grammar and punctuation, or vice versa? Develop an action plan to help you improve your writing skills.

5. Media *Documentary* Write a brief biographical sketch about John Diefenbaker and identify one or two of his important contributions to Canada. Present this information in a *Heritage Minute*-style documentary or on a Web page. If you choose to develop a Web page, include appropriate links to other sites.

The growing trade in animals, some of them rare species, poses dangers to public health and safety—and to the animals themselves.

Animal Wrongs

Magazine Article by Susan McClelland

At first, all that can be seen of Subira, a 2¹/₂-year-old lioness, are her amber eyes and a tuft of golden hair. Peering out from behind a shed at Aspen Valley Wildlife Sanctuary, 300 km north of Toronto, the big cat stands completely still, her head tilted and her gaze set on two people walking towards her pen. When the couple gets about 10 m away, Subira springs forward, closing the gap in huge bounds. Stopped by the wall of her cage, she paces back and forth, curiously sizing up the newcomers. When she recognizes her keeper, she turns kitten-like, languidly rubbing her back and side against the cage's steel meshing.

Such a cute image. Such a sordid story. Subira means "endurance" in Swahili, and the big cat has needed that quality in her initially miserable life. She was dumped into the exotic pet trade as a month-old cub—likely, authorities say, from an overstocked zoo. She was purchased at an auction in Alberta by a 17-year-old Vancouver girl, who soon realized she could not care for the growing lion and just locked it in a garage. She eventually sold Subira to two Penticton, British Columbia, men, but they, too, found lion ownership taxing. They couldn't find another buyer, however, and considered having the lion put down before Aspen Valley agreed to take the cat in.

When Subira arrived at the sanctuary, she was severely malnourished—at nine months of age, she weighed only 11 kg, the average size of a two-month-old cub. As well, the pads on her feet were cut, her nose was badly scratched and blood oozed from two large wounds on her forehead. She was in such a pathetic state that sanctuary founder Audrey Tournay felt compelled to take care of the lion even though her facility usually only rehabilitates animals native to Ontario. "I have seen many tragedies because of the wildlife trade," Tournay told *Maclean's*, "but I never get used to it."

A lion as a pet? It might sound outrageous, but there are few restrictions on ownership of wildlife, so the trade flourishes legally through classified advertisements in newspapers or trade magazines, at auctions and on the

Subira began life as a pet, an experience that nearly killed her. Photo by Rick Chard.

Internet. The majority of those exotic animals are imported birds and lizards that are sold by local shops to good homes. But more rare—and dangerous— imports are streaming into Canada, so the folks next door might someday acquire a wild cat, or a venomous snake or a rare monkey. That doesn't necessarily pose a problem if the animals are housed in enclosures that protect public safety, and if their owners are capable of caring for them. But too often, the animals suffer at the hands of ignorant or abusive owners. Lucky ones such as Subira are rescued and rehabilitated, but others end up dying prematurely from living in deplorable conditions, being killed for their body parts or sold to shooting ranches.

In Canada, there is little to stop that from continuing. The maximum sentence for cruelty to animals under the Criminal Code is six months in jail and a $2,000 fine. Some species are protected in certain provinces—Quebec has an Act Respecting the Conservation and Development of Wildlife, which, among other things, regulates animals in captivity. But there are no national endangered-species or animal-welfare laws. In fact, when the federal Liberals suspended Parliament prior to the 2000 election, the species-at-risk act, which would have offered some protection to wild animals on the Canadian Endangered Species List, died before gaining final approval. The suspension also killed proposed Criminal Code amendments that would have imposed longer sentences and heftier fines for animal abuse. "The public thinks there is more protection out there for animals than there is," says Shelagh MacDonald, program director for the Canadian Federation of Humane Societies in Ottawa.

There is more than just a shortfall of legislation. Traditional animal-welfare organizations such as local humane societies are generally geared to caring for domestic animals like cats and dogs. And the few wildlife sanctuaries, such as the one north of Toronto, are strained beyond capacity. "When they hear about abuse of captive wildlife, Canadians are outraged," MacDonald says. "What they don't realize is how much of this we actually see."

The trade of wildlife is a huge industry. No single agency keeps global statistics, but experts calculate that the legal side of the business is annually worth $15 billion worldwide, and millions in Canada. Law-enforcement agencies conservatively estimate the worldwide value of the illicit trade in wild animals at more than $10 billion a year. That makes the black market for things such as rare species and animal body parts worth more annually than the illegal traffic in arms. It is exceeded by the traffic in illegal drugs.

The pet trade has long been linked to narcotic smuggling. A U.S. fish and wildlife service report claimed that more than one-third of all cocaine seized in 1993 was connected to pet importation. That year, officials at Miami International Airport found several hundred boa constrictors from Colombia stuffed with 35 kg of cocaine. Most of the snakes were dead on arrival. Bruce Bagley, an international relations professor and drug-trade expert at the University of Miami, says narcotic smugglers frequently started out in the legal business of exporting animals. "Since the 1960s, Colombian drug lords have been involved in dealing wildlife," says Bagley. "They would get known by customs, so no one was suspicious later when cocaine got smuggled with the animals."

Usually, though, the pets themselves are the contraband, and because the United States is the biggest market, dealers often route their illicit cargo through Canada. In 2000, Michael and Harold Flikkema of Fenwick, Ontario, were convicted of smuggling as many as 12,000 tropical and rare finches from Africa into Europe and Canada, and then to the United States. "Enforcement at the borders isn't always secure," says Nathalie Chalifour of World Wildlife Fund, "making Canada a good conduit to the United States."

The problem is not new. Back in 1973, alarmed by the impact of the commercial trade on populations of rare animals, wildlife experts drafted the Convention on International Trade in Endangered Species of Wild Fauna and Flora—known as CITES. Today, Canada is one of 152 nations that are signatories to CITES, which, among other things, bans international trade in endangered species and attempts to control traffic in threatened species through a permit system. But while CITES has made it more difficult to legally trade certain animals, the industry has still grown exponentially. In Canada, 7,400 live animals were imported or exported in 1993 with CITES permits. By 1997, the most recent year for which Canadian import-export statistics are available, more than 25,000 CITES permits were issued.

Even conventional pets can be hazards. Dogs can bite; cats can scratch. But exotic species pose a far more serious threat to public health, particularly since there are no federal licensing standards for pet-shop operators. Salmonella bacteria, including strains resistant to antibiotics, have been found on pets such as turtles, snakes, iguanas and lizards. And some primates, which are increasingly popular as pets, are suspected by scientists of carrying a number of deadly viruses. In 1997, a 22-year-old lab assistant at Atlanta's Emory University died from herpes B after coming into contact with bodily fluid from a rhesus macaque. And there are fears that some primates even carry HIV and the Ebola virus. "HIV appears to have come from chimpanzees," says Darrel Cook, lab manager at the B.C. Centre for Disease Control in Vancouver, "the same with herpes viruses that don't cause problems for the monkeys but are fatal to humans." Cook added ominously: "There are all kinds of health risks in the wildlife trade. We just don't know what they all are yet."

There are other safety risks. In 1994, a 16-year-old boy in Hanover, Ontario, died of a broken neck after being bitten by one of his uncle's two Siberian tigers. In 1999, a 71-year-old woman in Clearview, New Brunswick, required 409 stitches to close gashes on and around her head after she was attacked by her neighbour's Eurasian lynx. The victim had stopped by the house to drop off a birthday present. And in spring 2000, a venomous saw-scale viper—considered one of the most deadly snakes on earth—caused the evacuation of a city block in Toronto when it slithered free from its terrarium. A single bite from a saw-scale viper can be fatal, and at that time the closest facility known to have antivenin was in the United States. The snake was eventually found behind a baseboard. Despite a Toronto bylaw banning the ownership of venomous snakes, the saw-scale viper was one of 13 reptiles and a tarantula that Kent Parsons kept in his apartment. Many of the snakes have since been put down by the local health authority, and Parsons was fined $14,000.

The proliferation of such pets has forced some governments to act. Since 1976, the Dangerous Wild Animals Act has required pet owners in Great Britain to license their hazardous animals and pass inspections ensuring that both the public and the animals are protected. Yet in Canada, such regulations are rare. Fewer than a quarter of all municipalities have an exotic-animal bylaw, and even one that does, King Township north of Toronto, is currently having to take legal action to force a local motorcycle gang to give up its pet lion. Still, Maple Ridge, about 45 km east of Vancouver, is at least attempting to implement a bylaw that would ban the ownership of dangerous animals, including venomous reptiles. The law would also prohibit the trading of some species, including big cats such as lions and tigers, bears and crocodiles.

Port Colborne, Ontario, a tourist town southwest of Niagara Falls, hadn't seen the need to outlaw private ownership of wildlife until recently. "If we ban these pets, the problems won't go away—people will still own these animals," says Mayor Vance Badawey. Yet the city's council is scheduled to debate its new exotic-pet bylaw. Why? Because of the arrival in 2000 of Michael Baran and his $2-million snake collection. Baran claims to have 3,000 venomous snakes, including East African gaboon vipers, green mambas, king cobras and blackheaded bushmasters, which he sells on his company's Web site for as much as $4,500 each.

His business, Dragon Farms, is located in a warehouse a block from City Hall. In the approximately 150-square-metre facility, the snakes reside in large terrariums stacked atop one another. Narrow corridors allow staff, who visit only twice a week, to get in to feed and water the snakes. One staff member told British biologist and snake expert Clifford Warwick the cages are cleaned only when they begin to smell rancid. "These snakes are living in deplorable conditions," says Warwick, who toured Dragon Farms. "And there is little preventing the animals from escaping to the street. Any number of scenarios can lead to a person touching or falling against mesh lids and being bitten." Baran, however, claims his collection poses no threat to the public because his snakes cannot escape. He also says the city is wrongfully bullying him to close his doors. "They can't dictate to me," he said. "It's as simple as that."

The poster animal for the worst aspects of the pet trade could be Oso, a grizzly bear. Oso was captured as a cub in the wild after a hunter killed his mother. His first home in captivity was a travelling circus, where, like most performing bears, he was declawed and had his front teeth removed. When he outgrew his cubby cuteness, he was sold to a man in Sudbury, Ontario, and when the man moved away, Oso was left behind, locked in a cage with no food or water.

Barely alive when he was discovered more than three weeks later, Oso was taken in and partially rehabilitated by people in Belleville, Ontario, who then sold Oso to a collector. Over time, his weight dropped to 136 kg from 340, and at one point in 1997, he was nearly sold for his organs. But he was rescued by Bear With Us, a sanctuary near Huntsville, Ontario. "No matter what people say, there is no education value to owning wildlife," says Michael McIntosh, founder of Bear With Us. "It's just a fulfilment of someone's ego."

In the summer of 2000, Oso died of a heart attack at age 15—less than half the usual lifespan of a grizzly. A veterinarian said the premature death was caused by years of abuse, although none of Oso's previous owners were ever charged. But that's how it goes in the wildlife trade. Animals are often sold with little regard for their welfare, or for the safety of the public at large. And without a serious commitment to legislative protection and enforcement in Canada, there is little hope for change.

Exotic Pets For Sale
Some wild animals are as easy to acquire, and occasionally as inexpensive, as common pets such as purebred dogs or cats. But even truly exotic animals, including rare species, are readily available. *Maclean's* surveyed classified ads, online providers and pet shops and found the following animals available:

Baby monkeys, marmosets, lemurs and capuchins	$2,500 to $10,000
Galah cockatoo (a parrot imported from Australia)	$3,000
Wolverine (endangered in some parts of Canada)	$30,000
Green iguana (endangered in some parts of central and South America)	$49.99
Cougar	$1,200
King cobra	$900

1. Exploring Meaning

a. Susan McClelland develops her article by extensive use of examples. What makes this an effective strategy? Which example had the most impact on you? Why?

b. Why is there a trade in exotic pets? What motivates the dealers? What motivates the buyers? Discuss solutions to stopping the trade.

c. Who are the people and organizations that benefit from the exploitation of wild animals? Are there others that the author does not mention?

2. Technique and Style *Organization* The last two sentences in the article provide an excellent conclusion because they clearly state the thesis. Briefly list the details in the article that support this thesis. Why has McClelland chosen to put the thesis at the end of the article rather than clearly stating it at the beginning?

Examine the first sentence of each paragraph. How does McClelland vary her sentence structure to increase the impact of the story? How does she grab the readers' interest and set the tone for the article in the introductory paragraph?

3. Film Study View clips from a number of films, both animated and live action, about animals. To what extent do these films shape people's views about animals? What do you think is meant by the phrase, "the Bambi syndrome"? Write a short essay expressing your opinion about how animals are either used in the making of Hollywood films or portrayed in Hollywood films.

The Unjiggable Cod

Poem by Marian Frances White

They say you can't fish here anymore
unless you're a tourist
just when a record number of women
take to the boats
sure Theresa McCann sold her washing machine for a
    punt
rowed away to laughter pealing from the wharf
that subsided when she hauled in an oversize catch
long before the cod moratorium, of course
beginner's luck, they called it
until the fishing season ended
and her catch outdid theirs

All winter the men fought to win her
at the stern of their boat
all winter the Feds plotted
to tie up the fishing nets for good
despite this she refused to exchange the punt
back for the washing machine
all winter she hauled her clothes to the shore
broke ice and scrubbed to the wail of the boats lapping

Nothing was the same, ever after
not the sound of punts lazily drifting out to sea
as if on vacation
nor the way the oars broke water
on a perfectly windless day
nor the screech of gulls crying hopelessly for caplin

The courting season ceased
tourists enjoy the bay now
talk of the regal line of boats anchored
as if for their viewing pleasure
drop anchor long enough to jig[1]
the elusive cod
an artifact of a time
long before washing machines
and tourists

Marine's Geometry by Jean-Claude Girardin. Oil on canvas.

---

[1] **jig:** to fish with a jig, which is a lure weighted with bright metal.

1. Exploring Meaning

a. What background knowledge or information does the reader need to understand the poem? Discuss the poem's context with a partner. Why can't the local fishers fish anymore? What is the cod moratorium referred to in the poem?

b. Describe Theresa McCann. Do you think you would like her? Why or why not?

c. What does the author mean by "The courting season ceased"? What has happened?

d. Choose one image from the poem and explain its meaning and significance.

2. Critical Thinking In a small group, discuss the current state of Canadian fisheries. In which areas of the country are moratoriums in place? How have the communities that have been affected dealt with the moratoriums? Beyond their concerns about changes to their way of life, what complaints might people in these communities have about the moratoriums? You may have to conduct background research to effectively answer these questions.

Write an editorial expressing your views on the issues raised in the poem and through your research. Ask a classmate for feedback on your editorial. Are the issues clear? Have facts and examples supported any arguments?

With a partner, discuss what you know about Louis Riel.

A Thousand Supperless Babes: The Story of the Metis

Play Excerpt by Suntep Theatre

Honoré Jaxon was Louis Riel's secretary. For more than sixty years he collected and kept together literally tons of manuscripts and notes from Riel's life and the Metis Nation. He kept them in a New York apartment where he served as janitor until 1951 when he was evicted at the age of ninety. The documents went to the New York City dump.

INTRODUCTION

SONG: *"Honoré" by James Keelaghan (Song begins, then fade in sound of the street.)*

Honoré's huddled near East Fifty-third
His life in a pile not too far from the curb
It's come down to this place, but he's not too deterred
Honoré's huddled near East Fifty-third

Honoré sits on the Lower East Side
He's lost about everything except for his pride
A man with a vision the vision's denied
Honoré sits on the Lower East Side

They used to say Honoré wasn't all there
He'd a penchant for speeches and thousand-yard stares
They said that he'd fought when some halfbreeds rebelled
Sometimes he would weep and he'd whisper "Riel"

> STREET SCENE: *Three* WORKERS *haul boxes out from backstage and stack them along the front of the stage (perhaps as the audience is being seated). This is an open stage with other actors creating the atmosphere of a New York City street by entering and exiting as hawkers, vendors, buskers, hop-scotchers, and just plain passers-by. Quick mini-scenes occur between them, until someone somewhere blows a whistle and they freeze.*

THE NARRATOR: It's New York City, December 13, 1951, and it's very cold. This is a brownstone building on the Lower East Side of New York City, an apartment building where the janitor has just been fired. Ninety-year-old Honoré Jaxon has been fired because he's too old to do his job. The workers that you see are haul-ing out all of his possessions from the basement. It's going to take them six hours to haul three tons of material out onto this sidewalk in New York City. When they're done, there will be a pile of boxes 11 meters long, 3 meters high, and 2 meters deep. In those boxes is a lifetime of work, a dream that he had, to save all that he could of the history of the Metis people. And so, over his lifetime, he col-lected photographs, journals, articles, anything he could find, to keep the story of the Metis alive. So it's New York City, 1951, and the old janitor is in the hos-pital with pneumonia while all his life's possessions are being hauled out onto the street . . . And sometimes he would weep and he would whisper "Riel."

SCENE: WORKERS

WORKER #1: I didn't know anyone could have so much garbage!

WORKER #2: Yeah, I can't believe the stuff this guy had. What a bunch of junk!

WORKER #3: It's gonna take forever to get this stuff out!

WORKER #1: Well, let's go for another load. (*#1 and #2 exit. #3 opens an old trunk and finds a dusty book. #1 and #2 return with another load.*)

WORKER #1: What are you doing?

WORKER #3: I found a book.

WORKER #2: A book about nothing, I suppose!

WORKER #3: Well . . . let's find out.

WORKER #1: Hey guys, let's have lunch, okay?

WORKER #2: Sounds great to me. (*They sit on boxes and open their lunch kits.*)

WORKER #1: What'd you bring for lunch?

WORKER #2: Sandwiches. I think I've got a coupla boiled eggs. Wanna sniff?

WORKER #1: No way!

WORKER #2: Oh, and a can of sardines. All right!

WORKER #3: Listen to this. "It is an incredible and moving story . . ." (*Voice fades as Narration begins.*)

The Capture of Batoche by Sergeant Grundy and other artists. Colour lithograph.

SCENE ONE

NARRATION # 1: It is an incredible and continuing story . . . the story of the Metis. It is a story that I, Honoré Jaxon, have dedicated my life to tell . . . in the hope that it shall serve as an example for the downtrodden of our world . . . and as a lesson to the privileged and powerful, that the voices of everyday people everywhere shall not be silenced . . . we shall be heard!

SCENE: WORKERS

WORKER #3: "We shall be heard!" There you go. What about that!

WORKER #2: What's he talking about?

WORKER #1: Who's the "Matey"?

WORKER #2: Yeah, really . . . who are the "Matey"?

WORKER #3: Listen. (*Reading.*) "You may indeed ask 'Who are the Metis?' " . . . There you go. Maybe if you sit down and listen long enough, your questions will be answered. (*Continues.*) "It is a question many have asked . . ." (*Fades.*)

NARRATION #2: It is a question that many have asked . . . a question that continues to be asked . . . a question that Metis people themselves will struggle to answer . . . if they are ever asked!

And so I have gathered about me a lifetime of work: the notes and diaries of my life among the Metis of St. Laurent and Batoche, the minutes of meetings that I recorded when I was secretary and friend to the great Louis Riel, the photographs and interviews and memories of my visits to Canada's North-West, and the secret stories that were told to me as I prepared to tell this story. A story that must be told. And so I will begin . . .

SCENE: WORKERS

WORKER #3: Sounds interesting, eh?

WORKER #2: Sounds like a bunch of garbage to me!

WORKER #1: Come on, let's get back to work.

WORKER #3: You guys finished lunch already?

WORKER #2: Yeah, let's go. (*#1 and #2 get up to leave.*)

WORKER #3: Well, I'm not quite done. I haven't had a chance to eat yet. I'll be right there. (*#1 and #2 exit. #3 continues reading.*) "The Metis people were created with one, and only one, purpose in mind . . ."

SCENE TWO

Narration #3: The Metis people were created with one, and only one, purpose, in mind—to serve the capitalist system.

As the fur trade expanded across this continent, the wealthy merchants of England and New France needed a labour force to do all the work. They needed men who would work long hours and the longest of days . . . who would travel long distances away from home and family . . . who would be instant friends of the Indians of the North-West . . . And all of this for the lowest of pay. In their own words, they needed a colony of "very . . . useful . . . hands."

And so it was a carefully calculated plan that white traders should befriend Indian women, and raise their children to serve the wealthy fur merchants of the North-West and Hudson's Bay Companies . . . a ready-made working class, bred and born . . . to be exploited by the capitalists.

Many fur traders already had families in the East or in Europe . . .

Tableau (*Trader and family, facing audience.*)

Narration #4: . . . but they were encouraged to take wives among the Indian women of the North-West . . . and to start new families.

Tableau (*Mother and children have their backs to the audience.*)

Narration #5: Of course, these new families could not be allowed in the white forts and settlements . . . so most traders eventually went away and left them on their own.

Tableau (*Only mother and children, facing audience. Trader's chair is empty.*)

Narration #6: And that is how the Metis were . . . conceived.

* * *

SCENE ELEVEN

Narration #31: They are a great people, the Metis . . . the mixed blood people of the North-West. Like other people the world over they have survived all that governments and the wealthy have thrown against them. You see, this is not a world where justice is given freely. It is a world of injustice and oppression, where "a thousand babes go supperless to bed that one monster's brat may spew on silk."

At the age of 90 years, my story is nearly over, but the story of the Metis continues on. In my lifetime, I have seen no struggle that has touched my heart and spirit like that of the Metis. Their survival, their struggle for equality, gives me great hope. And so I, Honoré Jaxon, ask that this book and all of my papers and photographs be given to the Metis people that they may teach each other, and others as well . . . of their great history.

WORKERS: FINAL SCENE

(WORKERS *#1 and #2 enter with the last of the boxes, just as* WORKER *#3 closes the book.*)

WORKER #1: Well, that's it. That's the last of the boxes.

WORKER #2: Good thing too! I'm tired!

WORKER #1: Well, let's call it a day. I'm going home.

WORKER #2: Me too. I've had enough.

WORKER #3: What about all this stuff? All these boxes, these books, these photographs?

WORKER #1: What about them?

WORKER #2: It's not our problem anymore. The city will take care of all this stuff.

WORKER #3: What do you mean?

WORKER #1: It's all going to the dump. Where did you think it was going?

WORKER #3: But somebody must want it. They can't just throw all this away?

WORKER #2: Why not? It's just garbage. Who would want it?

WORKER #1: Come on, let's go. Let's call it a day. (*#1 and #2 begin to exit.*) Are you coming?

WORKER #3: (*Looks at all the boxes.*) Yeah . . . yeah, I'm coming. I'll be right there. (WORKERS *#1 and #2 exit. The music begins.*)

> **SONG:** *"Honoré" (Final verses.* WORKER *#3 looks at the boxes, then at the book in her hands. She opens the book, leafs slowly through it, then closes it and places it carefully on the pile of Honoré's lifetime of work. She turns slowly away and leaves. Before she exits, she turns for one last look at the "archives" and then exits. The song fades.*)

Honoré's buried in some pauper's grave
Of his archives there wasn't much to be saved
Forty-nine boxes of books hauled away
And a deed for some land in a place called Duck Lake

Honoré was all he said so it seems
The last act of life left him far from his dreams
They took it away it can't be redeemed
Honoré was all he said so it seems

NARRATOR: The lifetime of work of Honoré Jaxon, what he had dreamed would become an archives for the Metis people, was loaded onto a truck and hauled away to the New York City dump. Jaxon died less than one month later, on January 10, 1952.

SONG: *"Honoré" (Final chorus)*

They used to say Honoré wasn't all there
He'd a penchant for speeches and thousand-yard stares
They said that he'd fought when some halfbreeds rebelled
Sometimes he would weep and he'd whisper "Riel"
Sometimes he would weep and he'd whisper "Riel"

VOICES (*The actors enter, one at a time, to speak out-of-role to the audience.*)

VOICE #1: We do not mourn the loss of Honoré Jaxon's lifetime of work.

VOICE #2: Instead, we celebrate both his story and the story of the Metis people.

VOICE #3: Our history does not just lie on a shelf, or in books, or in a basement full of cardboard boxes.

VOICE #4: Our history lies in the stories that are told to us by our parents and grandparents. It lies within us.

VOICE #5: Stories are gifts. They last forever. And they tell us who we are.

VOICE #6: The history of the Metis lives on in the memories of its survivors. We are those survivors.

VOICE #7: My name is Angela Johns and I am the great-great-granddaughter of Isadore and Judith Dumont. I am very proud of how my family fought for our Metis rights.

VOICE #8: My name is Janet Goller . . .

VOICE #9: . . . and I'm Celine Mauvieux. We are the great-great-granddaughters of Christine Pilon.

VOICE #8: We are very proud to pass on her stories.

VOICE #8 & 9: Our family heritage.

VOICE #10: My name is Leanne Lasher. I am the granddaughter of Philoman Pelletier Allary. My grandmother was a great lady in her community. Unfortunately, I didn't get a chance to meet her, but I know it's not too late to know about who she was.

VOICE #11: My name is Gina. I am the great-granddaughter of Alex and Angeline Gouldhawke. I know that my grandfather would be pleased to know his Metis grandchildren no longer have to hide on either side of the aisle.

Voice #12: My name is Tracy and it's my grandmother's story about residential schools that I told. There are many stories coming out about residential schools and the life and times back then. There are still many to tell.

Voice #13: (Narrator): My name is Ben. I am a Cree Metis from northern Manitoba. The word "Metis" has come to represent mixed-blood people all across Canada. Together we have many more stories to tell.

> **SONG:** *"When This Valley" by Don Freed (As they sing, the cast frames the screen and the final photographs of Metis men, women, children, elders. The lights gradually fade to black. During the last verse, the cast moves slowly together and joins hands across the stage.)*

When this valley's no longer a wound that won't heal
When its story is well understood
Let infinity fly where the blue of the sky
Meets the green of the river and gold of the straw
In the valley of old St. Laurent.

When this valley was young it was peaceful and free
And its citizens were friends to all
If a stranger was cold or hungry or old
They were taken well care of by an unwritten law
In the valley of old St. Laurent.

When the names of its people are held to the heart
Of a land that was built of their blood
Shamrock, thistle, oak tree, sweetgrass, fleur-de-lis
All entwined in a braid a hanged poet foresaw
In the valley of old St. Laurent.

1. Exploring Meaning

a. Before reading "A Thousand Supperless Babes," what did you know about the Métis people? What new knowledge did you gain from reading this play?

b. What does the title mean? Is it a suitable title for this selection? Explain. If you do not think this is a suitable title, think of another more suitable one.

c. What do Honoré Jaxon's boxes of documents, photos, and memorabilia of the Métis represent? What does the New York City dump represent?

2. Oral Communication *Monologue* At one point in the play, one of the voices says, "Our history lies in the stories that are told to us by our parents and grandparents. It lies within us." Think about your family history told to you by your parents, grandparents, or other family members. Prepare a three-minute monologue about your personal history. Present this monologue to the class.

Performance Tip: Pronunciation, articulation, and projection are all especially important in presenting a monologue. You may find it helpful to think of your voice as something tangible, like a ball, that you are throwing to an audience using the power of your lungs and diaphragm. Remember that volume is an important part of projection, but not all of it. Practise projecting a whisper across a crowded room.

3. Writing *Interview* Conduct research about Louis Riel. Think of five questions you would like to ask Riel if you were to meet him. Then, imagine how Riel would respond. Develop an interview from these questions and your imagined responses.

4. Drama *Performance* With a small group, plan a presentation of one of the scenes in the play. Consider how you will use your voice—volume, tone, pace, expression—to portray the emotion.

Guide to Communication

Contents

Guide to Communication

WRITING A REPORT

A written report documents facts, information, and sometimes opinions about a specific topic. In school, you may be asked to write a report either to show your teacher that you've done adequate research on your topic (and have presented the information in a logical way); or to present the information in a lively, interesting way to your teacher and other students.

The following information can be helpful when writing a report:

Organization

A report should be *organized logically*, so that a reader can easily follow what you are saying. Reports can be arranged in the following ways:

- by **feature** or **characteristic** (for example, a report comparing two makes of computer; or a report that describes a new machine or invention)
- by **time sequence** (for example, a report that looks at the history of Canada's involvement in the space program; or a report on the process of metamorphosis in insects)
- by **order of importance**—from most to least important, or from least to most important (for example, a report that examines the impact that a road will have on a wilderness area)

You can use more than one kind of arrangement in the same report, as in the outline that follows. Note, however, that the overall organization in the example is by feature.

TOPIC: SKATEBOARDING	
Main Idea	Supporting Details
I. History of skateboarding	*arranged by time sequence*
II. Benefits of skateboarding	*has most important ideas at beginning and end of the section*
III. Safety precautions	*moves from most important to least important*
IV. Buying a skateboard	*arranged from the least important choice to the most important choice (the kind of skateboard being recommended)*

Style

- Use formal language.
- Use the third person (*he, she, they, it*).
- Try to adopt a factual, objective tone (avoid using words with strong good or bad connotations) that will convince your reader of the accuracy of the information you are presenting.
- Linking words that make connections between paragraphs and between sentences within paragraphs will help to make the report flow more smoothly, and clarify the connections among ideas.

Format

- If the report is longer than two pages, add a cover page. Include the report title, your name, the teacher's name, and the due date. Check whether your teacher would like information on the cover page arranged in a certain way.
- Use headings to help make the information in your report easier to find. Set off headings using capital letters, boldfacing, italics, or underlining. Leave a line of space before and after each heading.
- Give a source for all of the ideas and quotations you used in your report, and include any necessary citations and footnotes. (See below for notes on quotations, citations, and footnotes.)

Quotations, Citations, and Footnotes

Quotations

- Beginning your report with a quotation is a good way to grab the attention of your readers. Consult some dictionaries of quotations for ideas. Larger collections of these may be found in the reference section of your library, while some smaller collections are available on the Internet. Remember to double-check all quotations found on the Internet for accuracy.

  Bartlett's Familiar Quotations is a good resource for quotations from literary and historical sources, but there are many other resources from which to choose. For example, *Colombo's Canadian Quotations* contains quotations by Canadian politicians, writers, celebrities, and public figures on a variety of topics.
- Although you should mostly write in your own words, using a direct quotation from a reliable source is a good way to support one of your ideas or arguments. Remember to credit the person whom you are quoting, setting his or her words in quotation marks, and giving a source for the quotation.
- Be careful not to change a quotation's meaning by taking parts of it out of context (that is, by using it in a way that was not intended). For example, if a movie reviewer sarcastically calls a movie "the most exciting action picture

since *The Sound of Music*," it would be unfair to quote him or her as saying the movie was a "most exciting action picture."

Citations

In reports and essays, either include citations within the body of the text, or add footnotes at the bottom of the page to list the source of quotations, charts, tables, diagrams, and all ideas other than your own.

Here are some general guides for writing citations:

- Place the author's name and the page number(s), if appropriate, in parentheses after the borrowed material. If the citation is at the end of a sentence, the period should follow the citation.

  "The Arctic is mostly water—with ice on top, of course—and that ice is never more than a few feet thick" (Armstrong 1).

- If what you have written tells readers which author you are crediting, you don't need to repeat that author's name in the citation.

  According to Jennifer Armstrong, "The Arctic is mostly water—with ice on top, of course—and that ice is never more than a few feet thick" (1).

  As Teri Degler reminds us, "Even if the average temperature went up only 10°C, some of the ice at the North and South Poles might melt and raise the level of the oceans" (15), which would be catastrophic for low-lying countries like Bangladesh.

- If you refer to more than one work by the same author in your report, include a shortened version of the title. For example, if you mentioned two of Alice Munro's short stories—perhaps "Miles City, Montana" and "Jesse and Meribeth"—you could refer to (Munro, "Miles" 119) or (Munro, "Jesse" 249) in your citations.

Footnotes

For footnotes, instead of placing information in the text, put a small raised number at the end of the cited material, and a footnote with the same raised number at the bottom of the page, separated from the text by a short line (about ten spaces long). Indent the first line of the footnote. Check out the example at the right:

The first time you cite a source, give the full reference. For all subsequent references, cite only the author's last name and the page number.

  [2]Armstrong 22.

"The Arctic is mostly water— with ice on top, of course—and that ice is never more than a few feet thick." [1]

---

[1] Jennifer Armstrong, *Shipwreck at the Bottom of the World: The Extraordinary True Story of Shackleton and the Endurance* (New York: Crown, 1998) 1.

Here are some other sample footnote references:

- **book with more than one author**

  [3] Ann-Maureen Owens and Jane Yealland, *Canada's Maple Leaf: The Story of Our Flag* (Toronto: Kids Can Press, 1999) 5–6.

- **work in an anthology**

  [4] Duke Redbird, "I Am a Canadian," *An Anthology of Canadian Native Literature in English*, eds. Daniel David Moses and Terry Goldie, 2nd ed. (Toronto: Oxford University Press, 1998) 120.

- **magazine**

  [5] David Jarzen, "Pollen Power," *Owl*, Mar. 1997: 12.

- **newspaper article**

  [6] Réal Gross, "Slug Found in Milk Bottle," *The Middleton Mercury*, 15 Oct. 2000: A1.

- **video or film**

  [7] Ole Gjerstad and Martin Kreelak, dir., *Journey to Nunavut: The Kreelak Story*, National Film Board of Canada, 1999.

- **CD-ROM**

  [8] "Film Animation," *The Canadian Encyclopedia*, World ed., CD-ROM (Toronto: McClelland & Stewart, 1996).

- **Internet text selection**

  Include the Web site's address and the date that you accessed the information.

  [9] "Communities Use Radar Satellite to Gauge Ice Breakup," *Nunatsiaq News*, Internet, 14 May 1999: http://www.(Web site address).

- **interview**

  [10] T. Jai Singh, personal interview, 10 March 2000.

ORAL REPORT

An oral report is a report presented out loud, in front of a group or an audience. Even though the content of an oral report can be similar to that of a written report, it can be presented in different ways, using a variety of aids—such as computer graphics, slides, and working models—to help clarify or reinforce specific points. Some common forms of oral reports are presentations, demonstrations, and speeches.

Purpose and Audience

The purpose of an oral report is the same as that of a written report. The audience may consist of your classmates, your teacher, or both. Occasionally, you may be asked to present an oral report to another class or group. In business, oral reports are often presented to managers or colleagues to give them a quick overview of a situation or plan.

Organization

Oral reports are usually organized in the same way as written reports.
- Ensure that you prepare your presentation in an organized, logical manner.
- Include relevant facts, details, and examples to support what you are saying.

Style

When you deliver an oral report, your audience will not have a chance to go back and reread if they miss something. Therefore, to help them follow your presentation, you can provide them with clues that will lead them to anticipate what you are going to say. Here are some suggestions:
- At the beginning of your presentation, state your thesis clearly and give your audience an idea of how you will go about proving or supporting it. For example:

    I believe that the wetlands must be saved for three important reasons.

    OR

    The main stages in metamorphosis are egg, larva, pupa, and adult. I will describe each of these stages in turn.

- Use linking words such as *first, second, third*, etc., to connect paragraphs and ideas.
- Every so often, summarize what you have said and what remains to be said. For example:

    So far, we have looked at the difference between the egg and the larva stage of metamorphosis. Now, we need to look at the last two stages in the process: pupa and adult.

- Repeat specific words or ideas several times throughout the presentation to reinforce key points.
- Don't try to include too much information in a single presentation. Where possible, present your information in groups of threes: three sections, three reasons, three stages, etc. Grouping information in this way helps the audience to remember what you are saying.
- Explain any technical terms you use to your audience.
- Use facial expressions, gestures, pauses, and changes in your tone of voice to draw attention to important points.
- Consider using slide shows, overheads, charts, posters, or the chalkboard if these will help your audience to understand your ideas and make connections.
- Leave a little time at the end of your presentation for questions.

YOUR RÉSUMÉ IS YOUR ADVERTISEMENT

Article by Janis Foord Kirk

Controversy swirls around résumés most of the time and a firm consensus has never emerged about what they should say, what they shouldn't say, how long and how detailed should they be.

Still, some common factors exist. Employers today, faced with hundreds of résumés, generally want yours to be direct, to the point, easy to read and targeted.

Many résumé theories abound. One theory is that job seekers today need at least two résumés. The first needs to be a short, concise, brochure-like document. The second can be much lengthier, providing considerably more detail and offered later in the interview process. The belief is, once employers are genuinely interested in you, they'll want to know more.

Regardless of its length, be sure that your résumé finds ways to provide employers with answers to some of the questions that generally preoccupy them as they screen résumés.

• Who are you and how can I contact you?
• What do you want to do? Are you qualified to do it?
• What experience backs up your application?
• What education, training and skills back up your application?
• What have you accomplished to support your goals?

The real power of your résumé will depend, in large part, on how well you answer the last of these questions; what accomplishments from your working, education or volunteer life support your objectives?

Writing Your Résumé

Before attempting to create your résumé, prepare a list of personal information, including name, address, telephone number, schools attended, graduation year (if applicable), and employment history. Then make a list of your skills and abilities. Be honest with yourself and resourceful, too. Include hobbies, volunteer work, and club memberships that may have helped you to develop different skills. If you have a short work history, these facts can help to "beef" up your résumé.

Once you've assessed your skills, the challenging part begins. The following list of suggested rules should prove helpful to you in the preparation of your résumé.

1. Present your résumé in a clear, well-laid-out manner, on quality white paper. Do not use "gimmick" paper, colours, or styles. Your résumé should include:
   • personal information (name, address, phone numbers, e-mail address)
   • career goal or objective
   • summary of skills
   • work history (volunteer work, babysitting, part-time jobs, summer jobs, school work programs, co-operative education)

- education
  - achievements (diplomas, trophies, prizes)

2. Input your résumé.

3. Do not date your résumé.

4. Put your career goal near the beginning. Since many people "scan" down the résumé, it is important that you "grab" their attention right away.

5. Keep your résumé neat and brief. If possible limit it to two pages. Use point form to list information. Compress lengthy sentences into short statements. Your résumé will be easier to read and understand if it is concise.

6. Do not make mistakes in spelling and grammar. These kinds of errors make your résumé look unprofessional and spoil your chance to make a good impression.

7. Be honest. No one wants to hire someone who lies or exaggerates. Your résumé must accurately recap your background. You may not change the fact that you performed certain duties during an employment period. You may not change dates either. When employers uncover the smallest of "errors," they then become cautious about the remaining information.

8. Do not make "negative statements." Any information that indicates you do not have the standard of quality wanted by employers will prompt them to continue their search by looking elsewhere. You cannot lie, but you don't have to give away "handicaps" that have no relationship or connection to the job for which you are applying. This is *very important* as employers make their final decisions based on the total amount of negative information they obtain during the whole screening process.

9. Don't include your salary requirements. Some employers may consider you "too expensive." Others may consider that your stated requirements are "too low." As a result, they may assume that your skills are not sufficient to do the job. If you are specifically asked to state your salary expectations for a particular job, put them in the covering letter.

10. Do not include references. If you are asked to provide references, list them in your covering letter.

11. Do not include your picture. If you are applying for a position where the employer can *legally* ask for your picture, then attach the picture to your covering letter. Human-rights legislation protects applicants from discrimination based on sex, race, or age. Your picture will give this information.

12. Carry your résumé in a portfolio or briefcase in order to keep its pages clean and fresh looking in appearance—another good impression!

You've already identified your strengths and skills. Now it's very important to transfer this information to your résumé. There are many styles of résumés to choose from. These include:

- **The Chronological Format:** Personal information and work history are arranged from the most recent to the least recent.
- **The Functional Format:** Abilities, skills, and accomplishments are highlighted. This style is best suited to students who are looking for that first job or for someone who doesn't have a lot of work experience.

Sample Résumé—Functional Style

ANISHA VIJH
92 Southdale Drive
Corner Brook, NF
A1N 1T6
(709) 555-1234
avijh@vianet.com

OBJECTIVE	Graphic Designer
PERSONAL PROFILE	• Dedicated, with a positive attitude • Communicates effectively • Works well under pressure • Willing to learn
EDUCATION	Sheridan College, Oakville, ON Bachelor of Design, 2002 Herdman Collegiate, Corner Brook, NF Senior High School Graduation Diploma, 1999
SKILLS	• Highly organized, able to perform many tasks at once • Thorough knowledge of design and design theory • Experience in Web design • Thorough knowledge of Quark, Photoshop, After Effects, InDesign, and HTML • Ability to adapt to new technologies
WORK EXPERIENCE	Internship at MAX Advertising and Design, 2002 Aerobics Instructor, McPhail's Fitness, 1999–2000
ACHIEVEMENTS	MVP Senior Girls' Volleyball, 2000 Member of Yearbook Committee Member of the junior and senior high school bands

Your Covering Letter

92 Southdale Drive
Corner Brook, NF A1N 1T6
(709) 555-1234

03 October 20__

Justin Hwang
Hwang Advertising and Design
P.O. Box 201
St. John's, NF
A1B 1S1

Dear Mr. Hwang:

Please consider this my application for the full-time position you advertised in *The Telegram*. I would like to become a graphic designer at Hwang Advertising and Design.

As a student in the Graphic Design Program at Sheridan College, I acquired the knowledge necessary to become a graphic designer in a small organization. Furthermore, I have had the opportunity to apply what I've learned in school during an internship at MAX Advertising and Design.

I would like to meet with you to discuss further my qualifications and will telephone you on Thursday, October 12 to arrange an interview.

I look forward to meeting you. Thank you for your time and consideration.

Sincerely,

Anisha Vijh

Anisha Vijh
Encl.

A covering letter is a *must* for any résumé. It's the introduction to your résumé—the attention-grabber.

Covering letters must always be originals for every position applied for. Photocopied "general" covering letters, with "specific" inserts aimed at a particular job, are definitely a mistake. They indicate that you could not take the time to compose a letter that applied to the job in question. Instead, you expect the interviewer to read through all of your material and sort out what applies to that particular job. Letters like this make a very poor first impression!

If possible, address your covering letter to an individual, using the *correct* spelling of the person's name and title. Using the form of address "Dear Sir or Madam" shows that you were not willing to spend the time and effort needed to secure the name of the *appropriate* company contact.

Your letter should be clean and neat, with no errors.

Try not to go beyond one page in length. In the first paragraph indicate why you are writing and what source of information led you to contact this company.

In the second paragraph, tell about your education and/or experience and how these relate to the open position. This paragraph should be your "hook." Stress the part of your background that would be a definite asset to the company to which you are writing. This hooks your reader's interest.

Finish by suggesting or, more assertively, by telling the reader that you will telephone to arrange an interview so that you may provide additional information about yourself. Tell the reader the date you will call; then mark that date on your calendar and make sure to follow through as promised.

PRE-INTERVIEW QUESTIONS

So now you've got that all-important job interview. Where do you go from there?

When you're applying for a job or getting ready to face an interview, most people worry about what questions they are likely to be asked. But if you're serious about landing the job, you should make sure that the toughest questions you face come from yourself.

To put your best foot forward in any job interview, you need to prepare yourself by facing up to some tough questions.

What is the message I want to get across to the interviewer or prospective employer? What three or four pieces of information about myself do I want to make sure I bring out?

Few candidates do much preparation for a job interview, but those who don't are making a mistake. You should never try to "wing" an interview—or any other important presentation. To make the best impression, you have to know exactly what you want to say.

Make a list of the points you want to get across. Think of your interests, your abilities, and your accomplishments. What have you done that can help this company move forward?

Whatever your message, think about the best way to communicate it. You have a few facts or stories you want to bring out, and you should never finish an interview until you've done so.

Your best chance will probably come when the interviewer asks you how you think you can contribute to the company. Be prepared.

You'd be surprised how many candidates act as if they never saw these questions coming. If you've prepared properly, you can turn these questions into opportunities to showcase your best material.

If the interviewer's questions don't seem to be heading in a direction that would let you cite your accomplishments, it's okay to subtly take the initiative. Answer any question the interviewer asks, fully and honestly, but don't hesitate to segue into areas that give you a chance to tell your story or underline your experience.

Ask yourself, "What are my 'must-haves' in this job? What do I need to learn about this company, my prospective manager, or my colleagues, so that I can determine if this is the place—and the opportunity—for me?"

Everyone has a bottom line when considering acceptance of a new job. Knowing your "bottom-line" demands is useful for evaluating any organization or job offer. You can do some preliminary research to find out what sort of future the company has, or ask around to learn what sort of person your boss might be.

But be realistic. Keep your "must-haves" down to three items. Tops. Any more, and you're not likely to be working soon.

Ask yourself, "What questions do I hope the interviewers won't ask?" And then prepare your responses to them—just in case.

Remember going into exams and praying that they wouldn't ask anything about photosynthesis, or the origins of World War I? Most people approach interviews the same way—aware that they have a few weak spots that they hope nobody will probe.

Everyone's weak points are different. Maybe there's a two-year gap in your résumé that you hope no one will notice. Perhaps you're not eager to explain why you've had six jobs in five years, or you always flub questions like: "What are your weaknesses?" Or maybe you just never know how to handle the question, "How much money are you looking for?"

Face up to your fears. Prepare for your interview by coming up with plausible, positive answers to questions like these. Good bosses and experienced interviewers have a way of sensing the weak points in any presentation, so presume that you'll need answers to all of your worst-nightmare questions.

Your average bookstore, or any one of hundreds of career-related Web sites (Yahoo! is a good place to start), will have lots of resources that can help you anticipate the tough questions you might be asked, and help you frame the most positive responses.

Finally, here's a question you should not ask yourself prior to an interview: "Do I really want this job?" Good question. But don't ask it too soon.

Many people do, and they often talk themselves out of exploring a potentially promising opportunity.

My advice: don't make up your mind prematurely. The point of a job interview is to help each party learn more about the other. Maybe, during the interview, you'll discover something that will impress you so much that commuting a little longer, or changing jobs for the same salary becomes much less of a concern. And the career you save may be your own.

Memo

A memo is a short, informal note used as a reminder, or to tell someone something important. However, although it is informal in tone, a memo should:

- be addressed to someone
- come from someone
- have a suitable heading
- be dated
- have a brief message that keeps to the point
- consist of complete sentences

Look at this example of a memo.

Memo

To: All Teachers at Vancouver Technical Secondary School
From: Principal Leah Belanger
Date: May 11, 2002
Re: Annual Spring Barbecue

All teachers are reminded of our annual spring barbecue this Friday. A sign-up sheet has been placed on the back of the staff-room door, and we will need volunteers to help with setting up the barbecues, cooking the food, and organizing the games. I hope you can all find time to get involved. Like last year, I have volunteered to sit in the dunk tank.

E-MAIL

E-mails (electronic mail) are written for the purpose of keeping in touch, sending urgent messages, expressing thanks, or offering good wishes, congratulations, or greetings to people you know well. They can either be formal or informal, but should not be used instead of letters and cards used for more formal occasions such as births, deaths, illnesses, graduations, or for offering thanks.

Here are some useful tips for e-mail writing:

- Adjust the tone of your e-mail to suit the situation. For workplace e-mails, use a more formal tone and conventional language. For friends or family, use a friendlier tone, making it sound as if you are speaking directly to the person reading the message.
- Only use slang, colloquial language, and other non-standard expressions if your reader will understand your meaning. However, avoid incorrect spelling and bad grammar.
- E-mail acronyms, such as FYI (for your information); BTW (by the way); TTYL (talk to you later); and HTH (hope this helps) are also acceptable as long as the reader understands what they stand for.
- Try not to use capital letters for whole words, as this is regarded as impolite.
- When you reply to an e-mail message, write full sentences, don't just type "yes" or "no."

- Avoid forwarding mass or "chain" e-mails to others; many people don't like receiving them, even if they're from a friend.

Look at the following examples of an e-mail message and an e-mail reply. Note that when you reply to an e-mail, you can either do so by pressing the "reply" button, in which case the original message will be returned to the sender, along with your reply; or you can type out a new e-mail reply message.

From: jszasz@northernlights.com
To: nlewis@smile.net
Subject: FYI hockey fans

Message:

Hi Naneesh,

A bunch of us are going to celebrate the end of Semester 1 exams by going to see the Oilers play. If you are interested, let me know. I'm organizing the tickets.

TTYL,
Jason

From: nlewis@smile.net
To: jszasz@northernlights.com
Subject: Re: FYI hockey fans

Message:

Hey Jason,

I'm definitely interested in the game. Of course, you know I couldn't say no! BTW, how much are the tickets? What date is the game?

Later,
Naneesh

BUSINESS LETTER

A business letter is a formal message written to an individual (other than a friend or relative) or business.

Purpose and Audience

People write business letters to complain, request that a particular action be taken, give information, order, sell, or convince the reader to do something. They are usually written to organizations or individuals whom the writer does not know well.

The following tips are useful when writing a business letter:

Organization

- Give your reason for writing the letter in the first sentence, then add the background information, details, reasons, or examples.

- End the letter by outlining what action you would like him or her to take and thanking the person.

Style
- Use a courteous tone, even if you are writing to complain about something.
- Use formal language and standard grammar, punctuation, and spelling.
- Use short sentences and say what you have to say directly and efficiently.
- Avoid any unnecessary words or expressions.

Format
- Include a **return address**. In business letters, this may be preprinted on a letterhead.
- Include an **inside address**. This is the address of the business or individual to whom you are addressing the letter. If you are writing to a company and don't have the name of the person to whom the letter should be directed, use Dear Sir or Madam, or the person's title: Dear Human Resources Manager. Note that there is no punctuation at the end of each line, and that the postal code is separated from the rest of the address by two spaces.
- Include the **date**, using numerals (for example, 15/4/01).
- Begin with a **greeting**, using a colon (Dear Prof. Wong:).
- Keep the **body** of the letter as brief as possible, breaking up your message into paragraphs to make it easier to read.
- Consider using one of the following more **formal closings**:

Yours truly,	Sincerely,	Best regards,
Yours,	Sincerely yours,	Regards,

- Type **your name** four lines beneath the closing, and put your handwritten signature in the space between these two elements.

There are several ways of setting up a business letter. The following are descriptions of two models:

- In **full block style**, you begin all lines at the left-hand margin and double-space between each element (for example, between the inside address and the date, between the date and the greeting, between paragraphs, etc.).
- In **modified block**, the return address, date, complimentary close, and your name and signature should begin at the centre of the page. All other lines begin at the left-hand margin. Use the same spacing as full block.
  Either layout is acceptable for any business letter you wish to send.
- If you are writing on paper that already has a letterhead, do not include a return address. Instead, write the date two lines below the letterhead, and then leave two to six lines before beginning the inside address.

Look at the sample business letter on page 318, written in modified block:

Halifax West High School
3620 Dutch Village Road
Halifax, NS B3A 2J2

15/1/02

Maggie Maclean
Maclean's Signs
300 Montgomery Drive
Halifax, NS B4F 1K8

Dear Ms. Maclean:

I am a member of the committee at Halifax West High School that is organizing a career day for Monday, April 3. The main objective of our career day is to have a variety of speakers who work in unique or non-traditional fields.

I am writing to ask if you would consider attending to discuss your career as a sign painter. Approximately 30–40 students will listen to your talk. In the half an hour that you have to speak, we would like you to discuss what you do, the education and skill background you have, and what you like and dislike about your position. After the half an hour, we will have 10 minutes for questions.

We will also be able to provide you with an overhead projector, video machine and TV, and/or a chalkboard, should you need any of these items for your talk.

Please let me know by the end of February if you will be able to visit our school and participate in our career day. I can be reached by phone at 902-555-5555 or by e-mail at dchang@loons.com.

Thank you for your time.

Yours truly,

David Chang

David Chang

Leaving Phone Messages

If you need to leave someone a phone message on voice mail, it needs to be brief, clearly spoken, and should include only the necessary information the other person needs to know in order to call you back.

Here are some tips for leaving phone messages:

- Your message should ideally not last longer than 30 seconds.
- Start to speak immediately after the "beep" so that you have enough time to record your message.
- Identify yourself. Remember that even if you are phoning someone you know well, he or she may not always recognize your voice over the phone.
- Speak clearly and slowly, so that the recipient can hear what you have to say the first time. If you do speak quickly, however, repeat important pieces of information, such as your phone number, so that the person has a chance to jot down the number the second time.
- Give only key information: your name, the time and date, your telephone number, who you want to speak to (if the number is a general number and not a personal voice mail), and, if relevant, what you want to speak to the person about in one, brief sentence.
- If you are phoning someone you don't know—for example, for an interview—it is important to let that person know why you are phoning. If you just leave your name and phone number, he or she may overlook you as a possible candidate for the job!

Author Biographies

Bauer, Joan Since she was a child in River Forest, Illinois, Joan Bauer wanted to entertain people and make them laugh. After a successful career in sales and marketing, she became a full-time writer, which has helped her accomplish her life-long goal.

Benchley, Peter Peter Benchley was born in New York City and raised in New Hampshire. After graduating with a degree in English from Harvard, Benchley worked as a journalist and speech writer before becoming a best-selling novelist with the publication of *Jaws* in 1974.

Boles, Derek Derek Boles was born in Montréal in 1949. An avid *Titanic* fan, Boles has been writing and speaking about the disaster for over twenty years.

Bradbury, Ray Ray Bradbury was born in Illinois but moved to California when he was fourteen. The winner of many awards, he has a crater on the moon named for one of his novels.

Brewster, Elizabeth Born in New Brunswick in 1922, Elizabeth Brewster has won several awards for her poetry, including the President's Silver Medal for Poetry in 1979 and the Saskatchewan Arts Boards Lifetime Award for Excellence in the Arts in 1995. Brewster currently lives in Saskatoon where she is Professor Emeritus at the University of Saskatchewan. She received the Order of Canada in 2001.

Callwood, June A prolific journalist and social activist, June Callwood is the recipient of many awards including the Order of Canada. She is the founder or co-founder of over fifty organizations including PEN Canada, Jessie's, and Casey House.

Canin, Ethan The author of several books, Ethan Canin was a graduate of Harvard Medical School before becoming a full-time writer. He splits his time between California and Iowa where he is on the faculty of the University of Iowa.

Carr, Emily Emily Carr was born in Victoria in 1871. After studying art in San Francisco, London, and Paris, Carr returned to the British Columbia wilderness she loved and became one of Canada's best-known painters.

Clark, Sally The recipient of several awards for her plays, Sally Clark has been playwright-in-residence at several theatres, including Theatre Passe Muraille, The Shaw Festival, and Buddies in Bad Times. She currently lives in Vancouver.

Coombs, Ann Known as "Canada's Faith Popcorn," Ann Coombs was born in Toronto in 1945. She is profoundly interested in change and spirituality in the workplace.

Crozier, Lorna Lorna Crozier grew up in Swift Current, Saskatchewan. In 1992, she won the Governor General's Award for her book of poetry *Inventing the Hawk*.

Diefenbaker, John Born in Neustadt, Ontario in 1895, John Diefenbaker was raised and educated in Saskatchewan. He was elected to Parliament in 1940 and in 1957 became Canada's 13th prime minister. Under his leadership, Canada passed its Bill of Rights and saw the appointment of the first woman to Cabinet and the first Aboriginal person to the Senate. Even having lost the leadership to Robert Stanfield in 1967, Diefenbaker served as an MP until his death in 1979.

Friedmann, Pavel Pavel Friedmann was born in Prague on January 7, 1921. In 1942, he and his family were shipped by the Nazis to the Theresienstadt (Terezin) Ghetto outside of Prague. Friedmann was shipped to Auschwitz where he was murdered on September 29, 1944.

Gordon, Sheldon Sheldon Gordon was born in Winnipeg, Manitoba on November 13, 1949. He writes for the *Imperial Oil Review.*

Gottlieb, Carl Carl Gottlieb is a well-known actor, director, and screen writer. He has acted in movies such as *M*A*S*H** and *The Jerk.* He directed *Caveman* and *Steve Martin Live,* and he won an Emmy for his writing on *The Smothers Brothers Comedy Hour* and a Golden Globe for *Jaws.*

Hall, Monty Monty Hall was born in Winnipeg in 1924. After graduating from the University of Manitoba, he became a TV news anchor before becoming the host of the highly successful game show *Let's Make a Deal.*

Hart, Johnny Creator of the comic strips *B.C.* and *The Wizard of Id,* Johnny Hart has won numerous awards including Best Humor Strip in America, National Cartoonist Society, 1967; The Reuben, Cartoonist of the Year, National Cartoonist Society, 1968; and the Seger Award, King Features, 1981. He lives in Endicott, New York.

Hiam, Alexander Alexander Hiam has worked in marketing for many years after receiving degrees from Harvard and U.C. Berkeley. He has written many books on marketing and marketing strategy including *Adventure Careers* and *The Manager's Pocket Guide to Creativity,* and has taught at the School of Management at the University of Massachusetts.

Holliday, Monica Monica Holliday is a student at Mount Forest District High School in Ontario.

Hossaini, Ali A resident of New York City, Ali Hossaini's writing has appeared in numerous publications including *Al-Ahram Daily* (Egypt), *Maclean's,* and *The Village Voice.* "Love," he says, "is the only reason to write."

Husted, Bill Born in Montana but raised in Arkansas, Bill Husted has had a varied journalistic career. After working at many jobs including a stint at the *National Enquirer,* he now writes a column on technology for the *Atlanta Journal-Constitution.*

Jackson, Marni Marni Jackson was born in Winnipeg, Manitoba. She was nominated for the 1993 Stephen Leacock Award and is the recipient of three National Magazine Awards. To relax while she's working, she plays the fiddle.

Joe, Rita Rita Joe was born on the Whycocomagh Reserve in Nova Scotia in 1932. She has received numerous awards for her work including the Order of Canada in 1990. Joe is an active poet and lecturer.

Laux, Dorianne Dorianne Laux was born in Augusta, Maine in 1952. She is Associate Professor and Director of the University of Oregon's Program in Creative Writing. She is the author of three books of poetry and the recipient of poetry endowments from the MacDowell Colony and the National Endowment for the Arts.

Le Dressay, Anne Anne Le Dressay was born in Virden, Manitoba in 1949. She started writing because she loved the sound and rhythm of language. She taught English and creative writing at Alberta community colleges for many years. She now lives in Ottawa and teaches English at the University of Ottawa.

MacLeod, Alistair Born in North Battleford, Saskatchewan in 1936, Alistair MacLeod moved with his family to Cape Breton when he was ten. He taught at Indiana University before moving to the University of Windsor where he is currently Professor of English and Creative Writing. He returns to Cape Breton every summer because it inspires him.

Maruki, Iri Iri Maruki was born near Hiroshima in 1901. After the bombing of Hiroshima and the loss of many family members, Maruki and his wife Toshi Maruki produced several art works illustrating the horrors of war. He died in 1995.

Maruki, Toshi Toshi Maruki was born on Hokkaido in 1912. Along with her husband Iri Maruki, she produced many pieces of art that illustrated the horrors of war. All of her art was influenced by the bombing of Hiroshima and the Battle of Okinawa. She died in 2000.

Menon, Vinay Vinay Menon was born in Akron, Ohio in 1970. He is a staff writer with *The Toronto Star.*

Naranjo-Morse, Nora A poet and potter who lives a traditional Pueblo life at Santa Clara Pueblo, Nora Naranjo-Morse has been called one of the most exciting Native-American artists of her generation.

Parker, Brant Brant Parker is the cartoonist responsible for *The Wizard of Id.* He was born in 1920 in Los Angeles. Before teaming up with Johnny Hart to create the award-winning comic strip, Parker honed his skills at many places including Walt Disney and America Greeting Cards. He was awarded the Reuben, Cartoonist of the Year in 1984.

Patch, Catherine Born in Toronto in 1947, Catherine Patch is a professional journalist who enjoys writing about the people she meets.

Petričić, Dušan Born in Belgrade in the former Yugoslavia in 1946, Dušan Petričić immigrated to Canada in 1993. He is the author of several children's books and his cartoons appear regularly in *The Toronto Star* and *The New York Times.*

Pietropaolo, Vincenzo Born in Italy, Vincenzo Pietropaolo was raised in Toronto. He has been an independent documentary photographer for over thirty years. His images have appeared in many books and magazines as well as on CBC and TVOntario.

Pivato, Joseph Joseph Pivato was born in Tezze sul Brenta, Italy in 1946. He works to preserve and publish the voices of Italian immigrants in Canada. Pivato lives in Edmonton and is a professor of comparative literature at Athabasca University.

Popcorn, Faith Faith Popcorn predicts with ninety-five percent accuracy future trends in North American society. She is a graduate of New York University and the New York School of the Performing Arts.

Quan, Betty Betty Quan writes for stage, radio, and TV. She graduated from the University of British Columbia and has served as playwright-in-residence at the Canadian Film Centre Television Drama Program and the Tarragon Theatre. In 1996, she was nominated for the Governor General's Award for Drama.

Roberts, Charles G. D. Born in 1860 in Douglas, New Brunswick, Charles G. D. Roberts was a schoolmaster in both Chatham and Fredericton, New Brunswick. He was knighted in 1935 and is the author of eleven books of poetry.

Sipress, David David Sipress left his graduate degree in Russian History at Harvard to pursue his life-long habit of cartooning. He lives with his wife in Brooklyn.

Souster, Raymond Raymond Souster was born in Toronto in 1921. He worked at the Canadian Imperial Bank of Commerce until his retirement. He is founding president of the Canadian League of Poets and served as its president from 1967 to 1971. He is inspired by the people and streets of Toronto and his friendships with the poets Irving Layton and the late Louis Dudek.

Strowbridge, Nellie Born in Port de Grave, Newfoundland and Labrador in 1947, Nellie Strowbridge has won numerous awards for her poetry.

SUNTEP The Saskatchewan Urban Native Teacher Education Program was founded in 1980. It is a four-year Bachelor of Education program offered by the Gabriel Dumont Institute in co-operation with the University of Saskatchewan. It places a strong emphasis on Métis and First Nation history and culture.

Suzuki, David David Suzuki was born in Vancouver in 1936. He is the author of over thirty books and has received numerous awards for his work, including the Order of Canada.

Thompson, Clive Clive Thompson was born in 1967. After graduating from the University of Toronto, he became a freelance writer and editor. He is currently editor-at-large of *Shift* magazine. In 2000, *The New York Daily News* named him one of the "50 New Yorkers to Watch in 2000."

Tynes, Maxine Maxine Tynes, recipient of the 1998 Milton Acorn People's Poet of Canada Award, was born in Dartmouth, Nova Scotia in 1949. She still lives there, writing and teaching high school. She has been a broadcaster, playwright, and high school teacher, but it is as a poet that Tynes has earned her reputation.

Updike, John John Updike was born in Shillington, a small town in Pennsylvania. After graduating from Harvard with a degree in English, Updike became a full-time writer. He has won numerous awards including two Pulitzer Prizes.

Valgardson, W. D. William Valgardson was born and raised in Gimli, Manitoba. Much of his writing, both for children and adults, deals with his Icelandic heritage. He taught high school English for many years before becoming a Professor of Creative Writing at the University of Victoria.

Walker, Alice Born in Eatonton, Georgia in 1944, Alice Walker was the youngest child of poor sharecroppers who were descended from slaves. A graduate of Sarah Lawrence University, her books and poetry have been translated into over a dozen languages and have won various awards including a Pulitzer Prize.

Watterson, Bill Bill Watterson was born in Washington D. C. in 1958 and was raised in Chagrin Falls, Ohio. He now resides in Hudson, Ohio with his wife and several cats. Creator of the vastly popular *Calvin and Hobbes* comic strip, Watterson was the youngest person ever to win the prestigious Reuben Award for "Outstanding Cartoonist of the Year."

White, Marian Frances Marian Frances White was born in Carbonnear, Newfoundland and Labrador in 1954. In 2000, she was the recipient of the Artist of the Year Awards given by the Newfoundland and Labrador Arts Council. Well-known as a poet, she is also famous for her yearly publication *A Woman's Almanac*.

Wyatt, Rachel Born in Bradford, England in 1929, Rachel Wyatt immigrated to Canada in 1957. She currently lives in Alberta and is the director of writing at the Banff Centre. A writer of both novels and plays, her work has appeared on stage as well as on the CBC and the BBC.

Zeman, Brenda A former track-and-field athlete, Brenda Zeman is now a writer. She also teaches a class in postmodern mythology at the University of Saskatchewan.

Glossary

Active Voice In the active voice, the subject of a sentence does the action. *The <u>dog</u> ran into the street.* Use the active voice when possible. It uses fewer words and is more precise than the passive voice. See **Passive Voice**.

Adjective An adjective is a word that describes a noun or pronoun: *He looked <u>pale</u>.* Adjectives as well as describing, can also limit a noun: *I read <u>two</u> books over the holidays.*

Adverb An adverb can describe a verb, an adjective, another adverb, or a whole clause or sentence. Adverbs usually tell how, when, where, or in what manner.

Alliteration Alliteration is the repetition of the same initial sound in words that are close together to create an effect: *The <u>s</u>un <u>s</u>ank <u>s</u>lowly.*

Allusion An allusion is a brief reference within a literary work to another literary work, or a person, place, event, or object from history, literature, or mythology. For example, saying someone has a "Midas touch" is an allusion to the myth of King Midas, who turned everything he touched to gold.

Antagonist The antagonist of a narrative or dramatic work is the main person in opposition to the hero or **protagonist**.

Apostrophe ['] An apostrophe can be used to
- show possession: *Pierre's hat*
- indicate a contraction: *I've, we're*
- replace missing letters in speech: *How 'bout you?*
- replace missing numbers in a date: *the Class of '02*
- show the plural of letter or symbols: *There are two a's in Alberta and two 0's in 2009.*

Appositive An appositive is a noun or noun phrase that relates to or explains a noun or pronoun that immediately precedes it. Appositives are set off with commas: *I am sending an e-mail to Katherine, <u>my third cousin</u>. Charles Schulz, <u>the cartoonist</u>, created* Peanuts.

Assonance Assonance is the repetition of similar vowel sounds in neighbouring words: *sweet dreams.* This technique is frequently used in poetry.

Bias Bias is an inclination or preference that makes it difficult or impossible to make a fair judgement in a particular situation.

Circular Structure Circular structure occurs when a phrase, line, or idea at the beginning of a text is repeated at the end of it.

Clause A clause is a group of words that has a subject and a verb.
- A **main clause** or **independent clause** expresses a complete thought and can stand alone as a sentence: *I forgot my keys.*
- A **subordinate clause** or **dependent clause** does not express a complete thought and cannot stand alone as a sentence: *Although he lost his keys.* The following examples show different types of clauses:
- **adverb clause**: <u>*When the dog barks*</u>, *the whole neighbourhood wakes up.*
- **adjective clause**: *Menta, <u>who sometimes babysits for us</u>, is taking a trip to Greece.*

- **co-ordinate clauses** which are clauses of the same rank: *I can make the salad and you can make the dessert.*
- **restrictive** or **essential clauses** are not set off by commas: *The CD <u>that you bought me</u> is defective.*
- **non-restrictive** or **non-essential clauses**: *The CD, <u>which I lost months ago</u>, isn't very good.*

Cliché Clichés are overworked expressions that no longer have much impact. It's best to avoid them in your writing. Writers, however, do sometimes use clichés to create effects: *sick as a dog, quick as a cat, under the weather.*

Climax The climax is the most important, and usually the most exciting, part of a story. All the action builds to this point. After the climax, the story winds down to its conclusion.

Colloquialism Colloquialisms are words or expressions that we use in everyday speech or informal writing, but that aren't appropriate in more formal writing: *Give me a break!; I've had it!*

Colon [:] A colon warns you that something is to follow. Use colons to:
- introduce a list
- begin a quotation in formal writing
- express time: *9:50, 21:00*
- separate the volume and page numbers of a magazine: *Food Lover's Digest, 4:17–19*
- after the salutation in a business letter: *Dear Ms. Palmer:*

Comma [,] A comma indicates a slight pause in a sentence. Most modern writers use as few commas as possible without confusing the reader. Use a comma
- between compound sentences (if sentences are short, the comma may be omitted): *<u>Carla concentrated</u>, but <u>no solution came to mind</u>.*
- with nouns of address: *David, shut the window.*
- with words, phrases, or clauses that interrupt a sentence: *We will, however, do our best to win. We were delighted, <u>when for the first time</u>, the baby walked.*
- with introductory words, clauses, or phrases: *<u>Naturally</u>, Jackie was pleased. <u>At last</u>, I was able to finish my book. <u>When we had finished eating</u>, we took a long walk.*
- between items in a series: *<u>Maria, Josef, and Patrice</u> went for a swim.* Some writers omit the comma just before the *and* or the *or* in a series. This is acceptable as long as it is done consistently and the sentences are still clear.
- to set off "which" clauses: *The coat, <u>which is red</u>, is too small for me.*
- in some forms of dates: *September 5, 2006* (BUT *5 September 2006*)
- in salutations of personal letters: *Dear Patrick,*
- to set off degrees and titles: *Dr. Irene Pepperberg, Ph.D.; Carl Heinz, M.D.*

Compound Adjective A compound adjective consists of two or more words that function as one word and expresses a single thought: *an up-to-date book, a five-storey building, a well-known author.*

Conflict Conflict is the problem or struggle in a story that the main character has to solve or face. Conflict is created in four classic ways: human against self, human against human, human against nature, and human against society.

Conjunction A conjunction is a word that connects other words, phrases, clauses, ideas, or sentences.
- **Co-ordinating conjunctions** connect two similar words, phrases, or ideas: *The dog barked, <u>so</u> I jumped.*

- **Subordinating conjunctions** signal that one idea is less important than, or dependent on, another: _Whenever_ the dog barked, I jumped.
- **Correlative conjunctions** come in pairs, each introducing one of the two things being compared: _Not only_ did the dog bark, _but_ I _also_ jumped.

Connotation/Denotation The definition of a word found in the dictionary is its denotation. Many words also have a connotation. This means that a word may have positive or negative associations, or a particular mood or slant in meaning, that affect what the word tells the reader: The words _giggle, laugh, titter, chortle,_ and _snicker_ all denote more or less the same thing, but each has a different shade of meaning.

Consonance Consonance is the repetition of similar consonant sounds within words: _wonder/wander._ Consonance is sometimes used as a technique in poetry.

Dangling Modifier A dangling modifier occurs when the word being modified is implied but doesn't appear in the sentence. When you use a phrase to begin a sentence, make sure the word that follows it is the word it modifies.
Dangling: While jogging, the CD player broke.
Better: While jogging, I broke the CD player.

Dash [—] A dash makes a strong break in a sentence. Dashes are useful for emphasis, but too many can make your writing disjointed and difficult to read. Consider using other punctuation, such as commas or parentheses, instead.

Debate A debate is a formal argument, often in a public setting, for and against an issue or question.

Diction Diction refers to the way an author expresses ideas in words. Good diction includes grammatical correctness, skill in the choice of effective words, and a wide vocabulary.

Dynamic Character A dynamic character is one who undergoes a significant and permanent change in personality or beliefs.

Editorial An editorial is an article in a newspaper or magazine, or a comment in a radio or TV broadcast, giving the opinion or attitude of the publisher, editor, or other speaker regarding some subject.

Ellipsis Points [. . .] Ellipsis points are a series of three dots that show something has been left out. Use ellipsis points to:
- show that words have been cut from within a quotation
- indicate that a sentence or thought has been left unfinished

Eulogy A eulogy is a tribute to someone who has just died, and is often delivered as a speech at a funeral.

Figurative Language Language can be literal or figurative. Literal language says what it means directly. Figurative language uses words to paint a picture, draw an interesting comparison, or create a poetic effect.

Foreshadowing Foreshadowing is a plot technique in which a writer plants clues about events that will happen later in the narrative.

Free Verse Free-verse poetry is written without using regular rhyme or rhythm. Images, spacing, punctuation, and the rhythms of ordinary language are used to create a free-verse poem.

Gerund A gerund is the form of verb that ends in -_ing_, used as a noun: _Walking is a good form of exercise._

Homophones Homophones are two words that are pronounced alike but are spelled differently: *hear/here*. Homophones can be confused easily in speech and writing.

Hyperbole Hyperbole is a deliberately exaggerated statement made for effect.

Hyphen [-] Hyphens are used in the following ways:
- to spell compound numbers from 21 to 99: *twenty-one*
- to spell out time: *the six-thirty bus*
- to spell out fractions: *one-third of a cake*
- in some numerical expressions: *a five-year-old girl*
- in many expressions formed with prefixes: *de-ice, ex-boyfriend, pro-Canadian*
- when a compound modifier comes before a noun, unless the first word ends in *-ly: rosy-fingered dawn* (BUT *carefully woven cloth*)
- in some compound words: *merry-go-round, jack-rabbit.* Note, however, that because many compound nouns are written as one word (*nighttime*), or as two words with or without a hyphen (*hand-picked, hand brake*) it's best to check your dictionary for the right form.

Idiom An idiom is a fixed, colourful expression whose meaning is different from the literal meaning of the words and is easily understood by people speaking the same language. *To be in hot water*, for example, means to be in trouble, not immersed in warm liquid.

Imagery Imagery is the pictures or impressions that writers create in the minds of their readers. To create these pictures, they use descriptive techniques such as figures of speech (simile, metaphor, personification, oxymoron), onomatopoeia, alliteration, and allusions.

Interjection Interjections are short words or phrases that express strong emotion, such as surprise, shock, sorrow, or excitement: *Hey!, Oh!, Ouch!*

Interview An interview is a good way to get expert opinions or advice on specific topics. They are also a great primary source. A **transcript interview** is an article that is set up in a question-and-answer format.

Irony Irony occurs when a statement or situation means something different from (or even the opposite of) what is expected. Another type of irony is called **dramatic irony**. It occurs in plays when the audience knows something that the characters do not.

Jargon Jargon is language that does not communicate. It is usually the language of a particular group or profession. For example, legal jargon refers to terms commonly used by those whose practise law.

Logo A logo is an identifying symbol used as a trademark in advertising.

Metaphor A metaphor is a comparison of two things that are not alike. The comparison suggests that they do share a common quality: *her words pierced my heart* (compares "her words" to the action of a knife or sword).

Misplaced Modifier Keep modifying words and phrases (adjectives, adverbs, prepositional and participial phrases) as close together as possible to the words they modify; otherwise you may create a misplaced modifier.

Misplaced: <u>Growling</u>, my hat was being eaten by the *dog*.
Better: <u>Growling</u>, the *dog* was eating my hat.

Narration Narration is the telling of an event or series of events. Narration is used in all types of writing, including narratives, plays, and poetry.

Narrator The narrator is the person or character telling a story. See **Point of View**.

Noun A noun is a word that refers to people, places, qualities, things, actions, or ideas. There are five main types of nouns:
- **common nouns** name general kinds of people, places, or things: *movie, dog, person*
- **abstract nouns** name ideas or qualities that cannot be sensed by sight or touch: *love, happiness*
- **concrete nouns** name things that can be touched: *foot, table, glass, book*
- **collective nouns** are singular in form but stand for a whole group: *class, team, bunch, family*
- **proper nouns** name specific people, places, and things: *Edmonton, Pauline, June*

Object The English language has three types of object. In the following examples, the direct object is in italics, and the indirect object is underlined.
- A **direct object** is a noun or pronoun that answers the question *what?* or *who?* about the verb: She bought a *skateboard.*
- An **indirect object** is a noun or pronoun that answers the question *to what? for what?* or *for whom?* about the verb: She bought <u>me</u> a *skateboard.*
- The **object of the preposition** is a noun or pronoun that comes at the end of a prepositional phrase: She bought a *skateboard* for <u>me</u>.

Onomatopoeia Onomatopoeic words are words that imitate actual sounds: *hiss, thud, bang, crash.*

Oxymoron An oxymoron is a combination of contradictory words that create a striking effect: *fiery ice, an intelligent fool.*

Paragraph A paragraph is a group of sentences that develops one aspect of a topic, or one phase of a narrative. Paragraphs are well developed if they are unified, coherent, and complete.

Parallel Structure In a sentence, two or more elements that are of equal importance, expressed in similar grammatical terms, are called parallel. The purpose is to emphasize ideas that are of equal importance.
Not Parallel: *Campers are taught hiking, swimming, and how to paddle a canoe.*
Parallel: *Campers are taught hiking, swimming, and canoeing.*

Parentheses [( )] Parentheses are used to set off comments or asides in a sentence: *They lived happily ever after (and so did the cat).*
- When necessary, use exclamation marks and question marks inside the parentheses, even in the middle of a sentence: *All of us except Keefer (Keefer is always optimistic!) were sure it was going to snow.*
- You can place whole sentences in parentheses. If the sentence stands alone, punctuate it as you would a regular sentence: *The French colony of Upper Volta, now called Burkina Faso, gained its independence in 1960. (Burkina Faso means "Land of honest men.")*
- Parentheses are also used within scripts to frame stage directions.

Parody A parody is a humorous imitation of a serious piece of writing. It makes fun by imitating.

Participle A participle is a verb form that can be combined with a helping verb—such as *be* or *have*—to form tense, but that cannot function as a verb on its own.
- The **present participle** of all verbs ends in *-ing* (*running, laughing, thinking, doing, being*).
- The **past participle** may end in *-ed, -en,* or *-t,* or various other ways (*called, given, bent, born*). It is the form of the verb you would use after *have.*
- A particle can also act alone as an adjective: <u>*Laughing*</u> *and* <u>*talking*</u>*, we ate* <u>*burnt*</u> *marsh- mallows.* When the participle is used as noun it is called a **gerund.**

Passive Voice In the passive voice, the subject of the verb receives the action: *The fire was extinguished.* Where possible, use the active voice. See **Active Voice**.

Personification Personification occurs when objects, ideas, or animals are given human qualities: *The sun smiled down on me.*

Phrase A phrase is a group of words that does not have a subject and a verb. There are four main types of phrases:
- a **noun phrase** acts as a noun: *Kate loves <u>to go camping</u>.*
- an **adjective phrase** acts as an adjective: *<u>Fading fast</u>, he crossed the finish line.*
- an **adverb phrase** acts as an adverb: *Clare crossed the threshold <u>for the last time</u>.*
- a **prepositional phrase** contains a preposition, and can act like a noun, an adjective, or an adverb: *<u>From downtown to my house</u>, is a two-hour walk.* (noun); *The carpet <u>in the den</u> needs to be replaced.* (adjective); *He accepted the award <u>with disbelief</u>.* (adverb)

Plot Plot refers to the events in a story. It usually has five elements: exposition, rising action, climax, falling action, and resolution.
- The **exposition** or introduction sets up the story by introducing the main characters, the setting, and the problem to be solved.
- The **rising action** is the main part of the story where the full problem develops. A number of events are involved that will lead to the climax.
- The **climax** is the highest point in the story where the most exciting events occur.
- The **falling action** follows the climax. It contains the events that bring the story to its conclusion.
- The **resolution** or denouement is the end of the story when all the problems are solved.

Point of View Point of view is the vantage point from which the author tells a story. The four most common points of view are *first person* (I, me, we), *omniscient* (all seeing), *limited omniscient* (all seeing from the viewpoint of a character or group of characters), and *objective* (he, she, they, it).

Preposition A preposition is a word that shows a relationship between a noun, called the *object of the preposition*, and another word that comes before it in the sentence: *The house <u>in</u> the valley was swept away <u>by</u> the flood.* Here are a few examples of some common prepositions: *above, at, before, behind, by, for, from, down, of, on, since, through, until*, and *with*.

Profile A profile is a concise description of a person's abilities, character, or career.

Pronoun A pronoun is a word that replaces a noun or another pronoun. It should be clear what the pronoun replaces (its antecedent).

Protagonist The protagonist is the main character in a story.

Quotation Marks [" "] Two main uses for quotation marks are as follows: for direct quotations, and for words that define or describe.
- **Direct quotations**. Use quotation marks to show that the words inside are a direct quotation. Very long quotations (over one hundred words or over three lines of your writing) that are indented from the body of the text, don't need quotations.
- Use a comma between the speaker's tags (Camilla asked) and the quotation unless the quotation ends with an question mark or an exclamation mark and the speaker's tag follows. *Camilla asked, "Where is the notebook you borrowed?"* OR *"Where," asked Camilla, "is the notebook you borrowed?"* BUT *"Where is the notebook you borrowed?" asked Camilla.*
- A period or comma at the end of a quotation goes inside the quotation mark: *"The trouble is," he muttered, "I can't get the time machine to work."*

- A semicolon at the end of a quotation mark goes outside the quotation marks: *Sarah announced, "I don't want any more cookies, thank you"; then she sank back down on the bed and slept until morning.*
- A question mark or exclamation mark goes inside the quotation marks if it relates to the quoted material, and outside if it applies to the whole sentence: *Theo called out, "Where are you going?"* BUT *I'm tired of hearing you say, "I'll clean it up tomorrow"!*
- **Definitions and Descriptions**. You can use quotation marks in place of italics or underlining to indicate a word is being defined or explained: *The term "downsizing" is a euphemism that usually means firing a lot of employees.*

Racist Language Racist language is any language that refers to a particular cultural group or ethnic group in insulting terms, but racism also exists in more subtle forms.
- Mention a person's race only if that is relevant to the context. If a person's race or ethnic origin is relevant, be specific:
Irrelevant/Vague: *A'isha is African.*
Relevant/Not Vague: *A'isha is proud of her Nigerian heritage.*
- Avoid making generalizations about any racial or cultural group:
Stereotype: *The Welsh are great singers.*
Better: *The Welsh have a long tradition of singing.*

Rhetorical Question A rhetorical question is one asked for effect, and that does not invite a reply. The purpose of a rhetorical question is to introduce a topic or to focus the reader on a concern.

Rhythm Rhythm is the arrangement of beats in a line of poetry. The beat is created by the accented and unaccented syllables in the words used in each line.

Run-on Sentence A run-on sentence is formed when two sentences are run into one another. To fix a run-on sentence, add the proper punctuation or change the wording to make it a single sentence or two sentences.
Run-on: *The sky is clear it is spring at last.*
Better: *The sky is clear; it is spring at last.* OR *The sky is clear, and it is spring at last.* OR *The sky is clear because it is spring at last.* OR *The sky is clear. It is spring at last.*
- When two sentences are separated by a comma, this is called a comma splice. Fix the comma splice the same way you would fix a run-on sentence.

Satire Satire uses humour, especially irony and sarcasm, to expose flaws or criticize someone or something. Usually, the purpose of satire is to point out weaknesses or foolish ideas.

Semicolon Use a semicolon
- to separate two related independent clauses: *I love watching TV after school; it relaxes me.*
- along with a co-ordinating conjunction to join main clauses, if one or more of the clauses already contains a comma: *I threw on my coat, picked up my wallet, and raced to the bus stop; but the bus had already left.*
- to separate items in a list when one or more of these contains a comma: *Walter has lived in Tokyo, Japan; London, England; and Edmonton, Alberta.*

Sentence A sentence is a group of words representing a complete thought. It contains a subject and a predicate.
- A **simple sentence** consists of one main clause: *Yukio built a house.*
- A **compound sentence** consists of two or more main clauses: *Yukio built a house, and he expanded the backyard.*

- A **complex sentence** consists of one main clause and one or more subordinate clauses: *While I was way*, *Yukio built a house.*
- A **compound-complex sentence** consists of two main clauses and one or more subordinate clauses: *While I was away*, *Yukio built a house and he expanded the backyard.*

Sentence Fragment A sentence fragment is a group of words that is set off as a sentence, but that lacks either a verb or a subject.

Fragment: *We went to the game on Sunday. Jessica and I.* (lacks a verb)
Revised: *Jessica and I went to the game on Sunday.*
Fragment: *Never did understand those engines.* (lacks a subject)
Revised: *I never did understand those engines.*
Fragment: *The water felt good. Cool and refreshing.* (lacks a subject and verb)
Revised: *The water felt cool and refreshing.*

Sentence fragments are acceptable in informal writing, dialogue, and spoken English, but they are not appropriate in formal writing.

Sexist Language Sexist language is language that degrades or unnecessarily excludes either women or men. It's best to avoid generalizing about males and females unless the claims are based on scientific facts.
- Whenever possible, replace words such as *fireman, policeman,* and *man-made* with non-sexist alternatives such as *firefighter, police officer,* and *fabricated.*
- Avoid using the masculine pronouns *he, him,* or *his* to refer to both men and women. Instead, try one or more of the following methods:
  - Use the plural.
    Inappropriate: *A good teacher can always command the respect of his students.*
    Better   *Good teachers can always command the respect of their students.*
  - Replace the pronoun with *the, a,* or *an.*
    Inappropriate: *Whoever holds the winning ticket has not claimed her prize.*
    Better: *Whoever holds the winning ticket has not claimed the prize.*
  - Substitute *one* or *you.* Use *one* in more formal writing.
    Inappropriate: *A man never knows when his time will come.*
    Better: *You never know when your time will come.*
  - Use *her or his, her or him,* or *she or he.* Note, however, that this method can start to sound awkward if used too often.
  - Sometimes the best way to avoid sexism is to change the wording of the sentences.

Simile A simile compares two things or ideas directly, using *like, than,* or *as*: *My ears buzzed like a bee.*

Slang Slang is very informal language that is invented or used in a particular way by a specific group and is rarely understood by those outside the group. Examples of slang from earlier times include *razzmatazz* and *tripping the light fantastic.* More recent expressions include *cool* and *bummer.* Slang should be avoided in formal writing. It can be used in advertisements or writing aimed at one's peers.

Slogan A slogan is a short catchy phrase used to advertise a product or service.

Stereotype A stereotype is an oversimplified picture, usually of a group of people, giving them all a set of characteristics, without consideration for individual differences.

Style Style is the overall texture of a piece of writing; the particular way in which the ideas are expressed. Style is made up of many elements including diction, figurative language, sentences, and tone.

Subject Complement A subject complement is a noun, pronoun, or adjective that comes after a linking verb. It tells something about the subject: *Miko is a boxer. It is she. Your eyes look clear.*

Subject/Verb Agreement A verb should always agree in number with its subject. Singular subjects take singular verbs, and plural subjects take plural verbs. When you are looking for the subject of the verb, remember the following tips:
- Prepositional phrases like *at school, under my desk,* and *with great sadness,* never contain the subject of the sentence:

  Wrong: *One of the cars were stolen.* (*cars* is not the subject)
  Correct: *One of the cars was stolen.* (the subject *one* needs a singular verb)
- *There* and *here* are not usually the subject of the verb: *There are many reasons why I like you.* (subject is *reasons*)
- If the subject has two parts, joined by *or, not,* or *either . . . nor,* make the verb agree with the part of the subject that is nearest to it: *Neither my brother nor my parents were at my recital. Neither my brother nor my sister was at my recital.*
- Some subjects look like they are plural, but they are really singular: *The Diviners is a remarkable book. The news is about to come on. Five dollars is not enough to go to a movie.*

Suspense Suspense is a feeling of tension, anxiety, or excitement resulting from uncertainty. An author creates suspense to keep readers interested.

Symbol A symbol is an object or person that represents a quality, idea, or condition. Some symbols are generally accepted, or even universal; others are used in specific stories or poems to mean specific things. A dove, for example, is universally a symbol of peace.

Tense The tense of a verb is the property that expresses time. English has five categories of tenses: present, past, future, perfect, and progressive. The progressive and perfect tenses may combine with other each and with the present, past, or future tense to form compound tenses.

Theme The theme is the central idea that is expressed directly or indirectly in a literary work. In non-fiction, or an essay, theme is more often used to mean the same as thesis.

Thesis A thesis is the main idea, position, or view of the essay writer; it is the hypothesis at the heart of a writer's work.

Tone The tone is the implied attitude of the writer toward the subject or the audience. Tone differs from *mood,* which describes more generally the emotional feeling of the work. The tone of a piece of work can be described as *angry, satiric, joyful,* or *serious.*

Transition Words Transition words indicate relationships between ideas. Writers use them to suggest links between sentences or paragraphs.

Verb A verb is a word that expresses an action or a state of being.
- A **helping verb** comes before the main verb and shows its tense, mood, and voice. Common helping verbs are *be, do, have, can/could, may/might.*
- A **transitive verb** needs an object to complete its meaning: *We love your work.*
- A **linking verb** connects the subject with the complement: *The car is blue.*
- An **irregular verb** does not form its past participle or its past tense by adding *-ing* or *-ed* to the infinitive form.

Index of Authors and Titles

Acknowledgments

Every reasonable effort has been made to trace ownership of copyrighted material. Information that would enable the publisher to correct any reference or credit in future editions would be greatly appreciated.

10-11 "Early Inklings" by John Updike. Reprinted by permission. © 2001 John Updike. Originally published in *The New Yorker*. All rights reserved. **14-28** "Star Food" by Ethan Canin. From *Emperor of the Air*. Copyright © 1988 by Ethan Canin. Reprinted by permission of Houghton Mifflin Company. All rights reserved. **30-32** "A Photographer at Work" by Vincenzo Pietropaolo and Andrew Gorham. Reprinted with permission from *The Globe and Mail*. **33-34** "Hard Edges, Soft Skills" by Ann Coombs. **36-38** "Mud Woman's First Encounter with the World of Money and Business" by Nora Naranjo-Morse from *Mud Woman: Poems from the Clay*, by Nora Naranjo-Morse. Copyright © 1992 Nora Naranjo-Morse. Reprinted by permission of the University of Arizona Press. **43-44** "Shoe Store" by Raymond Souster is reprinted from *The Collected Poems of Raymond Souster* by permission of Oberon Press. **47-48** "Summer Job" by Nellie P. Strowbridge. Reprinted by permission of the author. **50-52** "Screen Test" by Sally Clark. **54** "The Butterfly" by Pavel Friedmann from *I Never Saw Another Butterfly* by U.S. Holocaust Memorial Museum, edited by Hana Volavkova, copyright © 1978, 1993 by Artia, Prague Compilation © 1993 by Schocken Books. Used by Permission of Schocken Books, a division of Random House, Inc. **56-57** "Quint Tells His Story" excerpt from the screenplay *Jaws* by Peter Benchley and Carl Gottlieb. **59-62** "Facing Extinction" by Kevin Hall. **64-65** "Suitcase Lady" by Christie McLaren. Reprinted with permission of *The Globe and Mail*. **67-74** "The Cabin Door" by Charles G. D. Roberts. **78-82** "What Stays in the Family" by Lorna Crozier. Reprinted by permission of the author. **83-92** "Epic of Survival: Shackleton" by Caroline Alexander, *National Geographic Magazine*, November 1998. Reprinted with permission. **94-97** "Why Canada Has to Beat Its Literacy Problem" by June Callwood. Reprinted by permission of the author. **100-106** "How We Lived" by Mary Vincent from *Canadian Geographic* (Jan/Feb 2001). Reprinted with permission. **107-110** "My Father's Escapes" by Joseph Pivato. Reprinted by permission of the author. **112** "Another story altogether" by Anne Le Dressay. Reprinted by permission of the author. **114-115** "Remember?" from *Horses Make a Landscape Look More Beautiful: Poems by Alice Walker*, copyright © 1984 by Alice Walker, reprinted by permission of Harcourt, Inc. **117-119** "The Gift: How One Act of Kindness Changed a Life" told by Monty Hall to Robert Kiener. Reprinted with permission from the June 2001 *Reader's Digest*. **120-125** "To Everything There Is a Season" from *Island: The Collected Short Stories of Alistair Macleod* by Alistair Macleod. Used by permission, McClelland & Stewart Ltd. *The Canadian Publishers*. **127-129** "Babu Chhiri" © Times Newspapers Limited, London (May 2, 2001). **130** "Where I Come From" by Elizabeth Brewster is reprinted from *Selected Poems* by permission of Oberon Press. **133-142** "The Reluctant Black Hawk" written and abridged by Brenda Zeman. Reprinted by permission of the author. **144-146** "Naomi Segal-Bronstein: Children's Champion" by Sheldon Gordon. Reprinted with permission of the author. **147** "Roll Me Up; Roll Me Down/Mobile-Mobility" by Maxine Tynes. Reprinted by permission of the author. **150-152** "Twenty Thousand Ears" by Rachel Wyatt. Reprinted by permission of the author. **153-157** "Nancy Chew Enters the Dragon" by Betty Quan. **158-159** "The Role of Words in the Digital Era" by Kathe Lieber. **160-161** "Gutenberg Can Rest in Peace" by Pierre Renaud. **162-164** "Premiums: The Most Abused and Misused Medium of All!" from *Marketing For Dummies*® by Alexander Hiam. Copyright ©1997 IDG Books Worldwide Inc. All rights reserved. Reproduced here by permission of the publisher. For Dummies is a registered trademark of Hungry Minds, Inc. **172-176** "Citytv: Now Available in Assorted Cultures" by Kim Honey and Timothy Pratt. **177** "Identity Crisis" by Monica Holliday. Reprinted by permission of Monica Lauren Holliday. **179-186** "Video Ga Ga" by Vinay Menon. ©2001. Reprinted by permission—The Toronto Star Syndicate. **188-195** "Disaster as Popular Culture" by Derek Boles. Reprinted by permission of the author. **198-202** "It's All History Now" by Bill Husted. © 1999 Bill Husted. Reprinted by permission of *The Atlanta Journal-*

Constitution. **206-210** "The Flying Machine" by Ray Bradbury. **212** "As It Is" by Dorianne Laux by permission of Pushcart Press. **214-218** "Clocks, Computers and Why We Play God" by Jay Bookman. **220-223** "Virtual Therapy, Real Results" by Clive Thompson. Reprinted by permission of the author. **224-226** "Body Scanners" by Kimberley Noble from *Maclean's Magazine* [March 26]. © 2001. **228-232** "Zap! It's the Future" by Chris Wood from *Maclean's Magazine* [August 20] © 2001. **234-239** "Future Tense." **241-243** "Written in the Body" by Marni Jackson. Reprinted with permission of the author. **244-245** "Genome Sequence Just the Beginning" by David Suzuki. **248** "Justice" by Rita Joe. **250-259** "A Matter of Balance" from *What Can't Be Changed Shouldn't Be Mourned.* Text copyright © 1984 by W.D. Valgardson. Published in Canada by Douglas & McIntyre Ltd. Reprinted by permission of the publisher. **263-273** "The Truth About Sharks" by Joan Bauer. **276** "Floating Lanterns" by Iri and Toshi Maruki, translated by Nancy Hunter. **278-279** "At War With Oneself" by Ali Hossaini. Reprinted by permission of the author. **284-289** "Animal Wrongs" by Susan McClelland from *Maclean's Magazine* [January 22]. ©2001. **291-292** "The Unjiggable Cod" by Marian Frances White. Reprinted by permission of the author. **294-301** "A Thousand Supperless Babes: The Story of the Metis" by SUNTEP Theatre. Reprinted with permission.

Visual Credits

Front cover Daryl Benson/Masterlife. **9** J. Lannen/Stone/Getty Images. **12** J. Thornton/ Photodisc. **17** A. Ruggieri/Image Bank/Getty Images. **30-32** Vince Pietropaolo. **37** *Pearlene* by Nora Noranjo–Morse/Fine Art Collection/ Heard Museum, Phoenix, Arizona. **40-41** Dušan Petričić. **45** The New Yorker Collection 1999 David Sipress from cartoonbank. All rights reserved. **48** *Summer Fish* (1979) 26"x30"/oil on panel/private collection/ Toronto, ON/Courtesy Mary Pratt. **53** J. Stromme/Picturesque/PictureQuest. **57** Kobal Collection/Universal. **60, 61** Reprinted with permission of Knight Ridder/Tribune Information Services. **68** *Gothic Tree* by Cecil Day/Collection of the Newfoundland and Labrador Art Gallery. **76** *Crying Totem Pole* by Emily Carr (1928)/oil on canvas/Vancouver Art Gallery/ Emily Carr Trust VAG 42.3.53 (Photo Trevor Mills). **77** *Survivor Drifting* by David Blackwood/ Etching/Copyright David Blackwood. **81** Jane Sapinsky/Firstlight. **83** Scott Polar Research Institute. **85** Royal Geographical Society/6162. **99** *The India of Tehuantepec* by Alfredo Ramos Martinez/Christie's Images/Corbis/Magma.

100 National Archives of Canada/PA-10254. **101** (**top**) Notman Photographic Archives/McCord Museum of Canadian History/Montreal/ MP-0000.2082.2; (**centre**) Provincial Archives of Manitoba/N2473; (**bottom**) British Columbia Archives/A-01028. **102** CN Collection/Canadian Museum of Science and Technology/AB.H.02. 233593. **103** (**top**) CN Collection/Canadian Museum of Science and Technology/AB.1.1. X34972; (**centre**) CN Collection/Canadian Museum of Science and Technology/AB.H-10.2.44951; (**bottom**) Richard Harrington/ National Archives of Canada/PA-147029. **104** (**top**) Bob Anderson/Masterfile; (**bottom**) Todd Korol. **105** (**top**) Darwin Wiggett/Firstlight; (**bottom**) Peter Bennett. **106** Russ Burden/ Spectrum Stock. **115** Illustration by Christopher Myers from *Harlem: A Poem* by Walter Dean Myers/Published by Scholastic Press, a division of Scholastic Inc./Illustration copyright © 1997 by Christopher Myers/Reprinted by permission. **p. 123** *Bringing Home the Christmas Tree* (oil on masonite) by Eric Sloane (1910-1985)/Private Collection/Christie's Images/The Bridgeman Art Library. **127** Binod Joshi/AP/Canapress. **132** © estate of Ruth Pawson/Photo courtesy Saskatchewan Arts Board Permanent Collection. **140** *Big Boys Playing Hockey* by Allen Sapp/ Acrylic on canvas/Private Collection/John Kurtz Assiniboia Gallery. **146** Spyros Bourboulis. **149** R. Daly/Stone/Getty Images. **151** Craig Van der Lende/Image Bank/Getty Images. **166** Courtesy of Covenant House. **168-170** Annie Griffiths Belt/National Geographic Image Collection. **171** By permission of Johnny Hart and Creators Syndicate, Inc. **173** Eliana Aponte/ Archive Photos. **177** D. Bonesey/Stone/Getty Images. **180** H. Diltz/Corbis/Magma. **189** *The Titanic Sinking on 15th April 1912* by Harley Crossley/oil on canvas/The Bridgeman Art Library. **197** *Indefinite Divisibility* by Yves Tanguy (1942)/oil on canvas/Albright-Knox Gallery. **201** H. Lloyd/FPG/Getty Images. **204** *Prometheus Carrying Fire* by Jan Cossiers/Museo del Prado/Art Resource, New York. **207** Hulton Deutsch Collection/Corbis/Magma. **217** Kobal Collection/MGM. **221** Brian Hughes/Reprinted with permission – The Toronto Star Syndicate. **230** Leif Peng. **239** J. Rajs/Stone/Getty Images. **243** D. Hallinan/Masterfile. **247** R. Daly/Stone/ Getty Images. **255** Bill Hatcher/National Geographic Society/Firstlight. **261** CALVIN AND HOBBES © Watterson. Reprinted with permission of UNIVERSAL PRESS SYNDICATE. All rights reserved. **274** Cathy Thorne. **285** Rick Chard. **292** *Marine's Geometry* by Jean-Claude Girardin. **296** National Archives of Canada/C-002424.